£2·95

The Beginners Guide
to Good Gardening

The Beginners Guide to Good Gardening

David Carr

BLANDFORD PRESS
Poole   Dorset

First published in the U.K. 1979

Copyright © 1979 Blandford Press Ltd,
Link House, West Street,
Poole, Dorset, BH15 1LL

British Library Cataloguing in
Publication Data

Carr, David
   The beginners guide to good gardening.
1. Gardening
I. Title
635   SB453

ISBN 0 7137 0934 0

Set in 9/10pt Monophoto Plantin
by Keyspools Ltd, Golborne, Lancs.

Printed and bound in Great Britain by the
Fakenham Press Ltd., Fakenham, Norfolk.

Contents

List of Tables

Introductory Notes

The book is designed to help newcomers to gardening and amateur gardeners and is in two parts for ease of reference.

Part One is divided into eleven chapters. The first three chapters deal with Site and Soil, Propagation and Plant Care, and could usefully be read by beginners before practical gardening is attempted. The following six chapters discuss specific areas of gardening, viz. Greenhouses, Frames and Cloches; Flowers and Foliage; Fruit; Trees, Shrubs and Climbers; Turf, and Vegetables and Herbs. Thus all the information relevant to a specific branch of gardening can be found in one chapter. The chapters on Problems and on Tools and Equipment are most likely to be referred to when looking for information on a particular point. For this reason, and so that individual items in the earlier chapters can also be easily found, each chapter is arranged in alphabetical order.

An important feature of Part One is the use of tables to present information, and a List of Tables can be found on page vii.

Part Two, also arranged alphabetically, provides an extensive index of gardening terms with self-explanatory definitions and also a useful cross-reference system which directs the reader to more detailed information in Part One.

Part One

Chapter 1. Site and Soil

Acidify Certain plants, such as primulas and rhododendrons grow best in acid soils or potting composts.

Chalk or alkaline soils can be made suitable for these plants by incorporating finely divided flowers of sulphur at the rate of 280 g/m² (8 oz/sq yd). This should lower the pH level from 7.5 to 6.5 on medium soils, but an increase of up to one-third extra may be needed on heavy ground. Great or small amounts of sulphur can be given according to climate, soil type and plants being grown.

Potting composts can be made suitable for acid loving plants by omitting ground limestone from the mixtures.

Some proprietary composts are available which are suitable for acid loving plants or have the chemicals ready to mix as necessary.

Aeration The lack of air or oxygen in soils, composts and even in ponds is detrimental to plant growth.

Digging, forking and cultivation help to reduce compaction, break up any hard pan and let air into soils. Submerged aquatic plants, such as elodea in ponds and pools, release bubbles of oxygen in sunlight to aerate the water in which they grow. Fountains or jets of water playing on garden pools also have an aerating effect. Good aeration is necessary for fish to survive.

Turf which has become compacted through the use of rollers and heavy wear can be spiked or forked to loosen the ground and let in the air. *See* Chapter 8, Turf.

Aggregate culture This practice involves growing plants in a soilless rooting medium consisting of one or more of the following materials: gravel, peat, perlite, sand and vermiculite.

Although many gardeners use soilless seed, cutting and potting composts, few only practise aggregate culture. It consists of providing bitumen-lined tanks having 150–250 mm (6–10 in) depth of aggregate and of a convenient area. The plants are watered with dilute nutrient solution, either from surface level just above the aggregate or by sub-irrigation from below.

Proprietary ready-made nutrient mixtures are most convenient and need no elaborate preparation beyond measuring out and dissolving in water to the correct dilution.

Aspect When selecting suitable plants for any site, it is necessary to consider which compass direction it faces and the slope of the land. Sunny, south-facing slopes are quick to warm up in spring, producing the earliest crops whereas ground with a northerly aspect is cool,

1 Aspect. South-facing walls receive much more sunlight than those with an easterly or westerly aspect, which are shaded in the evening, *as here*, or in the morning.

3

often shaded, and plants are late to come into bearing. Sites which slope in easterly or westerly directions are intermediate in character, but cold east winds often damage tender shoots in spring.

Banks *See* Grading and levelling, this chapter.

Boundary The treatment of the meeting point between areas, levels or surfaces is an important consideration of garden layout and design.

Two main types of division which occur in gardens are physical barriers such as hedges or fences and visual divisions like timber and kerb edgings between lawns and paths, or flower beds with, say, low box hedge surrounds. Steps, terraces, and retaining walls are also forms of boundary between surfaces of different levels.

Any method of treatment should be practical, require little attention and be in keeping with the character of house, garden and surroundings. The use of screens, walling or trees to deflect or filter wind can considerably increase the range of plants which can be grown in a garden.

Clay burning This consists of heating or baking clay over a slow-burning fire until it becomes granular, hard and crumbles easily. It can then be scattered over the ground. This can be carried out by placing clay on a sheet of corrugated iron over a fire. Another method that is sometimes used is to place a 75–100 mm (3–4 in) thick layer of clay over a slow-burning bonfire leaving air holes at the top and bottom. Clay, once burnt, loses its sticky qualities and when re-wetted behaves like grit, sand or brick dust.

Climate This is the cumulative effect of weather at any specific place and exerts a powerful influence over plant growth.

The regional differences of temperature between northern and southern districts account for the variation in

hardiness and type of plants encountered in the respective areas. Plants which are considered hardy in the South, may not be so in the North.

Rainfall also affects the suitability of plants for various areas. Plums and blackcurrants, which prefer moist conditions, are best suited to wet, western districts, in the U.K. Dessert apples and pears which grow best in warm, sunny low-rainfall areas are more suitable for the southern and eastern regions of Britain than western.

Compost In order to maintain and improve soil fertility, considerable quantities of manure and compost need to be added to soil quite frequently.

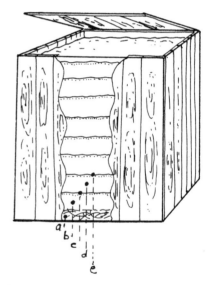

2 Compost – garden. The method of making compost in layers in a timber bin with the front cut away for east of viewing, is shown here: (*a*) coarse material (*b*) vegetable waste (*c*) manure OR sulphate of ammonia (*d*) as (*b*) (*e*) ground limestone.

Garden compost, so named to distinguish it from the potting type, is a manure substitute, obtained from the decomposition of plant remains. In gardens, compost can be made in ventilated boxes or bins. One practical way to make compost is to use a bin about 900 mm (3 ft) in diameter, or square and of similar height. Clean straw, leaves and non-woody plant remains (but excluding noxious weeds like docks or any diseased material) are stacked in layers alternating with activator and ground limestone.

To fill the container place a 50 mm (2 in) layer of rough, twiggy, or coarse material like bean haulm at at the bottom, followed by a 150 mm (6 in) layer of chopped, wet, plant remains. Scatter 200 g/m² (6 oz/sq yd) of sulphate of ammonia or proprietary activator over this layer. Spread another 150 mm (6 in) layer of wet leaves and remains over the first, watering as necessary to wet the mixture. Then evenly scatter ground limestone over this layer at the same rate as the fertiliser. Repeat the process with similar layers of vegetable matter, applying sulphate of ammonia (or activator) and ground limestone alternately after each 150 mm (6 in) layer, until the bin is filled. Water the compost as filling proceeds; finally cover the complete bin with plastic or a lid to keep the mixture moist and warm to speed up decomposition.

When the material has decomposed into a dark brown crumbly, sweet smelling mass, it is then ready for use.

Compost, potting The best known mixtures are the John Innes composts which consist of the following ingredients.

Seed and cutting compost. Composition parts by bulk: 2 of sterilised loam, 1 of horticultural peat which should be moist and granular, not dusty, and 1 of clean grit sand. To this mixture is added 20 g (¾ oz) of ground limestone, and 40 g (1½ oz) of calcium superphosphate per 36 litres (8 gal)

Potting compost. Composition by bulk: 7 of sterilised loam, 3 of horticultural peat and 2 of sharp sand. To each 36 litres (8 gal) of this mixture is added 112 g (4 oz) of John Innes base fertiliser, for No 1 Potting compost. Double or treble this amount is added to make John Innes Potting compost No 2 and No 3 respectively. John Innes base fertiliser, which is usually purchased in ready-made form, contains approximately 5% Nitrogen, 7% Phosphate, and 10% Potash.

Soilless compost. This can consist of peat with sand, or other material such as perlite or vermiculite, in varying proportions, plus balanced base fertiliser with added trace elements.

Charcoal. Fine grades of this can be added to seed and potting composts to prevent acidity, particularly where these are used for slow-growing plants. Add charcoal to compost in the ratio of 1 :20 by bulk.

The complete range of John Innes composts can be obtained ready for use as can the many soilless mixtures. These ready-mixed packs are most convenient where time and space are strictly limited.

Where composts are made at home, one or two points should be observed. When mixing two or more ingredients together, their moisture contents should be similar. Spread out the ingredients, preferably in shallow rectangular layers on a clean disinfected surface. Turn the mixture at least three times, using a spade or shovel first in one direction, then back, then returning to the first position.

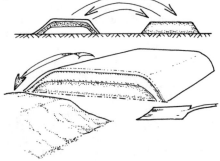

3 Compost – potting. Spread the ingredients, such as loam, peat, sand with fertiliser in layers before turning and mixing three times *as shown. Top*: this is side view. *Centre*: making the first turn.

Compound fertiliser *See* Fertiliser, this chapter.

Colour The colour of soil and surroundings is important for plant growth and development.

Darkening the soil with well-weathered soot from domestic chimneys has been shown to benefit early crops in various ways. Black or dark soils warm up more rapidly with sun heat than those that are white or light coloured, and can be 1–2°C (2–4°F) warmer.

Greenhouse indoor walls, supports and glazing bars as well as frames, should ideally be painted white for maximum reflection of light.

Cultivation Operations necessary for good soil management and which are carried out in gardens, are given below in alphabetical order.

Bastard trenching See Double Digging, below.

Cultivating This consists of breaking down the ground after winter digging, for example, using a three or five-prong cultivator. The method of use is a steady downward chopping and combing movement, drawing the curved tines through the soil towards the operator. This is also effective for loosening compacted ground, for breaking down soil ridges in spring and clearing ground of weeds.

Digging This is still one of the best and most beneficial operations in gardens, in spite of mechanisation. It provides a good opportunity for working in well-rotted manure, garden compost and peat or similar. There are several recognised variations of this process, each suited to the various conditions.

Double digging. This should be carried out ideally when starting on a new site and subsequently every third year. Excavate a trench about 250 mm (10 in) minimum depth and twice as wide, placing the excavated soil at one end to fill the last trench. Place a layer of organic matter in the trench and fork this in to a similar depth as the trench.

Repeat this process, and throw the soil from the second trench to fill up the first, inverting the soil as work proceeds. This operation is repeated until the area is double dug.

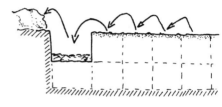

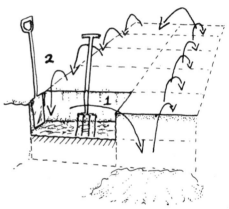

4 Cultivation. Double digging involves excavating a trench, manuring and forking the bottom. Repeat this process, throwing the soil from the second trench into the first and subsequently *as shown by the arrows.*

Single digging is carried out in a similar manner, but the second spit – spade depth – is left undisturbed.

Ridging. This consists of throwing the soil up into ridges in autumn. The aim is to expose as much soil surface area, of clay soils in particular, as is possible to the frost, snow and wind which will break up the soil. Dig out an area of soil 600 mm × 600 mm (2 ft × 2 ft) for a start to a spit depth, placing the excavated material where it can conveniently be used to fill the last section of trench. Working backwards, 600 mm (2 ft) at a time and in a similar width, throw the soil up into a ridge, incorporating manure and burying any weeds in the bottom. Repeat this process until the area being ridged is completed.

6 Cultivation. Trenching is similar to double digging, but is carried out in narrow strips, usually for one or two rows of crops, such as runner beans.

5 Cultivation. Ridging consists of throwing the soil up into long narrow ridges for frost to break down into a fine condition.

Trenching. This forms an important part in the successful growing of sweet peas, runner beans and celery, for example, and is another task for the spade. Trenching is basically similar to double digging, except that the trench is only half filled in during autumn digging. Winter weather breaks down the soil ready for sowing or planting after forking and/or cultivating in the spring.

Forking On stony and sometimes heavy soils, a digging fork is preferable to a spade, especially for spring preparation. This tool is excellent for incorporating manure into the bottom of trenches and for loosening or breaking down the ground in spring. A fork is ideal for digging out weeds by the roots, especially where the soil is dry.

Hoeing Hoeing is basically a means of chopping or cutting the tops off seedling

weeds, loosening compacted soil, and creating a dust mulch to conserve moisture.

Several types of hoe are available, each one suitable for particular purposes.

The Dutch or push hoe is used with a push and pull action, with the operator moving backwards.

The draw hoe has a blade at right angles to the handle and is used with a chopping action. The user moves forwards over the loosened soil. This hoe is used for taking out drills before sowing crops such as beetroot and peas. Both this and the heavier Canterbury hoe, which is used similarly, are suitable for use on heavy land.

Ploughing This consists of inverting furrows of soil, burying weeds and manure in the process, usually with a tractor.

Raking This operation is carried out with various patterns of rake for specific purposes.

Iron and stainless steel rakes used on soil are handled comb-fashion, back and forwards. This serves to break down soil lumps, create a fine tilth, level out minor undulations and work in fertilisers.

Wire rakes are best suited for use on turf,

7

for aeration, scarification and leaf gathering.

Rotary cultivation is essentially a mechanised operation and consists of shattering and pulverising the soil with rotor tines, usually in spring for seed bed or planting operations.

Drainage An important requirement for successful gardening. In fertile well-drained land, surplus water which is disposed of by drainage is termed gravitational. The moisture then left in the soil and of use to plants, is termed capillary moisture. The aim of draining land is to remove gravitational water, which would otherwise occupy the spaces between soil particles and exclude air. Air and water are both needed for good growth, healthy plants and fertile soil. Land which is waterlogged for any length of time quickly becomes infertile.

There are many ways of draining land, but the most commonly used methods in gardens are the sump and drainage pipes together with good cultivations.

A sump or catchpit is usually adequate for average purposes in gardens not exceeding 6 m × 6 m (20 ft × 20 ft). This consists of excavating a hole of 1.5 m (5 ft) minimum depth by 1 m square, and

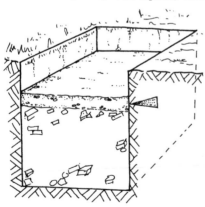

7 Drainage sump. In small gardens, a hole filled with clean brick rubble or stone with a thin layer of fine gravel, *arrowed*, and covered with good soil, works well.

filling this with clean builders' rubble to within 300 mm (12 in) of the top. Cover the rubble finally with a layer of top soil over a thin scattering of fine gravel, to prevent soil being washed into the sump. A drainage pit should preferably be sited at the lowest point in a garden to be effective.

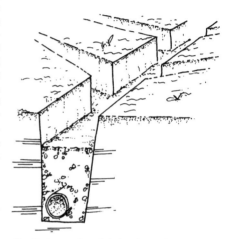

8 Drainage. Land drains in earthenware or plastic, laid herring-bone fashion in a bed of clean shingle. The best method for large areas.

Drainage by land pipes is the usual method of water disposal on larger areas. This consists of providing a herring-bone network of 100 mm (4 in) porous or 50 mm (2 in) plastic pipes at a depth of about 450 mm (18 in) in the ground, with 3 m (10 ft) or so between each row. The drains should have a minimum gradient or slope of 1:100, rising from a suitable outfall or main drain. The outlet should be sited at the lowest point for successful water disposal. The effectiveness of drain pipes can be increased by laying them in a 150 mm (6 in) layer of washed gravel before covering them with top soil.

Drainage of cold air This is another type of drainage problem. In late spring, sharp frosts often occur on clear nights

8

after a warm day. Cold or freezing air is heavier than warm, and behaves like water, filling up any depressions, or covering low-lying ground. Gardens which are completely surrounded by walls or thick impenetrable hedges can fill up with a layer of freezing air. This continues to build up during the night unless an opening is available for the cold air to drain away to lower ground. This downward movement of cold air can often be seen rolling down hillsides on spring nights and is referred to as a katabatic wind. The need for air drainage is most important where the blossoms of fruit trees can be damaged. Avoid having completely walled or fenced in fruit gardens.

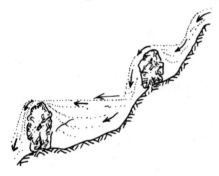

9 Katabatic wind. The waterlike movement of cold air down a hill, filling in hollow pockets, is a common occurrence on clear nights in spring.

Dressing The application of manures and fertilisers in a solid state to soils and potting composts is described as a dressing. Fertilisers which are dissolved in water and given to plants, are referred to as liquid feed. Two main types of dressing are recognised: base, and top or side.

Base dressings These include bulky manures, peat (or similar), as well as slow-acting fertilisers like bone meal and shoddy. Base dressings are usually applied during autumn and winter when the land is being dug or prepared well in advance of planting. This type of appli-

cation should be thoroughly mixed and incorporated with the soil, unlike top dressings which are spread on the surface. Base dressings perform two main functions: they maintain and improve the physical condition of clay and sandy soils as well as loam; they also provide necessary plant foods to sustain plants and soil bacteria. See Table of Fertilisers, this chapter, for list of materials used as base dressings.

Top or side dressings are so termed because they are applied to the soil surface beside the stem or crown of plants. Fertilisers such as Nitro-chalk which are used as top dressings are quick-acting stimulants and are applied during the growing season. A list of materials used for top-dressing purposes is given in the Table of Fertilisers.

See also Mulches, this chapter.

Earthing up This consists of drawing loose soil around the stems and roots of garden crops, such as celery, leeks and potatoes. It serves a number of purposes: extra earth around plant stems provides additional support from wind with crops such as kale and sweet corn; with leeks and celery, the exclusion of light ensures that the stems are suitably blanched, as well as giving extra protection in severe weather; in the case of

10 Earthing up. Fine soil is drawn from between rows of potatoes, *as here*, and worked around the plants in ridges or mounds.

potatoes, the extra covering of soil ensures that the developing tubers are prevented from turning green which occurs if they are exposed to light. Before earthing up, carefully fork over the space between rows, breaking up and stirring the ground. Use a draw hoe to work the freshly-loosened soil into a ridge or mound around the plant, taking care not to damage roots or stems.

Feeding One of the most common causes of lack of growth in plants is starvation, but overfeeding can also produce a similar effect. On average soils, which receive manure or compost in two years out of three only the main elements need be added for balanced nutrition. These are nitrogen, phosphorous in the form of phosphate, and potassium or potash. They are normally supplied in base fertilisers.

Nitrogen is present in all plant cells and a deficiency results in pale foliage and stunted growth with many small flowers and fruits. An excess produces lush, disease-prone growth with very few flowers, and the fruits are of poor colour.

Phosphorous promotes root formation and early cropping. Both excess and deficiency result in poor growth.

Potash is essential for the efficient working of the leaves and plant health generally, giving added hardiness. This element corrects the balance of excess nitrogen and improves the colour and flavour in flower and food crops. A deficiency often results in a form of scorching or browning around leaf margins. An excess of potash produces very hard and stunted growth.

In addition to the three major macro elements, crops also require boron, calcium, iron, magnesium, manganese, sulphur and others. These are usually referred to as trace elements because they are needed in very small quantities. Calcium is either present in chalk soils or supplied by lime additions. Applications of manure provide sufficient trace elements for most crops grown in soil.

However in aggregate culture trace element deficiencies have to be made good, usually in the form of proprietary trace element supplements.

Top dressing and liquid feeding are carried out during the growing season to replenish elements removed by the crops to ensure steady and continued growth and to prevent starvation. Liquid fertiliser can be applied to or through the roots, as in liquid feeding, or sprayed onto plant leaves, as in foliar feeding.

Fertility The maintenance and improvement of soil fertility involves satisfying individual plant needs for water, air, warmth, food, depth of soil, and freedom from plant poisons.

Fertilisers These are classified into various groups according to their nature and composition. Two main types are organic fertilisers, such as hoof or fish meal, and inorganic fertilisers like sulphate of potash.

Organic materials are obtained from the remains of living matter, animal and vegetable. These are often rather slower acting, but are believed by some people to have rather special qualities. These are frequently much more costly than inorganic fertilisers.

Inorganic fertilisers are obtained either as a result of some factory or chemical process, such as with sulphate of ammonia, or by the crushing of mineral rocks as with some phosphates. These materials are usually treated with acids or some other substance first.

Three other divisions are made as follows: complete or balanced fertilisers; compound or mixed, and straight fertilisers, all of which can consist of either organic or inorganic materials.

Complete or balanced fertilisers supply all the major essential elements, such as nitrogen, phosphorous and potassium, required by the plants. Complete fertilisers also contain essential trace or micro-elements, such as manganese and boron.

Compound fertilisers supply two or more essential elements.
Straight fertilisers supply only one.

Compound or straight fertilisers are particularly useful for top dressing to remedy some deficiency. Extra nitrogen for increased growth, or additional potash to balance excess nitrogen, are examples of how they can be used to advantage. Compound or straight fertilisers can be used to make up mixtures for any purpose or soil.

Grading and levelling These two important operations are normally encountered when making or remodelling a garden. Grading is the process of moving top and subsoil as necessary to the desired land form of gradients and contours. Levelling is the process of determining and marking out, usually by means of pegs, the vertical points to which soil, drains, paths and such like shall be placed. In the normal sequence of events where ground levels need to be changed, levelling precedes grading.

Grading In average gardens, as distinct from large scale operations where other considerations may apply, there are three important points to observe, among others. Where, for example, sloping ground is being terraced the amount of material to be moved needs to be kept to a minimum. Secondly, top soil should be kept separate from subsoil, and, finally, the top soil should be evenly distributed over the ground after the subsoil has been graded. Due attention should be given to the drainage of surface as well as soil water. To keep the amount of earth-moving to a minimum, the cut-and-fill method is sound practice where conditions allow. This consists, for example, of fixing a final surface level at roughly half-way up a slope. Excavated material above the level is used as 'fill' to raise the low ground. Keeping the top soil separate, one of the first tasks is to remove and stack this in a convenient place. Grade or move subsoils to the desired levels, consolidating filled or raised areas. Fork or loosen

Table of Fertilisers

Name	Use	Type	Complete	Compound or Mixture	Straight	Elements Supplied
Blood, Fish and Bone Compound	B	O	✓	—	—	NPK
Bone Meal	B	O	—	✓	—	NP
Dried Blood	TL	O	—	—	✓	N
John Innes Base	B	O/I	✓	—	—	NPK
Hoof and Horn	B	O	—	—	✓	N
Muriate of potash	B	I	—	—	✓	K
Nitrate of soda	TL	I	—	—	✓	N
Nitro-chalk	TL	I	—	—	✓	N
Proprietary complete	B	O/I	✓	—	—	NPK
Sulphate of ammonia	BTL	I	—	—	✓	N
Sulphate of iron	B	I	—	—	✓	Fe
Sulphate of magnesia	BL	I	—	—	✓	Mg
Sulphate of potash	BTL	I	—	—	✓	K
Superphosphate	BTL	I	—	—	✓	P

Key to type		Key to elements		Key to use	
O	Organic	N	Nitrogen	B	Base dressing
I	Inorganic	P	Phosphorous	T	Top dressing
O/I	Combined	K	Potassium	L	Liquid feed
		Fe	Iron		
		Mg	Magnesium		

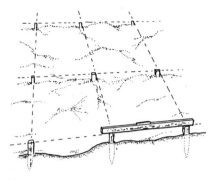

11 Levelling. When making a lawn, the high spots and hollows of the ground can easily be seen with the aid of some pegs, a straight edge and spirit level.

severely compacted subsoil, before spreading top soil over the area.

Levelling In most gardens this is restricted to working to existing levels, such as buildings, drives and roadways. In small gardens, levelling often consists of working with a spirit level, a 2 m (6½ ft) long straight edge, pencil, hammer and pegs. Starting at the highest fixed point, hammer in one peg and another about 2 m (6½ ft) away down the slope. Place the straight edge between the peg tops, and hammer in the second peg as necessary until the level is true, as checked with a spirit level. The difference in height between the existing soil surface and the top of the second peg is the change of level. More pegs are driven into the soil, 2 m (6½ ft) apart, in a straight line to the bottom of the incline. The height between each set of pegs is the difference of levels. When levelling an area differences are measured across a slope as well as down. When differences between the highest and lowest points are established, then the halfway level for cut-and-fill grading can be fixed. When levelling, it is necessary to allow a slight even fall of 1:60 to 1:100 for drainage purposes after grading the ground to its finished or surface level. Avoid inclines steeper than 1:4 for ease of maintenance.

Liming It is probably true to say that the majority of garden plants can grow well on slightly acid ground with a pH level of 6.5. Without the occasional addition of lime or calcium compounds, however, some soils would become excessively acid, infertile and deficient in calcium.

It is necessary to test soils before liming because an excess can also cause problems. The soil pH level, which is an indicator of the degree of acidity or alkalinity, can be measured in one of the following ways: by using a simple DIY soil test kit; by means of an electronic pH meter or by having the soil tested in a laboratory.

The amount of lime which should be applied depends on the crops to be grown, the degree of acidity and soil type

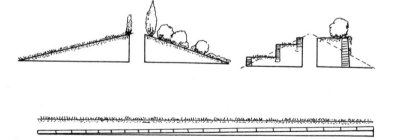

12 Gradient. Some critical levels or slopes for garden purposes. *Left to right*: mown grass, 1:4 maximum; planted banks are usually stable between 1:4 and 1:3; terracing and retaining walls are best where slopes are steeper than 1:3. *Bottom*: drains need a minimum slope of 1:60 to 1:100.

ing of loam stacks is becoming less frequent. Also, good quality loam is now a scarce commodity. Stack 50 mm (2 in) thick wet turves, preferably cut in spring, upside down in heaps. Apply a turf-thick layer of manure, if possible, between every three layers of loam. Where the soil is acid, alternate the manure with ground limestone, which is applied at the rate of 130 g/m² (4 oz/sq yd). The loam should be ready for use six to eight months later.

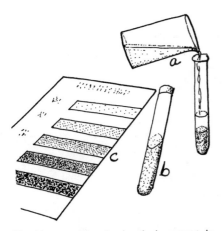

13 Lime testing. A chemical reagent is added to soil (*a*) and the resulting colour of the solution (*b*) is compared against a colour chart (*c*) by which the pH level can be determined.

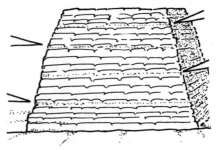

14 Loam stack. Wet turves are inverted and neatly stacked, and layers of manure are added, *arrowed left*. Add ground limestone to acid soils at intervals, *arrowed right*, as stacking progresses.

and the form of lime which is used.

Assuming a pH level of 5.5 in an average soil, then apply about 1 kg (2.2 lb) of ground limestone to 4 m² (4½ sq yd) to raise the pH to 6.5. Increase the rate by about one-third for clay soils. Lime is usually best applied to vacant land during autumn or winter. Calcium compounds react adversely with nitrogenous manures and fertilisers, and ideally should not be applied at the same time. Allow if possible a minimum lapse of 7–10 days between manuring and liming and between liming and applying fertiliser.

Lime can be applied as ground limestone, hydrated lime or burnt lime, but for practical purposes, ground limestone is by far the safest of these forms to use. Burnt lime is caustic and unpleasant to handle, and hydrated lime is intermediate between the two. With regard to calcium content, ground limestone contains about three-quarters the amount found in hydrated lime, or half that in burnt lime.

Loam stacking With the easy availability of ready-mixed compost, the mak-

Manuring The application of bulky organic material to soils is necessary to maintain and improve fertility. These dressings serve to open up and aerate clay soils, and improve the water-holding capacity of medium and light sandy loams. Soil bacteria feed on and break down organic matter to release plant food and dispose of harmful substances in the ground. There are various kinds of manures, as well as materials that are used as substitutes. Manures are usually best applied in autumn or winter, when they can be incorporated into the soil at the same time as digging. Manures should be well rotted otherwise they may cause a temporary shortage of nitrogen due to bacterial action on fresh material, unless extra fertiliser is added. Some crops such as peas, beans and onions need generous manuring, others

13

Table of Manures and Organic Substitutes

Name	Remarks
Compost	Variable quality depending on origin
Cow	Cold; better for sandy than clay soils
Guano	Concentrated; keep dry until used as a top dressing
Hop	A flaky by-product of brewing; tends to blow about; low feeding value
Horse	A hot manure; good for hot beds, heavy soils and mushrooms
Mushroom casing	A mixture of manure, chalk and peat; sometimes rather alkaline
Peat	Partially decomposed moss or sedge; slow to break down; little feeding value
Pig	Similar to cow manure
Poultry	Concentrated; keep dry to avoid loss of nitrogen, until used as top or base dressing
Pulverised tree bark	Fibrous; slow decomposing; low food value
Sewage sludge	Variable; avoid mineral contaminated sludge; best composted with straw before use
Sheep	Droppings are sometimes used to make liquid feed
Shoddy	Wool clippings; slowly decomposing; contains some nitrogen

such as parsnips and carrots need less for best results. The amount of manure needed for an area of ground varies according to crop, the fertility of the soil and its nature. A useful dressing is between one and two bucketsful (18–36 litres or 4–8 gal) of manure per m² (1¼ sq yd)

Manuring, green Also known as sheet composting, this practice consists of sowing mustard, Italian ryegrass or other seeds on vacant ground and digging in the resultant crop of foliage. Prepare the ground thoroughly, as for a seed bed, finally raking the soil down to a fine tilth. Sow the seeds fairly thickly at the rate of 35 g/m² (1 oz/sq yd), scattering them thinly on well-moistened soil. Lightly rake, and gently firm the seeds in. When the resultant seedlings are 150–200 mm (8–10 in) tall scatter sulphate of ammonia or nitrate of soda at the rate of 35 g/m² (1 oz/sq yd) before digging them in. The added fertiliser assists rapid decomposition of the compost material and prevents nitrogen starvation of the soil. This practice can be useful where manure is scarce and land can be spared for this purpose.

Marling This practice is occasionally carried out in autumn, on light sandy soils overlying natural marl. The usual method consists of excavating a trench to expose the underlying material, which is then dug out and thinly scattered over the top soil. This dressing is allowed to weather during winter and become mixed in. Avoid heavy applications at any one time or the land can be difficult to handle and work. Marl consists of a mixture of chalk and clay which improves the condition of sandy soils. Dried and powdered marl is sometimes very thinly scattered on sandy turf to help bind the soil. This practice is more usually applied to sports turf than private lawns.

Mulching This consists of placing a shallow 25–50 mm (1–2 in) layer of peat, manure or compost around the stems of plants on the soil surface. The main aims of providing a mulch are to prevent soil from drying out rapidly, to smother weed seedlings and to conserve moisture.

Water the ground well if necessary before applying the surface dressing, which is usually given in spring.

Riddling Also referred to as screening or sieving, this consists of rubbing and

14

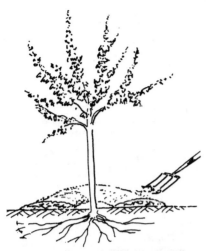

15 Mulching. This consists of spreading a thin layer of peat or similar material on the soil surface in a circle around plants. This conserves moisture and can be a convenient way of feeding.

sifting soil, peat or grit through riddles or sieves which have openings of various sizes depending on the purpose in hand. Soil for seed compost is passed through a wire mesh screen with 5–6 cm (3/16–¼ in) openings. Soil particles for final potting can be 12 mm (½ in) or less in diameter. Peat riddlings, which can be used for roughage in the bottoms of pots or boxes for drainage, are the coarse particles that have not passed through a riddle.

Rotary Cultivation *See* cultivation, this chapter.

Siting Considerable attention is usually paid to positioning tender plants out of the direct path of cold or prevailing winds. However, not always sufficient thought is given to siting plants, or buildings, in the best place to make maximum use of sunlight or shade. A number of points are worth noting.

Greenhouses which are used for raising plants during the winter months are best sited from east to west, but those used for summer crops only are better run from north to south.

Seedlings in winter need to be placed close to the glass for maximum light, but care needs to be taken to protect them from being chilled or frozen on frosty nights.

Winter vegetables are ideally situated in sunny south-facing positions.

In summer, rows of vegetables are usually best run from north to south, unless the area is heavily shaded by building or some other considerations apply.

Spring-flowering wall plants are often best sited on a south or west-facing aspect. North-facing walls are usually too shaded for winter and spring flowering plants as well as being cold.

East-facing walls are often exposed to freezing and chilling winds which can be very damaging to tender blossoms.

One important and sometimes overlooked point is that often tender, choice plants can survive when grown against a wall, where otherwise they would perish outdoors.

Soil classification Soils types are grouped together in various ways for a variety of purposes. Colour, climate, mineral content, drainage, the kind of vegetation carried, depth and other factors all enter into consideration. However, gardening is essentially a practical occupation, and a comparatively straightforward system based on fairly obvious features is recognised. There are five fairly distinct divisions with various intermediate stages. The five extreme and basic types are clays; sands and gravels; peat, moss or fen soils; chalk and limestone, and loam.

Clay soils are referred to as heavy, in recognition of the effort needed to cultivate them, especially when very wet or dry. These soils are sticky and glue-like with a smooth, pasty consistency when wet, they are impervious, holding rain water and draining slowly. In dry conditions they shrink, forming wide

16 Clay and Sandy Soils. The soil in the pot, *left*, contains a high proportion of clay, making it impervious and preventing free drainage, unlike the sandy mixture, *right*.

cracks in the ground and set rock hard. When well managed and drained, clay soils are very productive, being naturally rich in nutrients.

Sand and gravels are described as light soils, because of the comparative ease with which they can be worked under most conditions. These soils are usually free-draining, feel gritty and do not stick to tools or feet when wet as is the problem with clay.

Peat or fen soils also termed moss soils, are dark, fibrous and spongy when wet and sometimes dusty when dry.

Chalk and limestone soils are characteristically light or whitish coloured with increasing lumps of chalk or limestone as one digs towards the underlying subsoil. This type of land is usually neutral or alkaline with a pH of 7 or over.

Loams are intermediate in behaviour between clay and sandy soils, contain organic matter and are fertile. Heavy loams contain more clay and light loams contain more sand than medium loams.

Soil preparation The operations necessary to prepare the ground for any crop have certain basic similarities, but differ in detail to suit individual plant needs. The practical approach follows the sequence given below:

Weed clearing and disposal of rubbish.

Levelling and grading to desired contours.

Drainage of both soil and surface water, not forgetting air drainage.

Sub-soiling to aerate the lower levels.

Digging, manuring and soil improvement.

Liming and fertilising.

Cultivations to break down soil lumps and create a tilth before sowing and planting. The specific requirements of groups or individual plants are given in the relevant chapters. The aim of these various tasks is to eliminate or reduce any limiting factors to negligible proportions. The main requirements for growth are correct levels of temperature, moisture, air, light, food, space and freedom from poison or pollution: the elimination of weeds allows light and air to circulate, reduces competition for water, food and space as well as disposing of possible sources of pests and diseases; levelling, grading and drainage

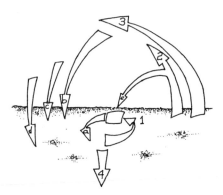

17 Plant food cycle. Soils lose and gain plant foods as follows. Losses: (1) by soil bacteria; (2) removed in crops; (3) nitrogen lost as gas into the air; (4) in soil drainage. Gains: (*a*) from bacteria; (*b*) nitrogen from the air; (*c*) given as manure; (*d*) supplied as fertiliser; (*e*) return of crop residues.

Table of Soil Types

Soils	Remarks
Clay	Slow draining, glutinous and heavy to work when wet, with smooth, greasy consistency. Shrink on drying, becoming iron hard. When well handled are rich and fertile but crops inclined to be late maturing.
Sand and Gravel	Quick draining, easy to handle, gritty to the touch, hungry, poor soils, inclined to be acid, needing feeding and liming. These, correctly handled, produce early-maturing crops.
Peat and Fen	These are dark and spongy when wet, containing much fibre, and are inclined to be dusty when dry. When carefully managed can be extremely productive.
Chalk and Limestone	Light or whitish coloured soils, containing lumps of chalk and limestone near the subsoil. Gritty or pasty when wet. Neutral or alkaline reaction with pH of 7 or over. These tend to be short of organic matter and need generous manuring. Excellent for members of the cabbage family.
Loam, light	Fertile soil, inclined to be sandy in texture. First class for carrots and parsnips.
Loam, medium	Average, medium texture, drains well, very fertile, producing excellent crops. Suits most kinds of garden plants.
Loam, heavy	Inclined to be slow draining, but fertile, containing more clay than other loams. Excellent for roses.

help to ensure a better balance of soil, air and moisture and coupled with cultivations ensure a greater soil depth for roots. Where crops have a good depth of soil, plants are better able to resist drought.

Sub-soiling In gardens this involves breaking up and loosening the earth or soil in the second spit at a depth of 25–50 cm (10–20 in). Double digging and ridging (*see* Cultivation, above) achieve this effect which is necessary for deep rooted crops, especially on shallow soils.

Chapter 2. Propagation

Aerial layering This is a method of not only increasing plants, but of producing well furnished plants more quickly than from, for example, seeds. Select a strong healthy tip or shoot about 450 mm (18 in) in length. Remove one or two leaves 250–300 mm (10–12 in) from the tip, and here make a slanting cut about half way through the stem with a sharp, clean knife. Encircle the stem at this point with damp, chopped sphagnum moss, enclosing this in a sleeve of plastic which is tied above and below the cut area. Support the tip with a cane or stick. Keep the plant warm and moist, syringing overhead occasionally. When roots appear in the moss, sever the parent stem just below the sleeve, which is carefully removed. Pot up the rooted layer in, for example, John Innes potting compost, keeping it warm, moist and shaded from strong sun until established. *Ficus decora*, better known as Rubber plant, is occasionally increased in this manner when specimens have grown too tall to house or when more plants are required.

Alpines Raised from seed, *see* Seed propagation, this chapter; raised vegetatively, *see* Vegetative propagation, this chapter.

Annuals *See* Seed propagation, this chapter.

Apical cutting A rather specialised way of propagating plants, also known as meristem culture. The cuttings consist of small pieces of cell tissue from the growing point or tip, some being only the length of a few cells in thickness. These small cuttings are grown in glass flasks or containers which have been well disinfected and grown on special culture solution. This method is carried out mainly with high-value crops like orchids, and then mostly to build up numbers of plants quickly as is necessary with new varieties. This is a 'laboratory' way of raising plants, presently carried out only by highly-trained staff.

Axillary cutting A growth or shoot which has originated from a leaf axil and can be prepared in various ways. *See* Cuttings, this chapter.

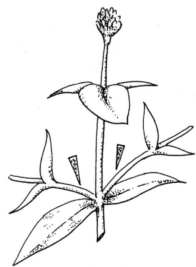

18 Axils. Two axillary shoots, *arrowed*, growing from the axils, the angles between leaf stalks and stem.

Base cutting Growths or shoots which have developed at or near soil level can be taken. These can be prepared in various ways, but are most commonly taken and trimmed as softwood cuttings. *See* Cuttings, this chapter.

Bedding plants These are raised mainly from seeds and softwood cuttings. This group of plants comprises hardy and half-hardy subjects. *See* Seed propagation and Cuttings, this chapter.

Bench heating *See* Mist propagation, this chapter.

Biennials *See* Seed propagation, this chapter.

Budding A method of raising plants which would not always be satisfactory when grown on their own roots. The success of this practice depends on uniting a bud graft with a suitable rootstock, the bud forming the scion.

This method of propagation has only limited appeal to amateurs because of the time required, and the difficulty of obtaining suitable root stocks. The essence of the technique is to insert a healthy, plump bud in a T-shaped cut, under the rind of an actively-growing rootstock during July and August. Obtaining a good bud consists of selecting a healthy pencil thick shoot of desired variety; removing a good bud by cutting about 12 mm ($\frac{1}{2}$ in) below it and

sliding the knife blade under the rind, behind the bud, coming out about 12 mm ($\frac{1}{2}$ in) above. A T-shaped cut is made in the rind of a pencil-thick rootstock. The prepared bud, with a short length of leaf stalk attached, is slid under the two flaps of rind which are carefully lifted in readiness to receive it. Bind the bud firmly in position using either budding/grafting tape or raffia. Under favourable conditions the bud should 'take', i.e. become united with the rootstock, in about three to four weeks.

Plants commonly propagated by budding include roses, apples, pears, plums, cherries, peaches, and various ornamental trees.

Buildings In addition to greenhouses and frame structures, many really keen gardeners have a potting shed. This serves as a soil and pot store as well as accommodation for seed sowing and pricking out. A form of building or structure which is becoming more widespread is a growing room. This consists of a heated and well insulated compartment which is internally lit with fluorescent tubes instead of natural sunlight.

Bulbs Plants which produce bulbs and corms (q.v. below, this chapter) can be increased by natural or assisted means.

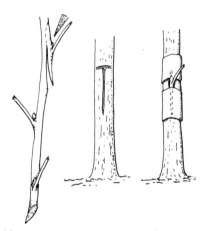

19   Budding. A bud, *arrowed*, is cut from a piece of scion wood and carefully slid behind the flaps of bark of the T-cut, *centre*. *Right*: the bud is held in place and kept moist with grafting tape.

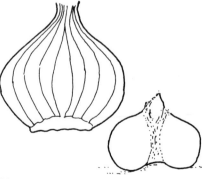

20   Bulb and corm. *Above*, a bulb cut in half to show the layers of scales, unlike the corm, *below*.

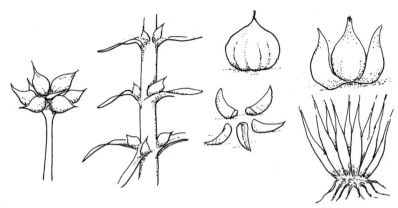

21 Bulbs, natural increase. *Left to right*: bulbils on a stem; lily bulbils in leaf axil; garlic bulb with cloves *below*; off-sets, *right*.

Natural methods.

Bulbils. Some plants, such as the Egyptian onion, produce small bulbs at the top of stems in place of flowers. With some varieties of lily, small bulbils form in the leaf axils. In good conditions these bulbils grow and mature, the smallest being treated like seeds, the others being set out in beds or containers to be handled similarly to the parent stock. One to four years is required to reach flowering size.

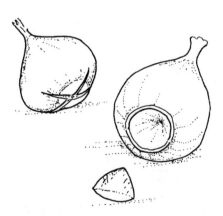

22 Bulb propagation. The production of bulbs or bulbils can be hastened by shallow cross cutting, *left*, or gouging out a small cone from the base *right*.

Cloves. Mature bulbs of, for example, garlic divide naturally into segments or cloves which when planted out at the right time, grow and develop.

Offsets. Many bulb crops, such as daffodils, narcissi and shallots, form bulb-like offsets which can be detached and planted out at the appropriate season.

Assisted means of increase Some varieties, of hyacinth for example, need encouragement to produce bulbs.

Cutting. If the base of bulbs are cut shallowly cross-wise when planting new bulbs will form along the line of the cut.

Gouging. This is a variation of cutting and consists of cleanly removing a cone shaped piece from the base of each bulb. This system produces more bulbs with some varieties, but leaves a larger wound for the possible entry of diseases.

Cacti This group of plants and the closely related succulents can be increased in various ways, both by seeds and vegetatively. *See* Cuttings, Grafting, Offsets and Seed propagation, this chapter.

Callus formation Fleshy cuttings of cacti, geraniums, and pelargoniums frequently root more readily if they are first left to dry. Lay them out in a single

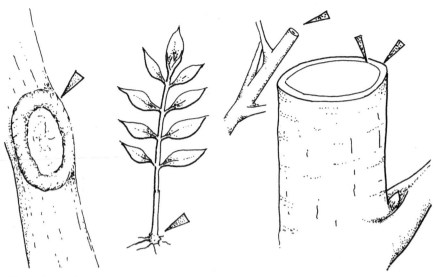

23   Callus. *Left*: a protective ring of callus, *arrowed*, growing over and covering a cut surface of tree stem. *Right*: callus, *arrowed*, covering the base of a cutting and from which roots are developing.

24   Cambium. *Top*: a cut shoot exposing the vital tissues, *arrowed*, in the centre, *shown* enlarged *below*. The inner circle, *arrowed*, is the cambium layer, covered by rind or bark, *arrowed*.

Table of Some Common Cacti and Succulents and their Propagation

Name	Method of propagation	
Astrophytum	Seeds and offsets	
Cereus	Seeds and stem cuttings	
Cotyledon	Seeds and leaf cuttings	
Crassula	Seeds and stem cuttings	
Echinocereus	Seeds and stem cuttings	
Echinopsis	Seeds	Seeds sown in spring.
Epiphyllum	Seeds, stem and leaf cuttings	Cuttings taken in
Kalanchoe	Seeds and stem cuttings	summer.
Lobivja	Seeds and offsets	
Rhipsalidopsis		
(Easter cactus)	Stem cuttings	
Schlumbergera		
(Christmas cactus)	Stem cuttings	

layer on newspaper for 24 hours in a shaded place before inserting them in a suitable cutting compost. This results in the early formation of a protective layer of callus tissue over the cut surface, lessening the chances of disease organisms entering the open wound.

Cambium This is a layer of actively growing plant tissue which occurs just below the rind or skin of most garden plants. When budding or grafting, it is most important that the cambium of the bud or scion comes into direct contact with that of the root stock.

Capillary attraction When propagating plants the ratio of water to air in the rooting medium is critical. Excess or deficiency of one or the other, such as excessive dryness or wetness, can be fatal to tender or delicate plants.

Boxes or pots of seedlings grown by conventional methods can be watered by standing them in a shallow container of water. Water is drawn up to the surface of the compost gently by capillary attraction which is far better for small seedlings than being deluged from above using a watering can.

Capillary benches These consist of shallow containers, lined with sand or capillary matting, which are kept constantly wet to act as moisture reservoirs. Plants growing in pots or boxes which rest on the wet sand or matting are watered by capillary attraction with the compost acting as a wick.

Cheshunt compound This is a copper-based fungicide which can be used to water pots or boxes of newly sown seeds to prevent damping off.

Chimaera Plants which when raised from root cuttings are not identical with the parent plant. They often occur in those with variegated leaves like certain varieties of pelargonium. However, when normal shoot cuttings are taken from the same plants, these grow and behave like the plant from which they were taken.

Chimaera, or plants which respond in this way, consist of two or more varieties. Due to the different cell arrangement between root and stem, the features of the inner or concealed variety are revealed. The popular, variegated golden form of Mother-in-Laws Tongue sometimes behaves like this when propagated from small below-soil surface 'toes'.

There is always a possibility of producing a new variety from plants that are not suspected of being a chimaera.

When propagating a treasured variety, it is safer in many cases to propagate from stem cuttings unless the choice kind is known to reproduce faithfully from root cuttings.

Clone Where a number of plants that are identical in all respects, termed clones, are required, it is necessary to propagate them vegetatively by cuttings or similar, from a single plant. Taking several cuttings from one chrysanthemum stool or a number of runners from one strawberry plant normally produces identical plants.

Conifers These are propagated only occasionally by amateurs, mainly because of the length of time required to produce sizable plants and often the lack of propagating material and facilities.

The methods which can be used are cuttings, grafting, layering and seeds, cuttings and layering providing perhaps the most convenient means of increase for people with limited time and space. For details *see* Cuttings, Grafting, Layering and Seed propagation.

Conifer Propagation

Genus	Method used	
Chamaecyparis Juniperus Thuja Taxus	Named varieties from cuttings Species can be increased from seeds	Cuttings taken late summer. Seeds sown in autumn or spring.
Abies Cedrus Picea Pinus	Named varieties from grafting Others by means of seed	Grafting in spring. Seeds sown in autumn or spring.

23

Container-grown Plants can be successfully raised and grown in various types of receptacle, including plastic, wood, clay and other ceramic material. The important considerations of any container are size and depth, hygiene, good drainage, ease and convenience of handling, and price.

Cool-house With pre-planning, many plants can be successfully propagated with a minimum night temperature of 4°C (40°F). Plants such as cabbage, cauliflower and lettuce can be sown in autumn, and overwintered in these conditions.

A small propagator can be used in conjunction with a cool house to germinate seeds needing a higher temperature, obviating the necessity to heat the whole house.

Corms These can be raised from seeds, and vegetatively by cormlets, sometimes referred to as spawn. As with bulbs, raising corms from seed is attempted by only a few amateurs. The uncertain results, the time involved and the plentiful supply of flowering-size corms all contribute to this situation. *See* Chapter 5, Flowers from seed. Corms of gladioli and crocus produce cormlets readily; these can be removed at lifting time, and

if sown like seeds in containers, under cover, can be grown on to flowering size. This takes from two to three years.

Cuttings The use of 'slips' or cuttings of various types, and seeds are the main methods of increase which are used by amateurs. In total, these probably account for 90% of the home production of plants. Cuttings are classed according to which part of a plant is used for propagation.

Bud or eye cuttings consist of a short length of stem with one or two plump buds or eyes, with or without a leaf attached. These vary in length from 25–75 mm (1–3 in) and can be used to raise vines when taken in autumn. Camellias and ivies can also be raised with this type of bud cutting, when a leaf is usually retained, unlike the vine which is rooted without a leaf – an eye cutting.

Leaf cuttings are used to increase various greenhouse or indoor plants such as Rex begonia and streptocarpus. This method consists of selecting a healthy vigorous leaf and cutting or nicking the leaf veins, and pegging or wiring the leaf blade onto some cutting compost. Leaf segments, consisting of small squares or rectangles of leaf blade, about 25–40 mm (1–1½ in) square are more convenient to handle. These are inserted edgeways to a

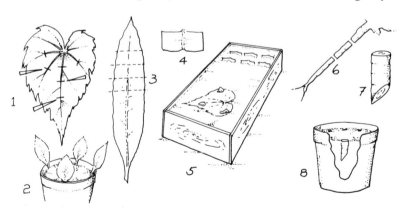

25   Cuttings. Leaf cuttings: (1) Begonia with cut veins, *arrowed*; (2) Saintpaulia, leaf stalk; (3) Streptocarpus leaf and (4) cut segment; (5) Begonia leaf held in place by small pebbles with sections of streptocarpus; (6), (7) and (8) preparing trimmed and potted root cutting.

depth of half their height in cutting compost, and then kept warm and moist. This is normally carried out in late spring or summer.

Leaf-stem cuttings look to all intents and purposes like a leaf cutting and consist of a leaf blade and stalk. With this type of plant material, the leaf stalk is inserted to half its length in cutting compost. Saintpaulias can be propagated in this manner.

Root cutting Plants with fleshy roots and leafy tops, such as some poppies and verbascum, are most conveniently increased this way. The parent plants are either lifted or soil is cleared away, to expose suitable roots during the resting season. Pieces of root, about 25–30 mm (1–1¼ in) long of pencil thickness, are prepared. This consists of washing the root in water if need be; making a square cut at the top and slicing the lower end obliquely. Insert the cuttings vertically 40–50 mm (1½–2 in) apart into pots or boxes of cutting compost, burying the tops about 12 mm (½ in) below the surface.

Stem cuttings Most stem cuttings can be grouped into two main types, namely heel and node, but there are many variations of technique.

A heel cutting consists of a shoot or growth at any stage of maturity to which is attached a piece of the stem from which it originated. When taking cuttings of this type, hold the selected shoot firmly, near its junction with the parent stem, pulling it off with a piece of wood or stem attached.

A node cutting is very similar in most respects to a heel type, except that the base is cut squarely immediately below a leaf joint.

An inter-node cutting is a third group, which is occasionally prepared. This resembles the node type, but the stem is cut midway between a pair of leaf joints. This type is sometimes used when raising clematis.

Stem cuttings also come into fairly well defined categories according to the degree of maturity of the wood or growth.

Softwood cuttings consist of young new growths such as occur on chrysanthemum or dahlia stools and fuchsias. Firm healthy shoots 50–100 mm (2–4 in) long, according to the type of plant, are selected. This type of cutting is cut below a node and the bottom one or two leaves are removed. Rooting of this and other kinds of stem cutting can be

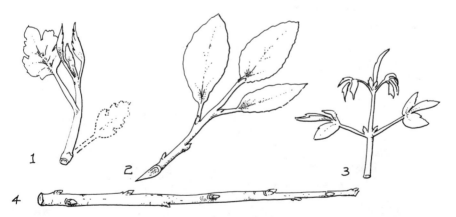

26   Cuttings. Different types of stem cutting as follows: (1) Softwood node cutting; (2) Semi-ripe heel cutting; (3) Semi-ripe internode cutting of clematis; (4) Dormant hardwood cutting.

27 Softwood cutting. This chrysanthemum, which was cut down in autumn, is starting to produce cuttings.

hastened by dipping the cut end in hormone rooting powder or liquid.

Semi-ripe cuttings are young growths in which the stem tissues are beginning to harden, and depending on the season and place, shoots in this condition usually occur during July. Cuttings of this type are particularly suitable for raising shrubs, many of which can be difficult to raise by any other means. Select firm, healthy shoots from 50–150 mm (2–6 in) long, which can be heel, node or internode. Trim the heels if need be, cut the others squarely and cleanly at the base. Remove the bottom leaf or two. Dip the base in hormone rooting preparation and insert the cuttings 100 mm (4 in) apart and up to one-third of their length in cutting compost.

Hard or ripe-wood cuttings consist of mature current season's growth, taken usually from about late September to mid-November. Firm straight lengths of ripened wood 200–400 mm (8–16 in) long are taken from healthy plants either with or without a heel. Where plants with prickles, such as gooseberries, are raised this way, remove the buds and prickles for two-thirds their length, starting at the bottom. Plant the cuttings

100–150 mm (4–6 in) deep in sandy soil in a sheltered spot. Hardy, outdoor plants can be grown on in a nursery bed in a sheltered corner until ready for planting out in their final positions.

Damping down or overhead Where soft propagating material of leaves, softwood and semi-ripe cuttings are being rooted, regular damping over with a fine syringe prevents them from wilting too severely.

Division This is a simple form of propagation which is used widely with herbaceous plants such as scabious, and Michaelmas daisies. Lift the roots during the dormant period, after flowering and before active growth commences in spring. Split large clumps into three, four or more well-rooted pieces, keeping the new outside growth, but discarding worn out old growth from the centre. Splitting can be carried out by pushing two garden forks into the clump, back to back, and using them as levers to force the pieces apart. With young crowns, lift them, shaking off the soil, and with a sharp knife cut each clump into two. After dividing, replant the split portions into well prepared beds.

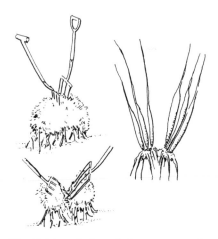

28 Division. *Left*: split large crowns by levering them apart with two forks. Small clumps, *right*, can easily be pulled apart.

26

Drill Seeds are sown at different depths and spacings, resulting in variations of sowing techniques. Outdoors, three or four variations are used. The V-shaped drill can be made with a draw hoe, rake or by pressing a piece of wood like a rake handle into a well prepared seed-bed. Vegetable seeds, such as beetroot, carrots and radish or hardy flowers like larkspur are sown in this type of drill. Mark out long rows with pegs and garden line. This type of drill is usually made on level ground, but in wet districts a V-furrow is made on a low ridge for best results with crops like swedes and turnips. The U-shaped drill, which is deeper and wider than the V-drill, is sometimes used for crops such as broad and runner beans and potatoes. This drill is usually made with a draw hoe. The flat bottomed drill is generally used when sowing garden peas. It is made by marking out each row with pegs and line and then taking out a 100–150 mm (4–6 in) wide and 50 mm (2 in) deep drill with a draw hoe.

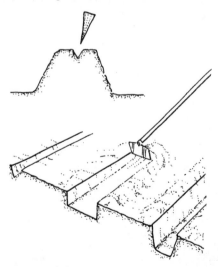

29 Drills. Seeds are sown in V-drills on ridges, *top*, or flat, *left*, and in flat bottomed type, *centre*, for peas, for example. Artichokes or potatoes are planted in 100–150 mm (4–6 in) deep drills, *right*.

F₁ and F₂ Hybrids F_1 and F_2 are simply symbols used to denote the first and second generations respectively of a cross between two plants of genetically distinct types. The preparation of hybrid seed is costly and beyond the capabilities of most gardeners because of the space, time and facilities needed. Hybrid seeds of this type are vigorous and uniform in habit. It is unwise to save seeds from these plants because succeeding generations are very variable.

Frames These have many uses for plant raising, in addition to their usual role of hardening-off indoor-grown plants. Seeds of different kinds can be started off, even in unheated frames from March to October, and seedlings can usefully be protected at any time of the year. Depending on variety, cuttings can be taken and started off between about March and November, providing year round use.

Germination *See* Seed propagation, this chapter.

Grafting This is seldom practised by amateurs, but it can be useful to understand why this technique is sometimes necessary and the points to note when handling grafted stock. Cacti, fruit and decorative trees as well as roses, are among the plants that are commonly grafted. Some named varieties of plants do not reproduce the characteristics of the parent when raised from seed, nor are they satisfactory when grown on their own roots. The three methods of grafting used, perhaps more than most are saddle graft, side graft, and whip-and-tongue. The success or failure of any form of grafting depends on matching up the cambium layers of rootstocks and scions.

Saddle graft This is used to increase various types of cacti and consists of making an inverted V– cut on the rootstock, ending in a point. A corresponding notched cut is made on the scion which 'sits' on the rootstock, and is

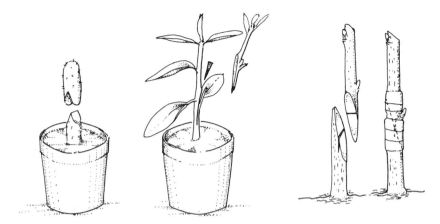

30   Grafting. *Left to right*: saddle graft; side graft, showing cut, *arrowed*, ready to receive scion; whip-and-tongue, before and after binding with grafting tape.

pinned in position, after which the cut surfaces are covered with grafting wax.

Side graft This technique is used for certain conifers, and consists of making a slanting side cut without removing the growing tip, on a pencil-thick rootstock just above soil level. A scion, of similar thickness, is prepared with a corresponding cut and is bound to the rootstock with grafting tape, after the two cut surfaces are matched up.

Whip-and-tongue graft This is perhaps the method most commonly practised, and is used mainly on deciduous subjects, including fruit trees and roses. Normally carried out in spring this consists of making an oblique cut about 40 mm (1½ in) long with a nick or tongue in the centre of the wood, on a pencil thick rootstock. Fruit trees are usually grafted outdoors. A scion is prepared with a matching cut and nick and secured to the rootstock with grafting tape. Cover the tape with grafting wax to prevent drying out.

Bench grafting is the term used for any form of grafting carried out indoors on pot-grown plants and where these are grown on under cover until established.

Growing room Precision growing of seedlings can be carried out in heated, ventilated and well insulated rooms, compartments or cabinets, which are artificially lit. The lighting provided by fluorescent tubes can be regulated as to quality, intensity and duration, giving very accurate control over growing conditions. Although this method of growing and raising plants has been known to be satisfactory for some years, the cost of installing and running has deterred its wider use among amateurs. However it is being increasingly used by commercial growers.

Irishman's cutting Slips or cuttings which are detached from parent plants and boxed or potted up with ready-formed roots attached are so termed. It is an often used practice, but not one to be recommended for exhibitors. The stems tend to be hard, preventing the development of top quality blooms.

Layering This method of propagation can be used on many woody plants where other methods have failed. This is usually carried out in autumn or spring and involves pulling down a shoot or growth to ground level, tying down and then covering a length of stem with fine soil. Low growing plants like creeping juniper are suited to this method.

28

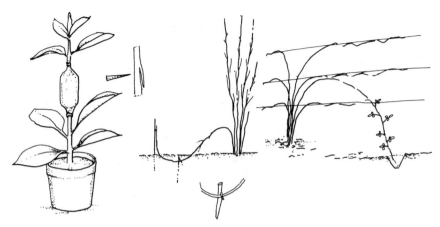

31   Layering. *Left*: air layering consists of covering a stem, *arrowed*, with moss, and keeping this in place with a plastic sleeve. *Centre*: normal layering with supple shoot pegged in place and covered with fine soil. Enlarged *below*. *Right*: tip layering of e.g. loganberry, with terminal bud pegged and covered with potting compost or friable loam.

Depending on the subject, the rooted layers can be severed from the parent plants in 12–24 months, or less.

Mist propagation A modern high-speed method of rooting cuttings which are raised under continuous or intermittent mist without heavy shading and with under-bench heating. Softwood and semi-ripe cuttings of many indoor and hardy woody plants can be rooted in 14–21 days where the bench is heated to 21°C (70°F). The advantage of this system is that cuttings can continue to make starch and sugar in sunlight, unlike heavily shaded cuttings. The mist prevents wilting.

Nutrient Film technique The raising of seeds and cuttings using this technique is still in its infancy, but would seem to offer some interesting possibilities for propagation. This technique consists of sowing seeds on a gauze-type material, continuously moistened with nutrient solution. Problems of anchorage of young plants and contamination need careful attention.

Piping A type of cutting, which is obtained from carnations and dianthus.

This consists of a young shoot which is snapped off at a node, trimmed as necessary and planted in cutting compost.

Proliferation A condition which occurs naturally with various plants including ferns. This describes the formation of living plantlets or bulbils on the leaves or elsewhere on mature plants. These, if pegged down into a cutting compost and kept moist, can form roots and then be severed from the parent plant and potted up.

Pseudo-bulb A swollen stem occuring among various types of orchids, which when split from the parent plants can grow and develop. *See* Vegetative propagation, this chapter.

Rhizome An underground stem, such as occurs with mint, which when removed can produce a new plant. *See* Vegetative propagation, this chapter.

Roguing A necessary practice of culling or weeding out unhealthy, inferior plants and those which are less desirable for some reason. This should be regularly carried out several times a year in the interest of space and plant hygiene.

Runner or stolon An overground shoot which can be pegged down, as with strawberries, to form rooted plants. These are severed from the parent and planted up as needed.

Seed propagation This method of raising plants for average garden purposes offers several advantages over, for example, cuttings. Seeds are comparatively cheap, enabling large numbers of plants to be produced at low costs. Variety of colour, shape and season, and the possibility of some really new or different plant is ever present with seed-raised plants.

Raising plants from seeds indoors These are normally best sown in boxes or pans containing seed compost of a loam or soilless mixture. Clean containers are given a shallow layer of rough peat or gravel over the bottom for drainage. Fill each container level with the rim or edge with compost. Where loam composts are used, press down lightly at the corners and edges of containers, finally smoothing the surface and putting on a level finish with a flat piece of shaped wood or firmer. The compost will now be 6–12 mm ($\frac{1}{4}$–$\frac{1}{2}$ in) below the rim of container. Soilless composts should be only very gently firmed to avoid undue compaction. For most purposes, a minimum depth of 50 mm (2 in) of compost is adequate. Small seeds are normally thinly scattered on the surface of well watered compost. Very small seeds like begonias are not covered with sifted compost as are larger seeds like pansies. When covering seeds, bury them no deeper than twice their own diameter. Large seeds like those of sweet peas are best spaced out singly about 25 mm (1 in) apart in boxes, or better still individually in small pots. Place a sheet of clean glass and a piece of paper over containers to exclude light and retain moisture. Keep the seeds warm and moist, removing the glass and paper when the seedlings appear. As soon as seedlings are large enough to handle, they should be pricked out into boxes or pots. *See* Chapter 5, Flowers *also* Chapter 9, Vegetables for individual details.

Raising seedlings outdoors Seeds are normally sown in drills at a time, depth and spacing to suit the individual needs of crop and gardener. One important consideration is that any seed bed should be well-prepared, level and without lumps or clods of earth. Occasionally some seeds such as radish are thinly sown broadcast and are very lightly raked in afterwards. In dry conditions water the drills before sowing and keep the ground moist as necessary. The resultant seedlings are either transplan-

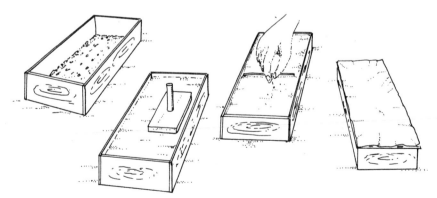

32 Seed sowing. *Left to right*: box crocked and ready; filling with compost and firming; sowing thinly after watering; finally covered with glass and paper.

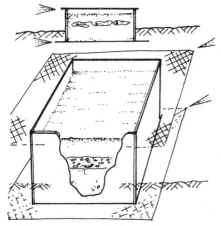

34   Seed or plant protector. *Top*: end view of seedlings inside the wire mesh guard. *Below*: the ends are covered with wire mesh also and the sides are level with the ground, preventing damage by animals.

33   Stratifying seed. Seeds are wrapped in muslin or laid loose, sandwiched between layers of sand and left outdoors. Place fine mesh gauze, *arrowed*, around them to keep mice and birds at bay.

ted or thinned to allow them space to develop. *See* Chapter 5, Flowers *also* Chapter 9, Vegetables, for individual details.

Stooling A form of layering, mainly practised by commercial growers for the production of fruit tree rootstock.

Stratification A pre-sowing treatment of certain seeds of, for example, members of the rose family to ensure even germination. This consists of putting seeds of plants like cotoneaster, crateagus, and rose between layers of sand in a pot or box outside. The action of frost and rain assists in breaking the dormancy of the seeds. It is advisable to protect the seeds with fine gauze, to prevent mice and vermin from feeding on them. After this treatment, sowing is carried out as normal, either in containers or in drills in a safe spot.

Suckers Shoots which occur at or near soil level. Those which occur from below soil level and develop roots can be severed from the parent plant and used for propagating purposes as with raspberries.

Tip layering Blackberries and loganberries can form plants at the tips of their growths or rods, if pegged into loose damp soil. When rooted these are severed from the parent plant and set out.

Tubers The potato is the best known example of this type of plant. The underground tubers are dug up and stored until required for planting.

Vegetative propagation The need to use methods other than seeds for raising garden plants arises for various reasons. Seed is variable and cannot be relied on to produce progeny of named varieties that are true to type. Some plants do not readily flower, or set seed, and other means have to be used to enable them to be increased. Various plants have adapted special structures enabling them to multiply in a variety of ways, and pass on all their features to successive generations. Vegetative increase can be effected by air layer; apical cutting – Meristem; bud or eye cutting; budding – various; bulbs; bulbil; corm; cormlet; division; grafting – various; layering; leaf cutting – various; offset; piping; proliferation; pseudo-bulb; rhizome; root cutting; scale; segment or clove; stem cutting – various; stolon; stooling; sucker; tip layering and tuber.

Chapter 3. Plant Care

Aerating Operations on soil, turf or in ponds to improve the degree of oxygenation.

Cultivations, such as digging, help to improve soil aeration.

On turf, this consists of vigorously scarifying the grass with a wire rake, first in one direction and then across the first sweep. The tearing and teasing out of old grass allows air and light into the turf. *See also* Chapter 8, Spiking.

With ponds aeration involves the removal of debris such as leaves from the water, and recycling water through a pump as with a fountain, returning the water in a jet or spray onto the surface. Where oxygenating pond weeds are present the need for artificial aeration is less, provided good hygiene is practised.

Bark ringing This consists of removing a single 6 mm (¼ in) ring of bark from the trunk of each unfruitful apple or pear tree. This is best carried out at blossom time. With a sharp knife, cut through the

bark, completely encircling the trunk. Make a similar cut 6 mm (¼ in) higher parallel to the first. Remove the ring of bark between the two cuts. Cover the open surface immediately with grafting or similar tape to prevent undue drying out. If the trees produce a good deal of blossom without setting fruit then bark ringing is unlikely to be helpful. *See* Chapter 10, Problems.

Blanching This practice consists of excluding light, either from ready-formed leaves and stems, with such as endives and leeks, or by creating dark conditions for leaves and stems to develop in. Chicory and rhubarb provide examples of the latter category. The object of blanching is to improve the colour, flavour and quality of crops.

Leaf blanching of crops, such as endive and dandelion, can be carried out simply and easily by placing an upturned pot or box over each plant when the leaves are dry. Where pots have drainage

35 Bark ringing. This involves making two parallel cuts encircling the trunk, removing a circle of bark and protecting the cut area with tape.

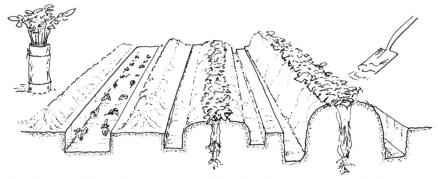

36 Blanching. Celery is blanched EITHER with collars of corrugated paper, *far left*, OR with soil, in three stages as shown : *left* crop planted in trench ; *centre* and *right* earthing as the crop grows.

holes, letting in light, place some clean, dry straw over each plant before covering.

To blanch stem crops, like trench celery and leeks, cover the stems with a collar of corrugated paper or place a drain pipe over so that the leaves project over the top. Tie the corrugated paper to prevent it from opening out and falling away. For average crops, not required for the show bench, celery and leeks are more commonly blanched by drawing fine, loose soil around the stems. Earthing up is better carried out in stages rather than all in one operation.

Blanching chicory is usually achieved by covering the roots with sandy soil before forcing begins. With rhubarb, this is often forced under greenhouse staging with sacking placed round to exclude light. Where rhubarb is forced and blanched with sun heat only, tall straw-filled buckets or boxes are placed over the dormant crowns.

Brutting This is an old but effective practice which can be used to make trees and shrubs flower and fruit more prolifically than if left alone. Wall trained apples, pears and chaenomeles (japonica) seem to respond particularly well.

In summer, but before mid-August, bend the young or semi-ripe growths

37 Brutting. *Left to right*: normal shoot; after bending; cut back after winter pruning.

downwards so that they snap, but do not break off. This bending should be about half way along the new growth. The immediate effect looks a little untidy, but provided the breaking is correctly done the leaves remain green. Most of the buds nearest the branch swell, but do not burst into premature growth. Also this method prevents excessive growth in wet seasons. In autumn, cut the shoots back as for normal winter pruning of spur-fruiting types of apples and pears. With chaenomeles, cut off the tips back to a good bud removing the broken or bent portion.

Bulb planting Flowering bulbs such as narcissi and tulips are most effective

34

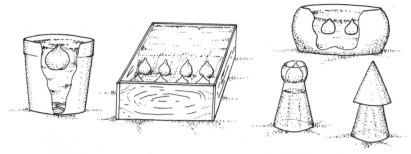

38 Bulbs planting. *Left*: single hyacinth bulb, just covered with compost in pot, cut away to show crocking and depth. *Centre*: tulip bulbs in process of being 'boxed up', the remainder being buried with compost before being plunged or placed in darkness. *Top right*: small bulbs in bowl, with side cut away to show depth of planting. *Bottom right*: single bulb being grown in water in glass holder. Paper cone is placed over bulb to provide darkness until rooting occurs.

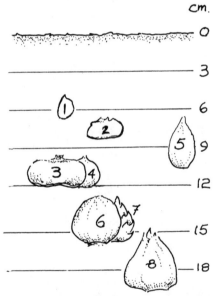

39 Bulbs planting depths. In average soils, bulbs and corms can be planted at the depths shown: (1) Galanthus (2) Crocus (3) Gladiolus (4) Tulip (5) Iris, Dutch (6) Hyacinths (7) Lilium (8) Narcissus.

when massed or planted in groups. When set out in beds and borders, bulbs are usually planted with a trowel at a depth roughly equal to three times their diameter. On heavy or wet soils it is sound practice to put a handful of sand under each bulb. The same is true of corms, such as those of gladioli. Some peat or leaf mould should be mixed with the top soil when covering bulbs or corms. Planting in grass involves the removal of a square or so of turf with a spade, or alternatively a turf plug can be removed with a bulb planter. The soil should be loosened, and have some peat or similar material worked in. Planting otherwise resembles that in beds except that the turf is replaced, covering the bulbs and corms.

Crown lifting This is a form of pruning often carried out on established ornamental garden trees, in which some of the bottom branches are removed. This practice can become necessary where the lowest branches are dead or diseased, conceal an attractive trunk from view, or are in the way of people or plants. The amount of pruning will depend on the circumstances, but any cutting is best done in autumn. Remove large limbs in sections if necessary and as described under lopping (q.v. p40).

Crown thinning A form of selective thinning of branches in trees with the aim of letting in more light and air. This is best carried out in autumn to avoid undue bleeding, which could occur if pruning took place in spring when the

35

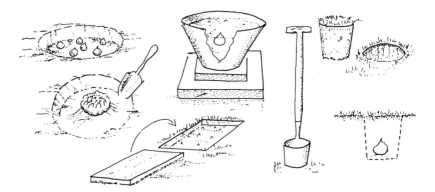

40 Bulb planting in open air. *Left*: a group of small bulbs and a single lily resting on sand before covering. *Centre top*: bulbs in container with side cut away to show details, and *below*, turf about to be replaced over bulbs. Bulb planter with, *top right*, earth plug removed and, *below*, bulb covered with plug and turf.

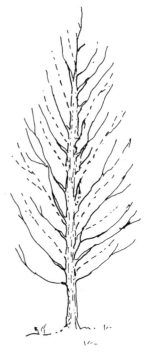

41a Crown lifting. Tree with lower branches cut away, indicated by broken lines.

41b Crown thinning. Tree with head thinned to let in light and air. The broken lines indicate removed branches.

sap is rising. Remove badly placed, diseased and crossing branches, burning any where there is risk of infection.

Damping down This consists of spraying water on floors, staging and walls of greenhouses, during warm sunny weather. This helps to maintain a humid atmosphere and prevent temperatures from rising excessively.

Damping overhead This is similar to damping down but includes syringing the plants and covering them with a film of moisture. Where this is carried out, it is wise to give the plant leaves time to dry before evening so that moisture does not encourage disease.

Deadheading It is desirable to remove old blooms as soon as flowering ceases, except where the seeds are needed, so that plant energies can be utilised to

De-blossoming Where spring-planted strawberries start flowering within a few weeks of being set out in their final positions, fruiting should be discouraged. This can be achieved by picking off the blossoms during the spring and summer. Strong heavy-cropping plants are produced which have been shown to out-yield those which are not deblossomed.

Defoliation This consists of removing the leaves of tomato plants to encourage early ripening of fruit with heavy foliage varieties. Defoliation is carried out as follows: cut leaves off with a sharp knife, flush with the stem; as the lowest truss of tomatoes starts to change colour remove all but one leaf beneath the cluster of

42 Deadheading. The old flower heads are cut back to new growth, just above a healthy leaf or bud.

produce fresh growth and flowers. Cut back the old stems to where fresh growth or buds are visible. This can be carried out to advantage on most ornamental plants as soon as flowering is over at any time of year.

43 Defoliating. Leaves are cleanly cut off close to the stem below trusses of ripening tomatoes.

ripening fruit; when the second truss of tomatoes begins to turn colour repeat the process with this and so on with subsequent fruit trusses.

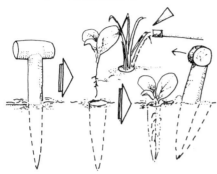

44 Dibber planting. *Left to right:* making the hole, inserting the cabbage plant and firming the soil around the roots. *Top:* leeks should be watered in, *arrowed*, and not firmed.

Dibber planting Small seedlings which have not developed a large root system, such as cabbage, can be quickly and successfully transplanted into their final positions using a dibber. On well-prepared ground at suitable distances and spacing, make a hole of sufficient depth and width to take each plant. Insert each plant into a hole so that the roots are not bent and the seed leaves are level with the soil surface. Then push the dibber into the ground alongside each plant so that with a lever action, soil is pushed to firmly hold roots and stem.

Disbudding This involves comparatively little effort but is often neglected. It consists of rubbing out all the surplus buds and shoots. Where large single blooms are required, each flower stem of chrysanthemums and dahlias, for example, is allowed to produce one flower from the best tip bud. All other buds are removed as soon as they appear and are large enough to handle.

Edging This is a simple though time consuming task, but very worth while for tidy lawns. Edging consists of put-

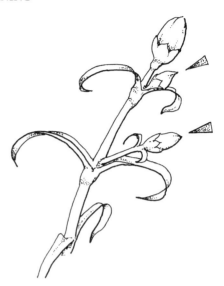

45 Disbudding. The terminal bud will produce a large bloom if the secondary or lateral buds, *arrowed*, are removed.

ting a perpendicular face on the edge or margin of a lawn. Place a straight-edged plank near to the line required. With an edging iron or a spade, using the plank as a guide, cut the turf vertically. Curved edges need to be marked out in sand, or scored with a stick before cutting. Subsequently when the grass grows over the margin, giving an unkempt appearance, use a long-handled pair of shears to trim the edges back to the hard shoulder.

Forcing *See* Chapter 4, Greenhouses, Frames and Cloches.

Grubbing This consists of digging out unwanted and undesirable plants, from weeds in lawns to the removal of old trees. The methods vary depending on the nature of the plant involved.

The occasional daisy or plantain in lawns can be lifted out with a two or three pronged grubber. Push the prongs under the base or rosette of leaves and, using the circular device which acts like a pivot, lever out the plant and roots.

38

This can be quicker, safer and cheaper than using weedkiller if only a few plants are involved.

Herbaceous plants can be dug out, complete with roots, using a spade or fork.

Woody plants, such as trees and shrubs, in the average garden are dealt with by sawing off the main branches before digging up by the roots. In confined spaces there is little or no choice, but to remove branches first. The same applies where stems prevent easy working around the various plants concerned. When dealing with small or medium-sized trees, the advantage of not sawing the trunk off at ground level before digging, lies in having the stem as a lever to pull this way or that as work proceeds. Large tree stumps can present a problem. Hand digging may not be practical and other means have to be found. Where costs and space allow, the hire of a mechanical stump chipper is always possible, but these machines should be used only by trained operators.

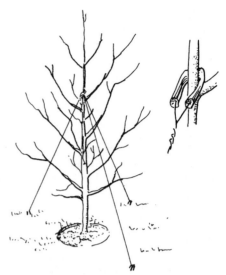

46 Guying. Medium to large sized trees can be supported by three wires attached high up the main stem and the other ends fastened to pegs spaced evenly round the tree. *Right*: a wire passed through a piece of hosepipe to protect the stem.

Guying This method of supporting tall, newly planted trees involves attaching three wires, high up on the main stem, and securing these to three pegs in the ground, spaced equally round the base. The tension of each wire should be the same so that the tree is not pulled out of position. Each wire should be passed through a short length of hose pipe, which is wrapped round the trunk. This prevents damage to the bark from bare wire, which might otherwise chafe the stem, especially during high winds.

Hanging basket Two types are frequently used, the traditional moss-lined wire basket or the ceramic or plastic container. These are suspended by wires or chains from brackets.

The traditional basket can be made up as follows. Rest the wire frame in a large, rigid plant pot or bucket for ease of handling. Line the bottom and sides with moss and part-fill with moist potting compost. Place a few plants, such as lobelia, around the sides, pushing the roots through gaps in the wires and moss. Position larger plants like pelargoniums centrally with other smaller plants like French marigold around, to create a domed or raised centre. Work compost in and around the roots as filling proceeds. Finally cover the soil between plants with moss to prevent drying out and for appearance. *The ceramic or plastic type* is treated rather like a window box. Place roughage in the bottom, for drainage, before part filling with moist compost. Place the largest plants centrally, finishing off with the smallest subjects around the edges. A moss covering for the soil provides an attractive finish.

Water the plants well after making up the baskets. And, if possible hang them up in a greenhouse or sheltered place for a few days before finally placing them in their flowering position. *See* Chapter 5, Flowers, for list of suitable plants.

Heading down Reducing the size of the crown of a tree should preferably be carried out in stages, and during autumn. It consists of a combination of crown thinning, and shortening branches back by half to two-thirds their length or as needed. The indiscriminate cutting back of all branches, leaving hat-peg-like stumps should be avoided. Ideally heading down should be carried out over a period of two years or so. Hard cutting back in one season often results in the production of water-shoots – vigorous, upright unnatural-looking growths.

Hoeing *See* Chapter 1, Site and Soil.

Lifting This is the operation of digging up plants before moving them to new positions. Most brassica seedlings and such as rose bushes are frequently lifted with little or no soil attached and are described as bare-root plants. Conifers and various other shrubs are best lifted with a good ball of soil attached to the roots. These are described as balled plants. In this case lifting consists of chopping round the plant with a spade and then sliding this underneath, and carefully lifting. Where plants are to be moved some distance, the roots are best wrapped in hessian or plastic to prevent drying out. Plants treated this way are described as balled and wrapped. Where plants are about to be moved, and the ground is dry, water the soil around the roots and allow to drain. Avoid lifting during frosty weather, or during very hot conditions. Preferably lift plants when they are in their resting phase. *See* Planting, this chapter.

Lopping Large tree limbs often have to be removed in the interests of safety, disease, old age or some other consideration. Remove large branches in sections if necessary, commencing near the tips and working in towards the trunk. When sawing, first make a cut under the limb about one-quarter to one-third way through. Then make a second cut, about 100 mm (4 in) further out than the first, sawing through the limb. Undercutting helps to prevent severe wood splitting which can enable diseases to make an entry. This cutting process is repeated with each limb, until only a short stump remains, near the trunk. Finally saw off the stump level with the trunk, and cut or pare off any rough edges with a sharp knife. Paint the remaining wound area with preservative.

Nicking and notching A practice which consists of regulating the development of buds by making either a

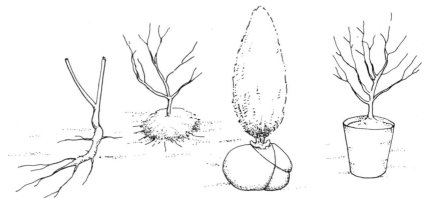

47 Forms in which plants are offered for sale. *Left to right*: bare root; balled; balled and wrapped; and container grown.

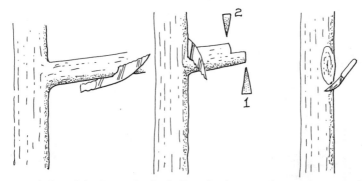

48 Lopping. *Left to right*: first under the limb; make the second cut above, *arrowed*, and saw off the stump close to the trunk. Finally pare off any rough edges with a sharp knife.

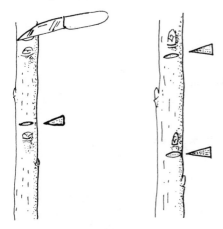

49 Nicking and notching. *Left*: notching above buds will usually stimulate them into growth and shoot formation. *Right*: nicking below a dormant bud will in many cases encourage the formation of fruit buds.

small nick below or a notch above a bud. This is usually carried out during May on trained forms of fruit trees. Nicking encourages the development of a fruit bud, whereas notching stimulates the bud to grow into a shoot.

Pinching Another term for removing the growing points or buds of plants. *See* Stopping, this chapter.

Planting This task, together with lifting, is carried out at some time by most people in the course of their gardening activities; often hurriedly and on hastily prepared ground. Land for planting should be well worked, free-draining, yet moist, manured and fertilised as necessary. When planting, the points to pay special attention to are the condition of the ground, the condition of the plants, weather conditions, the depth and size of hole, and support. Whether planting some small plants with a dibber, or preparing for a large tree, avoid planting on land that is frozen, waterlogged, or compacted and hard; break up any 'pan'. Plants should not be in a wilted condition. Trees and shrubs should preferably be dormant or nearly so, except where container-grown stock is used.

To ensure rapid establishment of newly-planted stocks, set plants out in mild, but cool shaded conditions which are ideal. Make sure the hole is deep enough to set plants out comfortably at the same depth in the ground as before the move. The diameter of each hole should be large enough to accommodate the roots with ease when they are spread out. Stakes for large trees should be in position before rather than after planting. Unless the top soil contains considerable quantities of organic matter, work in some peat with the soil as filling proceeds. Where the top soil is poor, it is advisable to prepare a good compost for

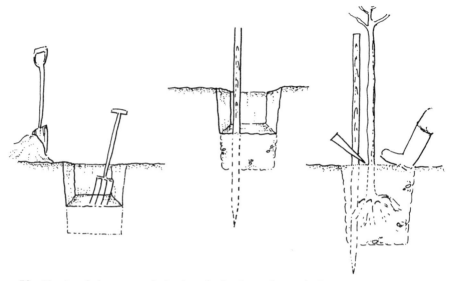

50 Planting. *Left*: prepare a hole of ample size, loosening up the bottom, and work in some peat or manure. *Centre*: stakes, where needed, should be hammered in before positioning trees or plants. *Right*: firming the soil as filling proceeds, making sure the level of planting is the same as in the nursery.

covering tree roots. A mixture of 3 parts loam, 1 part peat and 1 of sand, plus 140 g/m² (4 oz/sq yd) of John Innes base fertiliser for tree pits serves well. When filling make sure the soil is well worked in and around the roots, firming the ground after successive layers of fill are placed over the roots. In spring, place a peat mulch on the soil around newly-planted trees and bushes, to smother weeds and conserve moisture.

Pollarding This consists of cutting off all the branches of a tree, which in time forms a large knob, such as seen on old lime trees or willows beside water courses. This is usually necessary where large trees have outgrown their allotted space, as with street trees in towns. The need for this practice, which is costly in time and tends to encourage disease, can be avoided by planting small-growing trees in confined spaces.

Pollination and fruit setting The transfer of pollen from stamens to pistil is necessary for fruit and seed setting. This is an important aspect of growing fruit and seed crops. Early out-of-season tomato and strawberry flowers have to be pollinated by hand as have marrows and melons, to enable fruit to form. This can be carried out by dusting the flower centres with a piece of cottonwool, with tomato and strawberry. With melons and marrows, it is necessary to dust the open male flowers, those without embryo fruits immediately under the petals. Transfer some yellow pollen to the centre of the open female flowers, those with small fruits below the flowers. Greenhouse cucumbers are an exception and pollination results in poor quality fruits. Blossoms of fruit trees outdoors are normally pollinated by insects, but some varieties are unable to produce good pollen and need assistance from others. This is important with apples and pears, but even more so with cherries and plums. Some nurserymen produce family trees, having more than

42

one variety and including a pollinator. A family apple tree might consist of a few branches of Cox's Orange Pippin with, say, James Grieve as a pollinator variety. For successful fruit setting, especially where cross-pollination is involved, the pollen must be viable and compatible; the flowering period should be similar to the main variety. And insects or other means of pollen transfer are needed. *See* Chapter 6, Fruit for list of main and pollinator varieties. Where pollination is difficult, the use of hormone-type fruit setting sprays can be usefully applied to produce good crops. This often results in seedless, but otherwise normal, fruits.

Potting A general term used for putting plants in pots. The stage of growth, the manner of handling, the type of container and compost used all exert considerable influence on the subsequent development of plants grown in pots.

51 Pricking out. Seedlings should be handled carefully by the leaves, not the stems, lowering them into dibber holes in pots or boxes.

Pricking out is the first move with potting: it is carried out in the seedling stage.

Potting off consists of transferring young seedlings or plants from boxes to pots, often referred to as potting up.

Potting on is the moving on of plants from small pots into pots of increasingly larger sizes.

Potting up is a term also used when plants are dug out of beds and placed in pots. The important points to watch when potting are age and condition of plant; type and size of container; nature and compaction of compost; conditions when potting, and position of plant. It is sound practice to prick out plants as soon as they are large enough to handle. Tomatoes are best pricked out into pots as soon as the seed leaves are expanded. When potting on, this is ideally carried out as soon as plants are ready to move. This can be readily determined by knocking plants carefully out of their pots to see if roots are visible on the outside of the ball of compost. When this occurs move the plants into larger pots. When potting always make sure that plants are not wilting, water them first if need be to make sure the compost is moist. Potting is normally best carried out in the shade to escape undue drying out. Avoid using excessively large containers, especially with slow-growing subjects during the winter months, because the soil quickly becomes soured. Plastic, clay and fibre pots all have their uses. Plastic containers with a shiny finish are easy to clean. Peat pots are convenient, but not particularly cheap. It is important to use the correct compost, because plant needs vary at different stages of growth as well as between seasons. Slow growing plants require less food than vigorous rampant varieties. When filling clay or plastic pots, place gravel or peat riddlings to a depth of one-tenth the height of the container for drainage. Leave a similar space between the rim and compost surface for watering. When potting on slow growing plants in loam-based composts, a potting stick or rammer is used to force compost down the pot sides, filling in air spaces and consolidating the mixture.

Pricking out *See* Potting, this chapter.

Pruning The cutting back, and removal of shoots, stems, roots and other operations are carried out to control and regulate the amount of flowering, fruiting and extension growth. Some plants tend to be over-productive, exhausting their energies, others are shy cropping, needing to be treated differently.

The term pruning is usually reserved for woody plants, and stopping and side shooting are used to refer to soft, succulent growth. As a rule-of-thumb guide, hard pruning results in vigorous growth and light cutting the reverse. Pruning falls into three main categories: formative, routine and remedial.

Formative pruning involves hard cutting to encourage strong growth and the development of a framework of branches on trees and shrubs. Where plants are obtained from garden centres the initial formative pruning has usually been carried out. Trees are pruned to well defined shapes as indicated in the table.

Routine pruning Ornamental trees are best given the minimum of cutting.

As remedial pruning thin out crowded shoots and remove crossing and untidy growths. Any dead or diseased wood should also be cut out.

Fruit trees in gardens are usually wall-trained forms such as cordon and espalier apples and pears. Fan-trained peach and plum are grown on south-facing walls in favourable sites.

Bush trees are, perhaps, the most widely planted type nowadays after cordon fruits. Fruit trees are pruned by two main techniques: extension and spur methods.

Extension pruning is used on trees which carry fruit on the tips of branches, where normal spur pruning would result in loss of crop. With the extension or renewal methods, one-half to one-third of the number of whole shoots are cut back leaving the remainder untouched to carry the crop. The remaining shoots are pruned the following year.

Spur pruning, especially of wall-trained trees, is carried out in two operations. Summer pruning consists of cutting back new growths by one half to two-thirds. In winter these are shortened back to leave two or three buds on the new growth. Bush forms of plum are pruned as little as possible. With fan-trained peach and plum, new shoots are trained to replace fruited shoots.

Fruit bushes. Blackcurrants crop best on young wood; one quarter to one-

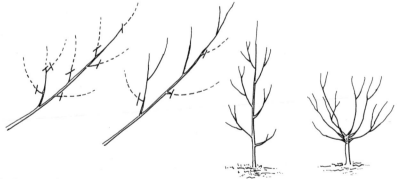

52　Pruning. *Left to right*: spur pruning; extension pruning; pyramid, and bush tree. The broken line denotes the branches which are cut out.

Table of Tree Pruning

Plant Group	Cordon	Es-palier	Fan	Bush	Half Stan-dard	Stan-dard	Tall Stan-dard	Double Cordon	Pyra-mid	Hori-zontal
Deciduous Tree	—	—	✓	✓	✓	✓	✓	—	—	—
Evergreen Tree	—	—	—	—	—	—	—	—	✓	—
Fruit Tree	✓	✓	✓	✓	✓	✓	✓	✓	—	—
Fruit Bush	✓	—	✓	✓	—	—	—	✓	—	—
Cane Fruit	—	—	—	—	—	—	—	—	—	✓
Shrubs	—	—	—	✓	—	—	—	—	—	—
Roses	—	—	✓	✓	✓	✓	—	—	—	✓

third of all shoots are removed, including the oldest fruited wood. Gooseberries and red currants are spur pruned after the style of apples, because these fruit on spurs on the older wood. For summer-fruiting raspberries cut out old fruited canes and tie in the new growths as shown in the diagram, leaving no more than five to each stool. Autumn-fruiting raspberries, such as September and Zeva are pruned in winter, when all growths are cut to ground level including the new.

Ringing *See* Bark ringing, this chapter.

Root Pruning A process involving the removal of some of the thickest and strongest growing roots of vigorous, but unproductive fruit trees. This practice is normally reserved for plums and cherries. In autumn, dig a semi-circular trench about 300–450 mm (12–18 in) wide, spade deep and approximately 600 mm–1.2 m (2–4 ft) from the tree trunk. Sever and remove thick sections of root as they are uncovered during digging. Paint over cut surfaces where these exceed 25 mm (1 in) in diameter, with a protective lead-based paint or preservative. With large trees carry out

53 Pruning. *Left*: summer pruning, cut the new growths by about half. *Right*: these shoots are shortened further as shown during winter pruning.

54 Pruning. Root pruning consists of digging a semi-circular trench, half one year, the remainder the next, cutting out thick roots. Replace fibrous roots and soil.

45

this operation over two years, removing a semi-circle of soil each year. Avoid damaging the fine fibrous roots which are covered over with loose fine soil and firmed, as the excavated soil is returned. If the summer following root pruning is hot and dry, water the tree roots occasionally and syringe the leaves in the evening after sunny days.

Side shooting This practice consists of cutting or rubbing out axillary growths, or side shoots, and is done with plants like tomatoes. The object of their removal is to divert the plant's energies to flower and fruit production and to growth of the main stem. Cut out any thick shoots close to the stem, and rub out small growths regularly as they appear.

peat and chalk mixture in beds or trays. This consists of breaking up block spawn into pieces about walnut size and planting them in spaces about 200 mm (8 in) square and 25–50 mm (1–2 in) deep, using a hand fork for convenience.

Spiling In hard shallow or stony ground, long rooted crops like carrots or parsnip are unable to form top quality roots without special measures. This practice consists of making holes in the ground with a crowbar, about 450–600 mm (18–24 in) deep and 75–100 mm (3–4 in) wide at the surface. The distance apart varies according to the crop being grown. Fill each cavity with John Innes Potting compost, or similar, on which seeds of long rooted crops like parsnips can be sown and grown to a high standard.

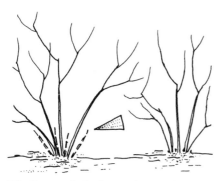

55 Snags. *Left*: long pieces of stem, *arrowed*, left after pruning, can harbour disease as they die back, unlike those, *right*, cut down to the ground.

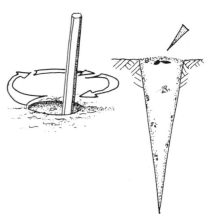

56 Spiling. Crops such as parsnips can be grown on shallow soils by making holes with a crow bar and filling these with fine soil or potting compost. Seeds, *arrowed*, are then sown over the prepared positions.

Snagging Sometimes short dead pieces of wood or snags can be found on shrubs or rose bushes where shoots have not been pruned to soil level or cut hard back to the stem. Cut out these bits of dead wood, using a pair of secateurs or strong-bladed sharp knife, to remove possible sources of disease and pests.

Spawning This is the operation in mushroom cultivation where small pieces of spawn are planted or set in fermenting manure and covered with a

Staking and tying A general term used for supporting a wide range of plants. The supporting stakes, sticks or canes should be strong enough to resist high winds, kept as inconspicuous as possible, be free from pests and diseases and cause no damage to crops. Tree stakes should be rammed or hammered into position before planting takes place. Two main methods are used for supporting trees in gardens; the single and the double stake. The latter is necessary for large trees on exposed sites. The single-stake method consists of using 40–50 mm (1½–2 in) thick wooden posts of larch or chestnut. These are positioned so that the top of the stake is 50–100 mm (2–4 in) below the bottom branches of each tree. Plastic tree ties can then be placed, one half-way up and another at the top of the stake. The double stake method involves planting trees mid-way between pairs of posts, spaced 300–450 mm (12–18 in) apart, and of similar height relative to the tree as with the single stake system. Two cross pieces of timber are fixed, one half-way up, and the other at the tops of each pair of stakes. The tree is tied to the cross members, using binding or cord, but wrapping a piece of hessian round the trunk first, to prevent chafing.

Steeping A method of watering delicate seeds or seedlings by immersing the seed container to about half its depth in a tray or bowl of water. Remove the container as soon as the compost is moist. This method is of greatest use for window-sill or frame culture where capillary watering facilities are not available.

57 Steeping. Small seedlings or dry pot plants can be watered by standing the pots or containers in shallow water until the compost is visibly moist.

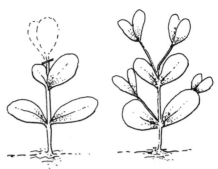

58 Stopping. Young plants or seedlings such as antirrhinums can be encouraged to become bushy by removing the growing points.

Stopping This is also referred to as pinching out, and consists of removing the growing points of main stems, side shoots or terminal buds. A sharp knife is preferred to using finger nails, which leave a ragged wound, liable to infection. As with side shooting, the 'tops' are best removed when small.

Sub-irrigation A system of watering plants from below surface level. This is used in aggregate culture where the rooting medium in water-tight tanks or containers is flooded, and the surplus liquid is drained back into a reservoir.

Summer pruning *See* pruning, this chapter.

Syringing Using a garden syringe to apply a fine overhead spray of water to plants, usually during fine weather, to reduce moisture loss and promote fruit setting.

Thinning A practice of removing small seedlings from their rows to give those remaining more space to develop. Ideally this should be carried out in two or three stages, starting as soon as the plants are large enough to handle, giving them increased space as they grow.

Fruits such as grapes and peaches also need thinning to permit the development of top quality fruit. Each peach fruit, for example, needs about

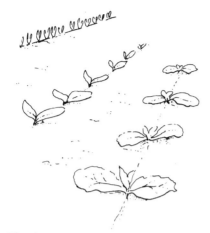

59 Thinning. Removing seedlings should be carried out in stages, leaving plants spaced further apart as they grow. *Left to right*: unthinned; after first thinning, and final spacing.

250 mm (10 in) square of wall area to grow to perfection.

Tilthing A process of forking over or cultivating the ground lightly, followed by combing through the soil with an iron rake. The breaking and working down of soil to a fine granular consistency.

Top draining This consists of removing surface rain water away from cultivated areas, usually by ditches at or near the ground surface. French drains are made by digging trenches which are filled with stone to soil surface. These can then be drained into a ditch, culvert or stream. The surface of the stone drain can then be covered with gravel to prevent fine earth from being washed in and blocking the flow of water.

Training This process consists of stopping, side shooting, pruning, or otherwise manipulating plants to control and regulate flowering, fruiting and growth. One common way to train plants is the cordon method, which can successfully be applied to greenhouse cucumbers and tomatoes, and sweet peas. This consists of training and supporting plants vertically or nearly so. One stem only is usual and side shoots are removed, or stopped as in the case of cucumbers. *See also* Pruning, this chapter.

Transplanting This consists of lifting plants out of a bed or border and planting them in new positions. The land which is to receive the plants should be well prepared and in good condition. Water plants before lifting, especially where the ground is dry. Excavate pits, and hammer in stakes before moving trees into position. Lift small plants carefully with a fork, and plant them with a trowel, making holes large enough

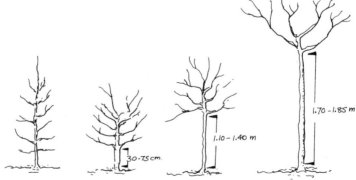

60 Training. Fruit trees in particular are pruned to form different shapes. *Left to right*: pyramid, bush, half-standard and standard.

48

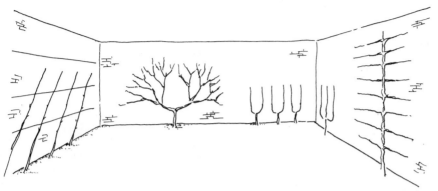

61 Training. Wall trained forms of trees and bushes deserve to be more widely grown. *Left to right*: oblique single cordons; fan; double cordon; triple cordon, and espalier.

to comfortably take the roots. When moving plants into new positions, set them out at the same depth in the soil as before the move.

Underplanting This consists of using low-growing subjects beneath the branches of trees and tall shrubs to cover bare earth. In this situation it is advisable to select plants which can tolerate

62 Underplanting. Low-growing plants, such as bulbs, *arrowed*, can be effective when planted below tall shrubs.

shade and competition for food and moisture, such as Rose of Sharon. *See* Chapter 7, Trees and Shrubs.

Watering One of the most important, but often incorrectly carried out of garden tasks. Three basic methods of

watering are commonly used: overhead, ground level and capillary or sub-irrigation.

Overhead watering is usually carried out in the open air, using sprinklers or spray lines. Outdoors, wet foliage is often less critical than in greenhouses, from the aspect of encouragement of disease.

Ground-level application consists of delivering water at or close to the soil surface through a hose pipe or watering can, using a rose to avoid compaction.

Sub-irrigation can be achieved by steeping container-grown plants in shallow water, using capillary benches and standing pots or containers on wet sand, flooding aggregate or gravel filled tanks, and draining off.

When steeping containers, these should be removed from the water after half an hour, to avoid stagnation, and, similarly, aggregate tanks should have the surplus water removed or drained. Important considerations are to start watering before plants wilt, to reduce the amount of watering in dull, cool or winter weather, and to avoid applying water to the soil faster than it can be absorbed. Where large quantities of water are needed in gardens, overhead or low level applications are usual. In the case of delicate seedlings, steeping or capillary watering are the safest methods. *See* Steeping, this chapter. Avoid

49

damaging blooms by wetting them, especially in strong sunlight.

Weeding The control of unwanted plants in gardens is achieved in various ways, including cultivations, the use of weed killers and natural means. On a garden scale the use of natural means, other than smothering seedling weeds by mulching, has very limited appli-cation. Cultivations such as digging, forking, hoeing, the use of cultivators and grubbers all have their places. The regular mowing of lawns also exerts a controlling influence on weeds of tall or upright habit. *See* Chapter 10, Problems, for the use of weed killers.

Winter pruning *See* Pruning, this chapter.

Chapter 4. Greenhouses, Frames and Cloches

Alpine Although hardy, many plants of this type are grown in unheated or cool greenhouses and frames, where the

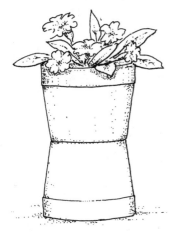

63 Alpine. Plant placed on upturned pot for extra light.

blooms are undamaged by weather. The plants can be grown in containers of suitable potting compost, in frames, watering as necessary. Various subjects can be easily moved into a greenhouse or dwelling when on the point of flowering to make the maximum use of cover. Successive batches are brought indoors and plants which have finished blooming are taken out again to maintain continuity of colour and interest.

The following table gives a short list of flowering subjects suitable for this form of cultivation.

Annuals Half-hardy and tender varieties of decorative plants which are usually treated in one of the following ways.

Sown under cover, pricked out, hardened off, planted and grown outdoors (many half-hardy annuals, which are used as bedding plants, like ageratum, are thus treated).

Table of Alpines

Name	Colour	Flowering Season
Androsace carnea	Pink	Apr–May
Arabis, various	Pink and white	Apr–May
Chionodoxa	Blue and white	Feb
Crocus, various	Blue, purple, white and yellow	Nov–Apr
Cyclamen coum	Pink and white	Oct–Feb
Draba, various	Yellow	Mar–May
Galanthus, various	White	Feb–Mar
Haberlea rhodopensis	Lilac and white	Apr
Iris danfordiae	Yellow	Feb
Iris reticulata	Blue/purple and yellow	Feb
Narcissus, dwarf various	White and yellow	Feb–Apr
Primula allionii	Purple, rose and white	Mar–Apr
Primula pubescens	Cream, mauve and white	Apr–May
Ramonda myconi	Purple and white	Apr–May
Saxifrage, various	Red, pink, white or yellow	Mar–May
Scilla, various	Blue and white	Mar–Apr
Soldanella, various	Cream and lilac	Apr–May
Tulipa, various	Red, white and yellow	Mar–May

51

Table of Popular Greenhouse Annuals

Name	Treatment	House type	Sow	Season of Colour	Feature/colours
Amaranthus caudatus Love-lies-Bleeding	i	Inter	Mar	Jul–Oct	Crimson or green tassels
Capsicum frutescens Ornamental Peppers	i	Inter/Warm	Feb	Aug–Dec	Cream, red or yellow berries
Celosia argentea cristata Cockscomb	i	Inter/Warm	Mar	Aug–Sep	Red or yellow crested heads
Celosia a. plumosa Prince of Wales Feathers	i	Inter/Warm	Mar	Aug–Sep	Red or yellow plumed
Clarkia elegans Clarkia	ii	Cool	Sep and Mar	Apr–May Jun–Aug	Pink and purple flowers
Impatiens balsaminea Balsam	i	Inter	Mar–Apr	Jul–Sep	Pink and red flowers
Petunia	i	Inter	Feb–Mar	Jun–Oct	Pink, purple red, and white flowers
Primula malacoides Fairy Primula	i	Inter	May–Jul	Nov–Mar	Lilac and rose flowers
Primula sinensis Chinese Primula	i	Inter	Apr–Jun	Nov–Mar	Flowers in shades of red, rose and wine
Reseda odorata Mignonette	i/ii	Cool/Inter	Mar–Apr; Jul–Aug	Jul–Sep Mar–May	White and yellow flowers
Salpiglossis Scalloped Tube Tongue	i	Inter	Apr and Jul–Aug	Jul–Oct Apr–Jun	Various brilliant coloured flowers
Salvia splendens Scarlet salvia	i	Inter	Jan–Mar	Jun–Oct	Pink or scarlet bracts
Tagetes, various Tagetes, African and French marigold	i	Cool/Inter	Feb–Apr	Jun–Oct	Brown, orange, red and yellow flowers
Thunbergia alata Black-eyed Susan	i	Inter/Warm	Feb–Mar	Jun–Oct	Cream and purple flowers
Torenia fournerii Torenia	i	Inter/Warm	Feb–Apr	Jun–Sep	Black, blue, purple and yellow flowers
Zinnia, various	i/ii	Inter	Apr	Jul–Sep	Orange, pink, scarlet and yellow flowers

Key i Indoor raised pricked out plants   ii Indoor raised but thinned out   i/ii Either method may be used
House Type Cool Cool house temperature 4°C (40°F) minimum   Inter Intermediate house 10°C (50°F) minimum
Warm Warm house 16°C (60°F) minimum

Sown under cover such as cloches, thinned out, hardened off, uncovered and grown on without protection (some hardy and half-hardy annuals, which are grown for effect or for cut-flower purposes, can be raised thus.)

Sown indoors, pricked out, potted on as necessary and grown under cover.

As above but the seedlings are thinned, not pricked out, and are eventually potted on as needed (Plants treated in either of these ways include some of the most popular and colourful greenhouse plants, details of which are given in the Table of Popular Greenhouse Annuals.

Augergine *See* Vegetable and Salad crops, this chapter.

Beans *See* Vegetable and Salad Crops, this chapter.

Bedding Plants Half-hardy and tender varieties are raised under cover by means of seeds and cuttings; for details of methods used *see* Chapter 2, Propagation.

In the following table are listed some common subjects together with their sowing times or dates for taking cuttings. All should be planted out in late May or early June when the danger of frost is past.

Begonia *See* Pot plants, this chapter.

Biennials While many garden plants in this group are hardy and can be successfully raised outdoors, there are some half-hardy and tender varieties which need protection. The method of cultivation is similar to that used for half-hardy and tender annuals, except that biennials, unlike annuals, flower in the succeeding year after sowing.

Bonsai A specialised branch of gardening which is widely practised in Japan and involves growing diminutive trees in containers. The success of this form of cultivation relies on maintaining plants in good health and shape, while preventing them from making strong growth by manipulating roots and shoots. This can be achieved by a combination of restricting the roots in small containers, reducing the flow of sap by winding wires round stems and branches, and avoiding overfeeding plants. Anyone who is seriously contemplating taking up Bonsai would be well advised to see tree specimens at leading shows, and if possible observe an experienced practitioner at work.

Bottle gardening A method of cultivation which consists of growing plants and crops in glass or plastic containers, enveloping shoots and leaves as well as roots. Bottle gardening is carried out to provide colour and effect indoors as well as to produce salad and vegetable crops. Carboys or large, clear glass containers are part-filled with a 50–75 mm (2–3 in)

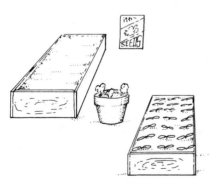

64   Bedding plants. *Left to right*: seeds; cuttings; plants pricked out; hardening off in frame.

Table of Bedding Plants

Name	Sowing date	Cuttings taken
Ageratum	Feb–Mar	—
Alyssum	Feb–Mar	—
Antirrhinum	Jan–Mar	—
Aster	Mar–Apr	—
Begonia	Nov–Jan	Feb–Mar
Chrysanthemum	Jan–Mar	Feb–Apr
Coreopsis	Feb–Mar	—
Dahlia	Feb–Mar	Feb–Mar
Fuchsia	Jan–Mar	Sep and Mar
Heliotrope	Feb–Mar	Aug and Mar
Impatiens	Mar	Feb–Mar
Kochia	Mar–Apr	—
Lobelia	Jan–Mar	—
Matthiola, 10-week stock	Feb–Mar	—
Mesembryanthemum	Feb–Mar	—
Nemesia	Mar–Apr	—
Nicotiana	Feb–Mar	—
Pansy	Feb–Mar	Sep
Pelargonium	Dec–Jan	Jul–Sep
Petunia	Jan–Mar	—
Phlox, annual	Feb–Apr	—
Salvia	Jan–Mar	—
Tagetes	Feb–Mar	—
Verbena	Jan–Mar	—

Table of Biennials

Name	Treatment	Sow	Flower	Remarks
Calceolaria hybrids Slipper flower	GB	May–Jul	May–Jul	Orange, pink, red and yellow shades. Excellent as pot plants.
Brompton Stocks	HHB	Jul–Aug	May–Jun	Lilac, pink, red and white flowers. Suitable for cut or pot work.
East Lothian Stocks	HHB	Jul–Aug	May–Jul	Lilac, pink, red and white flowers. Suitable for cut or pot work.
Trachelium	GB	Jun–Jul	Jun–Aug	Blue flowers, excellent for pot plant.

Key   GB   Greenhouse biennial
        HHB   Half-hardy biennial

Table of Suitable Bottle Garden Subjects

Name	Height (cm)	Remarks
Calathaea insignis	23	Leaves, dark and light green variations.
Calathaea makoyana Peacock Plant	45	Leaves, bluish-green with purplish markings.
Cryptanthus bivittatus	8	Reddish-pink leaves with green margins.
Ficus pumila	45	Small, dainty mid-green leaves, trailing habit.
Ficus radicans variegata	10	Green with cream leaf margins.
Helxine Mind-your-own-business	3	Mat-forming plant with small bright green leaves.
Maranta leuconeura	15–20	Bluish-green leaves with purple markings.
Maranta massangeana	10–15	Bluish-green leaves with reddish markings.
Peperomia magnoliaefolia	15	Mid-green leaves with cream margins.
Pilea cadieri	30	Green with metallic grey.
Pellaea rotundifolia	30	Dark green maiden-hair-like leaves.
Pteris cretica	30–45	Soft green fern foliage.
Tradescantia	10–15	Variegated foliage plant, trailing habit.

layer of rooting medium such as John Innes No 1 compost or equivalent to eight parts of which has been added one part by bulk of fine charcoal. Slow-growing foliage plants as listed are ideal for decorative purposes.

All plants in this list will grow satisfactorily at a minimum room temperature of 10°C (50°F). The container or glass jar should have a minimum open-ing of 50–75 mm (2–3 in). Use a paper funnel when pouring in soil to keep the sides and neck clean. Use two sticks for planting, one to cover the roots while the other holds the plants upright. When the plants are in position, cover the surface with fine pea gravel.

The food production side of bottle gardening consists of sprouting seeds in scrupulously clean glass containers, but

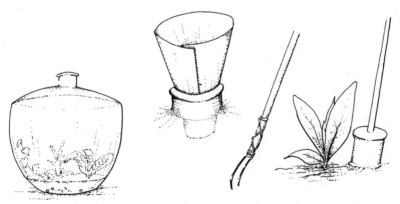

65   Bottle gardening. *Left to right*: part-filled carboy; paper funnel for filling; home-made fork on cane; bobbin on cane for firming compost round plants.

55

without any soil or compost. Jam jars, which are sealed with clean muslin held in place with an elastic band, serve admirably. In essence, the method consists in germinating a small quantity of seed, kept moist by rinsing in clean water, in each jar. The muslin allows the seeds to breathe. For satisfactory germination, a temperature of 13–19°C (55–65°F) is needed to produce ready-to-use sprouts in 4–8 days. Rinse the germinating seeds in water at least twice each day. Seeds which can be used in this way include Alfalfa, Fenugreek, Mung Beans and Triticale.

66 Bottle gardening. Placing seed in jar; half-grown crop; Mung beans ready for use.

Bulbs Many plants produce swollen storage organs and this feature is not confined to those which form true bulbs. Corms and tubers are also specialised organs for food storage, enabling plants to build up reserves, and in many cases to flower early in the year when other plants are not in bloom.

Indoor bulbs, corms and tubers are usually grown in containers. John Innes potting compost No 1 is an excellent rooting medium. When growing or forcing bulbs, corms and tubers, allow them to form a good root system for 8–12 weeks, in cool conditions before increasing the temperature. Plant these well in advance of the flowering period to allow time for good root development. *See*

Table of Bulbs. Set bulbs and corms much shallower than when growing outdoors, by just covering with compost. Winter and spring-flowering bulbs and corms are potted or boxed up in August or September. Place the containers on gravel or cinders in a shaded place outdoors or on the floor of a cool, dark cellar, but protect them from mice. Cover the outdoor containers with a 10 cm (4 in) layer of sand or peat after planting and watering. Keep the bulbs moist and bring them into light and warmth, a few at a time, when growth is apparent. Some of the bulbs and corms can be moved under and then kept in unheated frames until the buds show colour, to provide a long flowering season. Consult the catalogues of reputable suppliers for suitable varieties, which are not discussed here, because these change fairly rapidly. In the Table of Bulbs are listed some popular bulbs and corms together with cultural details.

Cacti These form a large and interesting group of plants, many of which are easily cultivated. These are usually grown for one or both of two main purposes: for colour and effect, or as a plant collection. Although these plants are easy to grow, they need free draining composts and care should be taken to avoid over-watering.

Well-known members of the Cactaceae family include those listed in the Table of Cacti.

Culture Remove and dry the 40–75 mm (1½–3 in) long cuttings for 24 hours on a shaded bench before inserting two or three of each round the edges of 75 mm (3 in) pots filled with cutting compost. Root the cuttings at 19–22°C (65–70°F) in a lightly shaded position. Pot up the rooted cuttings singly into 75 mm (3 in) and then into 100–112 mm (4–4½ in) pots of John Innes No 2 potting compost. The young plants of Kalanchoe should be stopped once or twice to make them bushy if this does not occur naturally. Those listed in the Table of Cacti should

Table of Bulbs

Name	Flowering Season*	Colours	Pot up	Move Indoors
Crocus	Jan–Mar	Blue, lilac, white and yellow	Sep–Oct	Nov–Jan
Daffodil	Dec–Mar	Orange, white and yellow	Aug–Oct	Nov–Mar
Freesia	Jan–Mar	Blue, lavendar, pink, purple, white, wine and yellow	Aug–Nov	Oct**
Hyacinth	Dec–Mar	Blue, pink, red, white and yellow	Aug–Nov	Nov–Mar
Iris	Feb–May	Blue, purple, white and yellow	Aug–Oct	Dec–Apr
Lilium	Apr–Jun	Orange, pink, white and yellow	Aug–Oct	Oct**
Muscari	Feb–Apr	Blue	Aug–Nov	Dec–Feb
Narcissi	Dec–Apr	Cream, white and yellow	Aug–Oct	Nov–Mar
Tulip	Dec–Apr	Orange, pink, purple, red, white and yellow	Aug–Nov	Nov–Mar

Key * Flowering season is controlled to some extent by variety as well as treatment.
** All bulbs can benefit from frame cover from November onwards, but freesia and lilium should be covered during October and subsequently.

Table of Cacti

Name	Flowering Season	Colours	Cuttings Taken	Winter Temperature
Epiphyllum hybrids	May–Jun	Cream, pink, red and white	May–Jul	6°C (41°F) min
Kalanchoe blossfeldiana	Feb–May	Pink, red and yellow	May–Aug	6°C (41°F) min
Rhipsalidopsis (Easter Cactus)	Mar–Apr	Crimson shades	May–Jul	13°C (55°F) min
Schlumbergera (Christmas Cactus)	Dec–Feb	Crimson shades	May–Jul	13°C (55°F) min

be ready for flowering within 6–18 months of taking the cuttings. Repot the plants after flowering, and protect from strong sun. Water sparingly during winter, but increase this during the summer months. With good care and attention, the young plants should flower and grow for several years without much trouble. Many cacti can be raised from seeds, but named varieties have to be increased by cuttings, or even by grafting on to seed-raised plants. John

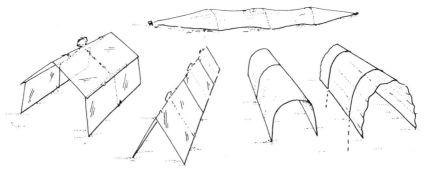

67   Cloche types. *Left to right*: barn; tent; rigid 'U'; semi-rigid. *Above*: tunnel.

Innes No 2 potting compost is a suitable medium for most kinds of cacti for average purposes.

Cloches The range of subjects which can be successfully grown with the aid of cloches is extensive.

The Barn Cloche is perhaps the most versatile and can be used according to one of three techniques: firstly, some crops such as lettuce are raised or planted under cloches, where they grow and eventually mature; other crops such as beetroot, tomatoes, sweet peas and runner beans are sown or planted and protected for the early part of their growth; finally, crops such as autumn strawberries, anemonies and endive are started off in open ground, but are covered with cloches to protect them at maturity.

The most practical way to use cloches is the technique known as strip cropping. This consists of providing two or three parallel strips of ground, each sufficient to take one row of cloches, with a pathway. This ensures the minimum of transporting of cloches, so that as a crop finishes on one strip, the cloches are moved onto the adjoining one. The soil preparation and cultural details of cloche crops are similar to those grown in open ground, except that the timing of operations are different. *Consult* Table of Cloche Crops. Covered crops also need more generous watering and liquid feeding than those grown in open air,

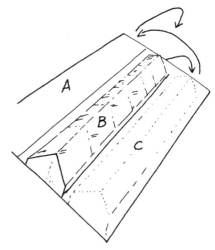

68   Strip cropping. Each row of cloches should be allocated three strips of land for ease of handling and maximum use. *Here* cloches on strip B are moved successively onto C, then A, and back to B.

due to the more favourable growing conditions.

Cool House Plants which grow and thrive in greenhouses and conservatories where a minimum night temperature of 4°C (40°F) is maintained are described as cool house subjects. The ventilators are opened when the temperature rises above 10–13°C (50–55°F) and closed again when it falls to these levels again.

Diseases of greenhouses, frame and cloche crops. *See* Chapter 10, Problems.

Table of Popular Cloche Crops

Crop		Sow	Cover	Harvest
Bean, French		Apr–May	Apr–Jun	Jul–Oct
Bean, runner		May	May–Jun	Aug–Oct
Beetroot		Apr	Apr–May	Jun–Jul
Brussels sprouts		Mar–Apr	Mar–Apr	Oct–Jan
Cabbage		Feb–Mar	Feb–Apr	Jun–Aug
Carrot		Mar–Apr	Mar–May	Jun–Jul
Cauliflower		Oct	Oct–Apr	Jun–Jul
Cucumber		Jun	Jun	Aug–Sep
Endive		Jul	Aug–Nov	Oct–Nov
Leek		Mar–Apr	Mar–Apr	Oct–Feb
Lettuce		Oct	Oct–Apr	Mar–Apr
Lettuce		Mar–Apr	Mar–May	May–Jul
Marrow	P	May–Jun	May–Jun	Jul–Sep
Onion, salad		Sep	Sep–Apr	Mar–May
Pea, round seeded		Oct–Nov	Oct–Apr	May–Jul
Radish		Mar–Apr	Mar–Apr	Apr–May
Spinach, summer		Mar–Apr	Mar–May	May–Aug
Sweet corn	P	May–Jun	May–Jun	Aug–Sep
Tomato	P	Jun	Jun and Sep	Aug–Sep
Strawberry summer	P	Aug	Dec–Jun	May–Jun
Strawberry autumn	P	Sep	Aug–Nov	Aug–Nov
Anemone	P	Jul–Sep	Sep–Apr	Oct–Nov and Mar–Apr
Calendula		Aug–Sep	Sep–Apr	May–Jun
Cornflower		Aug–Sep	Sep–Apr	May–Jul
Godetia		Aug–Sep	Sep–Apr	Jun–Jul
Larkspur		Aug–Sep	Sep–Apr	Jun–Jul
Myosotis	P	Oct	Oct–Apr	Mar–May
Nigella		Aug–Sep	Sep–Apr	May–Jul
Polyanthus	P	Oct	Oct–Apr	Mar–May
Scabious		Sep and Apr	Sep–May	Jun–Jul
Sweet pea	P	Mar–Apr	Mar–Apr	May–Sep

Key P Plants or corm used.
N.B. Harvesting date depends on many factors, such as variety, season, soil, sowing and covering dates and can therefore only be approximate.

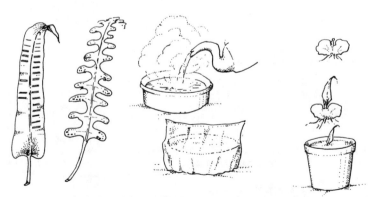

69 Ferns from spores. *Left to right*: fronds showing spore cases; sterilising compost before sowing; pan sealed in plastic bag; young fern.

Some Popular Ferns

Name	Minimum temperature (°C)	Height (cm)	Propagation
Adiantum Maidenhair Fern	4	30–45	Division and spores
Asplenium bulbiferum	7	45–60	Leaf bulbils
Nephrolepis Boston Fern	10	45–75	Stolons
Polystichum Japanese Holly Fern	4	60–90	Division and spores
Pteris Ribbon Fern	7	30–45	Division and spores

Popular Foliage Plants

Name		Minimum Temperature °C	Height (cm)	Propagation
Begonia rex		13	30	Leaf cutting
Chlorophytum		7	25	Plantlet
Cissus	C	9	60–2.5 m	Cutting
Codiaeum		16	3 m	Cutting
Cryptanthus		10	10	Offshoot
Dieffenbachia		16	60–1.2 m	Cutting
Dracaena		16	45–60	Cutting
Ficus benjamina		13	1.8 m	Cutting
Ficus elastica		16	1'5 m	Cutting with leaf-bud cutting
Ficus pumila	C/T	9	1.5 m	Cutting
Hedera	C/T	4	1.5 m	Cutting
Monstera	C	10	6	Tip cutting
Peperomia		13	15–20	Cutting
Philodendron	C	13	1.8 m	Cutting
Pilea cadierei		10	30	Cutting
Sanseviera		10	45	Sucker
Tradescantia	T	7	10	Cutting

Key C Climbing plant
     T Trailing plant without support.

Ferns A large group of foliage plants, many of which require shade and moist conditions.

Varieties which are commonly used as house plants can be satisfactorily grown in containers of John Innes No 1 or No 2 potting compost, or equivalent. Propagation is usually by spores or division. *See* Chapter 2.

Foliage plants These are grown for their leaves, which can provide colour and interest for a longer period than flowering plants. Many foliage subjects can be successfully grown in shaded situations which would be unsuitable for flowering plants. A long season of colour and tolerance of shade make these plants very popular for household decoration. The habit of growth of foliage plants varies from trailing to climbing, with intermediate bushy types.

All plants listed in the table will grow well in containers of John Innes No 2 potting compost. Water sparingly during winter, but more freely during summer, when syringing with clean water should be carried out to create moist growing conditions. Re-pot the plants in spring and summer into larger containers as they grow. Shade plants from intense sunlight. Apply an occasional feed of liquid fertiliser from about one month after potting or re-potting. Stake and tie tall plants such as Codiaeum, Ficus varieties and climbers. Varieties of Hedera, or ivies and *Ficus pumila* look attractive when trained over a light framework of canes or wires. Propagation of most of these plants can be carried out successfully between May and July. Root the cuttings in moist, shaded conditions, placed around the edges of pots of sandy compost, at a temperature of 19–22°C (65–70°F). When rooted, pot up cuttings into 75–100 mm (3–4 in) containers of John Innes No 2 potting compost and reduce the temperature to the levels needed by the individual varieties.

Frames Most of the crops which can be successfully grown under cloches, can also be cultivated in frames. *See* Table of Cloche Crops. In addition, these are better insulated from severe cold than cloches. Frames can also be heated and used for low-growing greenhouse crops such as bulbs, lettuce, cucumbers and melons. Unheated frames are widely used for raising various seedlings and for hardening off greenhouse-raised bedding and vegetable plants.

Hot bed Out-of-season crops are always sought after. However, the traditional hot bed of fermenting manure has been largely superseded by electric soil-warming cables. The scarcity of fresh manure and the labour involved in turning and making up 30 cm (12 in) deep layers of fermenting material each season, has resulted in the present position. Electric soil-warming cables once laid are ready for use for many years. The quantity of manure, peat or similar material needed annually to maintain soil fertility is much less than

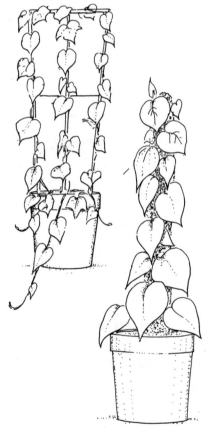

70 Foliage plants. *Left*; ivy trained over canes. *Right*: Philodendron growing up moss pillar.

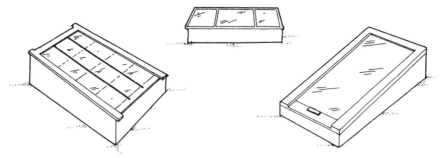

71   Frames. Three types of frames with lights. *Left to right*: traditional wooden or English; light-weight metal; and Dutch light.

that required for making a traditional hot-bed. It is used for growing early crops of cucumbers, marrows and lettuce.

Intermediate House Applied usually to greenhouses which are maintained at a minimum temperature of 10°C (50°F). During the day, when temperatures rise above 16°C (60°F) open the ventilators and close down again as soon as temperatures drop to this figure. For suitable crops *see* Tables of annuals and pot plants.

Orchids This group of plants is large and varied, attracting many enthusiasts. The newcomer to orchid culture is wise to start with a few easy subjects such as Cymbidiums and Paphiopedilums until some practical experience is gained.

Orchids can be divided into two main groups: epiphytes which develop aerial roots, and terrestial orchids which grow in soil-based composts. Plants belonging to the second group are less demanding than the epiphytes.

Cymbidiums The hybrids are more widely grown that the species, and the cool-house varieties are useful to start with. This group forms pseudo-bulbs above the compost. When these start to form roots, divide them, usually between March and May, and repot at about the same level as before. Provide at least a 25 mm (1 in) layer of clean pieces of broken pot or brick for drainage in

100 mm (4 in) pots or more for larger containers. Pot the divisions firmly into a well-aerated compost consisting of $1:\frac{1}{2}:\frac{1}{2}:1$ parts by bulk of fibrous loam; Osmunda fibre; peat fibre; live sphagnum moss. Add a 75 mm (3 in) potful of fine bonemeal plus a 125 mm (5 in) potful of medium grade charcoal and mix well in with each two 18 litre (4 gal) bucketsful of compost. Maintain a minimum 9°C (48°F) in winter rising to 15°C (58°F) minimum from April to September. Water sparingly in winter and freely in summer, when syringing and damping down should be carried out. Feed the plants occasionally with dilute, balanced liquid fertiliser during summer. Shade the plants from February to October and ventilate when the house temperatures rise more than 5°C (9°F) above the minima, but avoid draughts. Many of the hybrids produce flowers between February and June in shades of green, lavender, pink and purple.

Paphiopedilum Hybrids of *P. insigne*, better known as Lady's Slipper Orchid, are grown more widely than the true species. This type is usually increased by division of large plants between February and May. This orchid does not produce pseudo-bulbs, but forms clumps of arching leaves. The composts, watering, feeding, and general care are similar to the conditions needed for Cymbidiums. The flowers which appear between September and February are produced in shades of green, white and yellow with brown or purple spots and markings.

Perennials The majority of greenhouse flowering and foliage plants, excluding annuals and biennials are half-hardy or tender perennials. *See* Foliage, *also* Pot plants, this chapter.

Pests *See* Chapter 10, Problems.

Pot plants In the Table of Pot Plants are listed some colourful and popular plants which can be grown in a heated greenhouse. All these can be grown successfully in John Innes potting compost No 2 except where indicated to the contrary in the notes. All should be shaded from strong sunlight.

Specialist flowers While many flowering plants could be placed into this category, four crops stand out for special mention. These are chrysanthemums, dahlias, perpetual-flowering carnations and roses. The methods of cultivation which are given here are still widely used by amateurs. The modern commercial practices are not discussed because the requirements and aims are quite different.

Chrysanthemums
Early flowering varieties are raised under cover from cuttings, planted out in beds or pots in May depending on location and are flowered outdoors.
Mid-season types are similarly raised, but are grown in pots, which are brought indoors in September before frosts threaten, and flower by about mid-November.
Late varieties flower after the mid-season crop, and are treated in a similar manner.

Chrysanthemums are also classed according to their flower shape. The most outstanding are: incurves, reflexing, giant decorative, decoratives, singles and spray types. The life cycles of most chrysanthemums follow a similar pattern. After flowering the stools are cut back and overwintered indoors. Cuttings are taken in spring, hardened off and planted out. Feeding with dilute liquid fertiliser is carried out with all types. Stopping is necessary and large varieties are disbudded to produce the big single blooms.

Staking and tying is a very important part of growing chrysanthemums. Stake and tie tall varieties as they grow, at 15–20 cm (6–8 in) intervals.

72 Chrysanthemum. Large blooms individually staked and tied.

Dahlias Given below are the main groups in cultivation, which are classed according to flower type.
Border varieties. These are sub-divided as follows.
Single-flowered. These produce a single outer circle of florets around a central disc.
Anemone-flowered. This type forms a single ring of petals around an inner circle of florets.
Collarette. These are similar to the single-flowered, but form a collar-type

Table of Pot Plants for Greenhouses

Name	Conditions needed	Start	Season of colour	Colour	Remarks
Begonia, fibrous rooted	I	S. Jan–Mar	Jun–Oct	Crimson, orange, pink, red, white and yellow	Summer-flowering, are usually discarded in autumn. Sow afresh each year.
Begonia, tuberous rooted	I/W	T. Apr	Jul–Oct	Crimson, orange, pink, red, white and yellow	Dry off the tubers after flowering by laying pots on their sides for 14–21 days. Store them in a frost-free place, after removing pots, soil and compost.
Chrysanthemum, charm	CH	S. Jan–Mar	Oct–Dec	Crimson, orange, pink, red, white and yellow	Usually treated as annuals, and are started from seed each season. Any plants with unusual coloured flowers can be used to provide cuttings for taking in February or March. Seedlings or cuttings should be stopped two or three times to produce bushy plants. Stake and tie plants, which also need potting on as they grow.
Cineraria	CH	S. Apr–Jul	Dec–May	Blue, mauve, pink, red and white	Grow best with a long season of steady growth, plenty of water and ventilation on all reasonable occasions. Treat as a tender biennial.
Cyclamen	I/W	S. Aug–Mar	Nov–May	Pink, red and white	The best plants are usually obtained from an autumn sowing in warm conditions, and overwintered in an intermediate or warm house. Keep seedlings well shaded and ventilated during summer and syringe freely. The best blooms are produced on young corms.
Euphorbia (Poinsettia)	W	C. Apr–May	Dec–Feb	Pink, red and white	After flowering, lower the temperature to 7°C (45°F). And place pots on their sides under the greenhouse staging until late March or April, when the plants stools can be used to provide cuttings. Repot the stools, raise the temperature to 16°C (60°F) and syringe freely. Take and root 100–150 mm (4–6 in) long cuttings at 19–22°C (65–70°F) after dipping them when prepared into fine

Fuchsia	CH & W	C. Oct and Apr	Apr–Sep	Pinks, purple and white	The old fuchsia plants can be rested between October and February at a minimum temperature of 4°C (40°F), raising the temperature to 10–13°C (50–55°F) to produce new growth. Cuttings taken in October need intermediate or warm conditions of 13–19°C (55–60°F) minimum during winter. Plants raised this way grow larger than those raised from cuttings taken in spring. Where bushy plants are required, stop them at the six-leaf stage, but leave standards unstopped until the desired height is reached. Feed plants with dilute liquid fertiliser during the summer months from about three weeks after the potting on, which should be carried out as young plants outgrow their containers. Stake and tie regularly as plants grow.
Hydrangea	I/W	C. Mar–Jun	Apr–Aug	Blue, pink red or white	After hydrangeas have flowered, remove old blooms and place plants outdoors until early September when they should be covered with frames or brought indoors. Early flowering in April can be obtained by providing warm conditions from December onwards. Where lower temperatures are maintained flowering is delayed. Node cuttings of unflowered shoots, about 100 mm (4 in) long can be taken between March and June, and rooted, three around the edges of each 75 mm (3 in) pot. Where pink varieties are to be blued, add 120 g (4 oz) aluminium sulphate to each two 18 litre (4 gal) buckets of John Innes No. 1 potting compost. Stop rooted cuttings at the six-leaf stage to promote four to six

breaking. Where short plants are required, incorporate a proprietary growth-retardant when potting up rooted cuttings.

Table of Pot Plants for Greenhouses—*continued*

Name	Conditions needed	Start	Season of colour	Colour	Remarks
					good break shoots. Pot on the young plants finally into 125–150 mm (5–6 in) pots, stake and tie plants as they grow. Move the young plants outdoors in August to ripen the wood, bringing them in again in September.
Impatiens (Busy Lizzie)	I	S. Mar–Apr	Jun–Oct	Cerise, orange, pink, purple, scarlet and white	Treat Impatiens in similar manner to the summer flowering, fibrous-rooted begonia.
Pelargonium	I	C. Jul–Sep	May–Oct	Crimson, orange, pink, purple, scarlet and white	Keep pelargoniums on the dry side, particularly during winter and avoid over feeding with dilute liquid fertiliser. Propagation is by node cuttings 50–100 mm (2–4 in) long, selecting these from healthy plants only. Stake and tie tall varieties as they grow.
Primula obconica	I	S. Feb–Jun	Dec–May	Blue, crimson, lavender, pink, purple and white	Treat *Primula obconica* as an annual, and discard old plants when flowering ceases.
Saintpaulia (African violet)	I/W	C. Jun–Sep	All year	Blue, pink, purple and white	Avoid potting saintpaulias into containers which are too large. Healthy plants can produce flowers for two, three or more years with care. Feed plants occasionally with dilute liquid fertiliser. Avoid spilling water onto the leaves which can be marked easily. Propagation is usually by leaf-stalk cuttings.

Key
CH   Cool House 4°C (40°F) minimum
I   Intermediate House 10°C (50°F) minimum
W   Warm House 16°C (60°F) minimum
I/W   13°C (55°F) minimum
S   Seed sowing
T   Tubers started off
C   Cuttings taken

ring of upturned florets around the disc.

Paeony-flowered. This type consists of several circles of florets around an 'eye' or discs, producing blooms which are more full in effect than single varieties.

Decorative. Blooms of this type are fully double without a central disc, and are divided into classes according to size. These are usually listed as large, medium, small and miniature.

Ball. These are globe shaped, double and classed into ball or miniature according to size.

Pompon. These form small compact, tightly-arranged, fully double balls, which are more compact than the preceding.

Cactus and semi-cactus. These form distinctive, double blooms with quilled or rolled petals. Varieties of this type are further divided according to size in a similar way to decoratives.

Bedding dahlias. These are usually single, or semi-double and are raised from seed sown in March each year. Seedlings are treated as for rooted cuttings – pricked out, hardened off and planted out.

To propagate, border varieties can be raised from cuttings 50–75 mm (2–3 in) long, taken in spring. These are best rooted, either singly or about four round the edges of 75 mm (3 in) pots, filled with cutting compost. Keep them moist and in warmth, about 13–16°C (55–60°F). Prick the rooted cuttings out singly into pots of John Innes No 2 potting compost or equivalent. Harden-off the young plants in frames before planting outdoors, after the danger of frost is past.

Planting and aftercare. The ground should be well dug and manured. Apply and rake in 100 g/m² (3 oz/sq yd) of balanced fertilisers 10–14 days before planting. Allow 30–75 cm (12–30 in) between dahlias, depending on variety. Stake tall kinds with three canes each, and tie securely. Keep plants well watered and weed free. Disbud large-flowered varieties, and feed with balanced liquid fertiliser. Spray occasionally against aphid. In autumn, lift tubers after cutting down the tops to 20–25 cm (8–10 in), and store in a frost-free place during winter.

Perpetual-flowering carnation is a particular type of dianthus and is not subdivided like the chrysanthemum.

Cuttings about 75 mm (3 in) long from healthy plants, are rooted in sandy compost in spring. The rooted cuttings are potted singly into 75 mm (3 in) pots of John Innes No 2 potting compost. These young plants are potted on progressively into larger pots. The growing point is removed when plants are 100–150 mm (4–6 in) high to induce breaking. All plants are supported either by canes or posts, wires and strings.

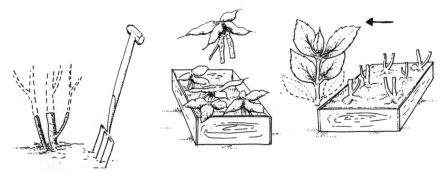

73 Dahlia. *Left to right*: top growth removed, stool ready for lifting; stools inverted, to drain water from stems and boxed up in spring for production of cuttings and, *arrowed*, trimmed cutting.

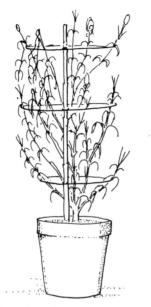

74 Carnation. Supported with cane and wire rings.

Disbudding is carried out to produce good-sized flowers. Regular feeding with diluted liquid fertiliser can be carried out every 10–14 days to advantage. Ventilate when temperatures rise above 13°C (55°F). Flowering plants are usually discarded after two or three years. *Roses* Hybrid tea varieties can be potted up in John Innes No 2 potting compost. The plants are brought indoors in January and are given similar conditions to carnations. Disbudding is carried out where large blooms are required. Feeding with liquid fertiliser commences as the buds start to show. The pots are moved outside in June and the plants are watered and fed until autumn when the stems are cut half way down as with outdoor H.T. varieties, and re-potted if necessary. In January, the plants are cut back hard and brought indoors again.

Vegetable and Salad Crops
Aubergines (Eggplant) This crop can be

grown in a broadly similar manner to tomatoes. Sow the seeds thinly in pots or boxes of John Innes seed compost and germinate in moist conditions at 22°C (70°F). Prick out the seedlings as soon as large enough to handle, singly into 90 cm (3½ in) pots. This crop can be planted in well prepared beds and borders at the spacing indicated in the table, although many gardeners grow them successfully in 150–200 mm (6–8 in) pots of John Innes No 2 potting compost. Stake and tie plants as they grow, preferably training them on single stems as cordons. Feeding can commence when fruits start to swell at the bottom. Remove side shoots as they arise, and

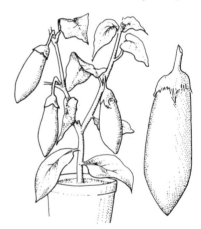

75 Aubergine. Limit pot-grown plants to three or four good fruits.

limit the number of fruits to three or four. Damp down floors on sunny days and ventilate at 22°C (70°F). Pick fruits as soon as they are large enough to use.
Cucumber Sow the seeds singly, placing them edgewise 12 mm (½ in) deep in 90 mm (3½ in) pots of John Innes No 1 potting compost. Germinate the seeds at 19–22°C (65–70°F) in moist, shaded conditions. Pot on the seedlings into 125 mm (5 in) pots of John Innes No 2 potting compost as soon as the seed leaves are expanded. Plant out when the seedlings have developed four or five

Table of Popular Indoor Crops

Crop	Sow	Space (cm) between rows	Space (cm) between plants	Harvest
Aubergine	Jan–Feb	75	40	Aug–Sep
Cucumber				
Greenhouse H	Feb–May	120	60	May–Oct
Greenhouse U/H	Apr	120	60	Jul–Oct
Lettuce				
Greenhouse H	Aug–Mar	25	25	Oct–May
Greenhouse U/H	Aug–Oct and Mar	25	25	Oct–Nov and Apr–May
Marrow	Mar–Apr	90–120	60	Jun–Oct
Melon	Feb–Apr	90	60	Aug–Sep
Sweet pepper	Feb–Mar	75	40	Aug–Sep
Tomato				
Greenhouse H	Jan–Mar	75	40	Jun–Oct
Greenhouse U/H	Mar	75	40	Jul–Oct

Key H   Heated crop
       U/H Unheated crop

true leaves onto mounds of prepared compost. One good mixture consists of equal parts of well-rotted manure and John Innes No 2 potting compost. Train the plants vertically as single cordons, tying each stem to a cane or stick at 15–20 cm (6–8 in) intervals as they grow. Stop the laterals or side shoots at the second leaf and the sub-laterals at one leaf, removing the main growing point when it reaches the top wire. Remove the male flowers, those without embryo fruits, before they open, to prevent pollination of flowers which spoils the table quality of cucumbers. Damp down frequently in warm weather to create humid conditions. Shade these plants between April and September. Top dress the mounds with a 25–50 mm (1–2 in) layer of prepared compost when the white roots start to appear on the surface. Cut fruits as soon as they are large enough to use to encourage continued cropping.

Lettuce A reliable method of growing indoor lettuce is to sow seeds thinly in boxes of John Innes Seed compost. Prick out seedlings 40 mm (1½ in) apart into boxes of John Innes No 2 potting compost as soon as they can be handled. Never allow the plants to dry out and give them as much light as possible, but ventilate when the temperature rises above 13°C (55°F). The ground for lettuce should be fertile, well limed with a pH of 6.8–7 and be free draining. Rake soil down to a fine tilth, level and even without lumps, and water the bed 24 hours before setting out the lettuce. Plant out the seedlings when four or five leaves have developed, but do not set them too deep.

N.B. Where the glass or plastic of greenhouses does not come down almost to floor level, it is better to grow the lettuce in boxes or containers not less than 100 mm (4 in) deep. These should be placed on staging.

Marrow Early crops of trailing varieties of courgettes or marrows can be grown in a similar manner to cucumbers, but with two main differences. They prefer

69

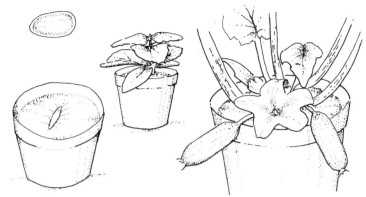

76 Marrow. *Left to right*: seed placed edgeways and covered after with compost; seedling ready for planting; fruiting plant in large pot.

less shading than cucumbers and the other requirement is that the female flowers of early crops of courgettes and marrows need to be pollinated. This consists of dabbing a piece of cotton wool into an open male flower – one without a fruit below, and transferring some pollen into the open female flowers, those with embryo fruits below. *Melon* The cultivation of this crop is similar to cucumber with one or two differences. With melons the aim is to

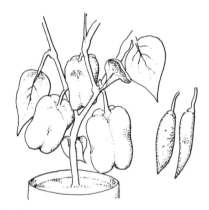

78 Sweet Pepper (Capsicum). Allow no more than four fruits on pot-grown plants. Chilli peppers on *right*.

pollinate four to six flowers all on the same day, and restrict the crop to three or four fruits. When these begin to mature, drier conditions are needed to assist ripening. Melons require only very light shading.

Sweet pepper (Capsicum) The method of cultivation broadly follows that of aubergine.

The principal difference is that the fruits can be picked green without loss of quality.

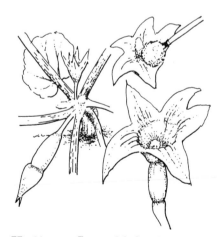

77 Marrow. *Top and Left*: taking pollen from male flower on cotton wool. *Right*: female flower ready for pollination.

Tomato Young plants are raised by sowing seeds in pots or boxes of John

79 Tomatoes. Being grown by ring culture method. Note bottomless pots of compost resting on moist gravel.

Innes seed compost or similar. Germinate them in a moist, shaded position at 19–21°C (65–68°F). Prick the seedlings out into 90 mm (3½ in) pots of John Innes No 2 potting compost as soon as these can be handled. Plant out the seedlings when 125–150 mm (5–6 in) high, into well prepared borders of fresh or sterilised soil. Alternatively they can be planted singly into 25 cm (10 in) pots of compost or into growing bags. With the ring culture method they are planted in bottomless pots for support while the roots have room to spread in a large tray of gravel. Train the plants as single cordons up vertical canes or strings. Remove side shoots as these occur. Start feeding the plants with dilute liquid fertiliser every 7–10 days until the final truss is fully developed. Damp down on sunny days during the summer and lightly syringe overhead as the first two or three trusses are in flower to assist fruit setting. Pick tomatoes as soon as they turn colour to help other fruits to swell unless required for showing, when they are allowed to ripen fully on plants. Remove the main growing point of plants in mid-August, just above the second leaf over the top flower truss. Fruits which form after that date do not have sufficient time to develop and ripen.

Chapter 5. Flowers and Foliage

Alpine *See* Rock plants, this chapter.

Annual A plant which belongs to one of the three major groups of annuals, biennials and perennials.

Annuals complete their life cycle in one year or less from the time seeds are sown, through the flowering period, to setting seeds and dying. Another feature of this group is the soft nature of the stems, which do not become woody. Although annuals are classified according to their use, they are also grouped according to hardiness, which influences their method of cultivation. Garden annuals originate from many parts of the world and from different climates such as alpine, temperate and tropical. These groups are hardy, half hardy and tender. *Hardy annuals* These plants can nor-mally be cultivated outdoors, but plants which are hardy in one place may not be so in another. Although truly hardy

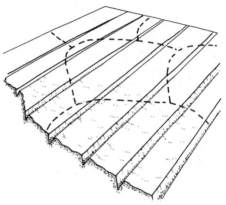

80   Hardy annuals. Sow in drills in patches for best effect.

Table of Plants Treated as Hardy Annuals, Summer Flowering

Name	Height (cm)	When Sown	Purpose		Colour
Calendula	45–60	Apr–May	B	C	Orange and yellow.
Candytuft, annual	15–25	Mar–May	B		Cerise, pink and white.
Clarkia	45–60	Mar–May	B	C	Cerise, pink, purple and white.
Clary	35–45	Apr–May	B	F	Pink, purple and white.
Cornflower	60–75	Mar–May	B	C	Blue, pink, purple and white.
Cynoglossum	40–45	Mar–Apr	B	C	Blue.
Godetia	30–75	Mar–Apr	B	C	Crimson, pink, red and white.
Larkspur	60–90	Mar–May	B	C	Blue, pink, purple, red and white.
Linaria	20–30	Mar–May	B		Blue, crimson, pink, yellow and violet.
Nasturtium, dwarf	25–40	Apr–May	B		Gold, rose and scarlet.

Key   B   used in beds or borders
C   used as cut flower
F   used as cut foliage

73

Table of Popular Plants Treated as Half-hardy Annuals, Summer Flowering

Name	Height (cm)	Space between Plants (cm)	Purpose		Colour
Ageratum	10–40	15–20	B		Blue, pink and white.
Alyssum	8–10	15	B		Pink, purple and white.
Antirrhinum	20–80	20–30	B	C	Crimson, orange, pink, scarlet, white and yellow.
Aster	20–75	20–30	B	C	Cerise, pink, purple and white.
Dianthus	30	25–30	B		Crimson, pink, scarlet and white.
Lobelia	10–20	15–20	B		Blue, carmine, lilac and white.
Marigold African	30–75	30	B		Gold and orange.
Marigold French	20–35	15–23	B		Gold, orange and red.
Mesembryanthemum	8–13	30	B	R	Crimson, orange, pink and white.
Nemesia	20–30	15	B		Blue, crimson, orange, pink and scarlet.
Petunia	15–30	30	B		Pink, purple, scarlet and white.
Phlox, annual	15–30	15–20	B		Crimson, pink, purple, scarlet and white.
Salvia	25–35	25–30	B		Pink, purple, scarlet and white.
Sweet pea	180	15	(B)	C	Blue, crimson, lavendar, pink, purple, red and white.
Tagetes	10–23	15–20	B		Crimson-red, gold and orange.
Verbena	15–30	30	B		Crimson, pink, purple and red.

Key   B   used in beds and borders for display
      C   used as cut flower
      R   used in rock gardens

annuals can survive outdoors in summer and winter, gardeners treat many plants as hardy, including some half hardy subjects so long as they can be sown and grown outdoors successfully.

Cultivation. Most hardy annuals can be grown successfully on light or medium soils which are fertile, free draining and form a good seed bed. The ground should be dug or forked, working in a bucketful, 18 litres/m² (3.5 gal/sq yd) of well rotted manure or peat. Lime the ground if need be to raise the pH to about 6.3, but allow a 10 day minimum interval after manuring. A few days before sowing rake in 70 g/m² (2 oz/sq

yd) of a balanced fertiliser. Break down any lumps of soil and create a fine tilth or crumb condition, with an even, level finish. Sowing is usually carried out in spring or autumn, in shallow V–drills which are moistened if necessary before seeding and lightly covered with fine soil afterwards. Annuals for cutting are usually sown in straight rows and those intended to provide splashes of colour in beds are sown in patches. Hardy annuals are usually thinned out rather than transplanted. Support tall varieties with pieces of twiggy brushwood, pushed among seedlings when only part grown. Keep the ground moist, weedfree and

Table of Arrangers Flowers

Name	Type and treatment	Cutting season	Feature
Amaranthus caudatus Love-lies-Bleeding	HHA	Su–Au	Crimson or green tail-like tassels.
Asclepias (Blood Flower or Milkweed)	HHP	Su	Unusual reddish or whitish flowers followed by decorative fruits.
Atriplex hortensis rubra (Red Mountain Spinach)	HA	Su	Tall stems of red foliage.
Cleome (Spider flower)	HHA	Su	Attractive pink and white spider like flowers, borne in clusters.
Echinops (Blue Globe Thistle)	HP	Su	Globular metallic blue seed head.
Eryngium (Sea Holly)	HP	Su	Spiky silver and blue-grey foliage and flower spikes.
Eucalyptus globulus (Blue Gum)	HHP	Year round	Scented grey foliage.
Helianthus (Italian White)	HHA	Su	Distinctive white sunflower-type blooms.
Molucella (Bells of Ireland)	HHA	Su	Curious small green, bell-shaped flowers clustered on the flower stem.
Nicotiana 'Lime Green' (Tobacco Plant)	HHA	Su	Long tubular flowers with star shaped arrangement of petals in yellowy lime green.
Ocimum Dark Opal (Blue Basil)	HA	Su	Scented purplish-blue leaves and stems.

Key HA Hardy annual Su Summer
     HHA Half-hardy annual Au Autumn.
     HP Hardy perennial
     HHP Half hardy perennial

hoe regularly. Remove the dead blooms promptly to encourage continued flowering.

Diseases and pests. *See* Chapter 10, Problems.

Half-hardy annual Plants in this category are or can be grown outdoors for part of their life cycle, but need a longer growing season than a temperate climate provides without protection.

Cultivation. Most half-hardy annuals or plants treated as such are best started off in greenhouses, frames or indoors on a window-sill. These seedlings are pricked out, then hardened off under frames in readiness for planting outdoors when the danger of frost is past, in late May or early June. The ground is prepared in the same manner as for hardy annuals, but the beds or borders are best given a good watering before planting in dry weather. Soak the seedlings, allowing the compost in the containers to drain before setting the young plants out in their flowering positions, preferably in dull, mild conditions. Stake and tie tall plants inconspicuously and as necessary with canes and string, or support with brushwood pushed into the soil. Keep the plants well watered and weedfree.

Deadheading of old blooms should be carried out regularly to prolong the flowering season.
Diseases and pests. *See* Chapter 10, Problems.
Tender annuals are best grown indoors apart from a few days in mid-summer when they can be placed and left outside. *See* Chapter 4, Greenhouses, Frames and Cloches.

Arrangers' flowers Certain uncommon flowering and foliage plants, which are particularly in demand for floral arrangements. Plants in this group are usually distinguished by some special or attractive features. Annuals, biennials and perennials are all represented in this category.

Bedding plants Decorative flowering and foliage subjects which are grown mainly for outdoor display in beds and borders as well as in containers of various kinds, such as window boxes. Bedding plants are normally set out into beds in the spring or autumn and when flowering ceases, they are usually cleared completely. Bedding plants are broadly classified according to their season of flowering as set out below.
Plants used for bedding purposes come from all the major groups of annuals, biennials and perennials.
Cultivation The beds and borders are prepared as for hardy annuals, but the plants are usually set out when part-grown or as bulbs instead of seeds. The arrangement of bedding plants in beds and borders is a matter of personal preference, but certain guide-lines may be helpful when preparing bedding schemes. Place tall plants at the back of beds against walls with the smallest

subjects at the front. With island or circular beds, tall plants are best set out in the centre and surrounded with dwarf edgings. Colour contrasts can be effective, such as blue and pink, or crimson

81 Bedding plants. Island bed, surrounded by lawn and flanked by borders. *Bottom*: section of bed, lawn and border.

with gold. Scarlet salvias with grey-leaved senecios are usully very impressive for a summer scheme. The planting and subsequent treatment of bedding plants are similar to those of their respective groups, such as annuals and biennials.

Biennial A member of the second major group of garden plants. Biennials normally require two years to complete their life cycle from seed sowing, growing, flowering through to finally setting seed and dying. Biennials in common with annuals are classed into hardy; half-hardy and tender categories, in addition to their uses.
Hardy biennials These can be sown and grown successfully in open ground. In a sheltered, sunny position for preference, prepare a seed bed. Dig or fork the

Type of bedding plant	Flowering season	Planting time
Spring	Spring	Autumn
Summer	Summer	Spring or early summer
Autumn	Autumn	Summer

Table of Spring Bedding Plants

Name	Type	Colour	Height (cm)	Category
Arabis	HP	Pink and white	15	E
Bellis	HP	Pink, red and white	10–15	E
Cheiranthus	HB	Gold and orange	30–40	M
Daffodil		See Narcissus		
Hyacinthus (Bu)	HP	Blue, crimson, pink, white and yellow	15–25	E
Myosotis	HB	Blue, pink and white	12–30	M and E
Narcissus (Bu)	HP	Orange, white and yellow	25–40	M
Pansy, Winter flowering	HP	Blue, purple, white and yellow	15–23	M and E
Polyanthus	HP	Blue, pink, red, white and yellow	15–20	M and E
Tulip (Bu)	HP	Pink, purple, red, scarlet, white and yellow	15–60	M
Wallflower	HB	Bronze, crimson and gold	25–45	M

Key M   Main plaints in bedding scheme   HP   Hardy perennial
     E   Suitable for edging or surround   HB   Hardy biennial
     Bu Bulbs

Table of Summer Bedding Plants

Name	Type Treatment	Colour	Height (cm)	Category
Alyssum	HHA	Pink, purple and white.	8–10	E
Antirrhinum	HHA	Orange, pink, red, white and yellow.	20–80	M
Begonia	HHP	Orange, pink, scarlet, white and yellow.	15–30	M and E
Dahlia	HHP	Orange, lilac, pink, purple, red and white.	30–75	M
Dianthus	HHA	Crimson, pink, scarlet and white.	30	M and E
Fuchsia	HHP	Crimson, pink, purple and white.	30–90	M and D
Kochia (F)	HHA	Green turning crimson.	50–90	D
Lobelia	HHA	Blue, carmine, lilac and white.	10–20	E
Marigold (African)	HHA	Gold, orange and yellow.	30–75	M and E
Marigold (French)	HHA	Crimson, gold and orange.	20–35	E
Pelargonium	HHP	Crimson, orange, pink, purple, scarlet and white.	30–90	M and D
Perilla (F)	HHA	Metallic bronze.	60	D
Petunia	HHA	Cerise, pink, purple, scarlet and white.	15–30	M and E
Salvia	HHA	Pink, purple, scarlet and white.	25–35	M and E
Tagetes	HHA	Crimson-red, gold and orange.	10–23	E
Verbena	HHA	Crimson, pink, purple and red.	15–30	M and E

Key D   Dot or spot plant   M   Main plants in bed or border
     E   Suitable for use as edging   HHA   Half-hardy annual
     F   Foliage plants   HHP   Half-hardy perennial

Table of Autumn Bedding Plants

Name	Treat-ment	Colour	Height (cm)	Category
Ageratum	HHA	Blue, pink and white.	10–40	E
Alyssum	HHA	Pink, purple and white.	8–10	E
Aster, various	HHA	Cerise, pink, purple and white.	20–75	M and E
Chrysanthemum dwarf	HHP	Bronze, crimson, pink, and yellow.	45–60	M
Chrysanthemum aureum (F)	HHA	Gold foliage.	10–12	E
Clary,-*Salvia horminum* (F)	HA	Pink, purple and white.	38–45	M and E
Marigold French	HHA	Crimson, gold, orange and red.	20–35	E
Senecio cineraria (F) (*Cineraria maritima*)	HHP	Grey foliage.	20–60	M and E

Key E   Edging
     F   Foliage plants
     M   Main bedding plant

HA   Hardy annual
HHA   Half-hardy annual
HHP   Half-hardy perennial

ground, incorporating a bucketful of peat, 18 litre/m^2 (3 gal/sq yd) and adding ground limestone if necessary, to bring the pH up to about 6.5. Rake in 35 g/m^2 (1 oz/sq yd) of calcium superphosphate, creating a fine tilth or crumb structure. By using peat and superphosphate, creating a fine tilth or crumb usual interval between manuring and liming or before adding fertiliser. Sow the seeds in moistened drills, 6–12 mm ($\frac{1}{4}$–$\frac{1}{2}$ in) deep, and 25 cm (10 in) apart and cover with fine soil. Keep the ground moist, weedfree and hoe regularly. Transplant the seedlings, when 50–75 mm (2–3 in) tall, into nursery beds, prepared as for sowing hardy annuals. Space the seedlings 150 mm (6 in) apart, leaving 300 mm (12 in) between rows, treating the nursery bed as the seed bed, watering, weeding and hoeing as needed.

Table of Hardy Biennials

Name	Height (cm)	Sow	Colour	Final space between plants	Flowering Season
Anchusa italica	90	Apr–Jun	Blue.	30	Jun–Jul
Campanula Canterbury Bell	40–75	Apr–Jun	Blue, pink and white.	30	Jun–Jul
Erysimum	15–20	May–Jun	Yellow.	20	Apr–Jun
Lunaria Honesty	60	May–Jul	Purple and white.	30	Jul–Sep
Myosotis Forget-me-not	20–30	May–Jul	Blue, pink and white.	15	Mar–Jun
Dianthus Sweet William	20–45	May–Jun	Pink, scarlet, purple and white.	20–30	Jun–Jul
Cheiranthus Wallflower	23–45	May–Jun	Crimson, gold, orange and red.	20–30	Apr–Jun

During September and October set out the seedlings in their final position in firm level beds or borders, prepared as for hardy annuals. Keep the plants weedfree and firm them into the soil again where lifted by frost. Staking and tying is rarely needed with biennials, but should if necessary be attended to. Dead-head old blooms to ensure continuity of flowering.

Half-hardy biennials Two plants, which are sometimes treated thus are Brompton Stocks and digitalis. Both subjects can be raised by sowing in May on a prepared seed bed and covering with frames. Prick out the seedlings into a sheltered nursery bed for their summer quarters. Plant the digitalis in their final positions as for hardy biennials, but protect Brompton Stocks with frames during winter and plant them out in March.

Bog garden plants With the size of the average garden becoming increasingly small, the opportunities for bog and water gardening diminish. Bog plants include various types of moisture-loving subjects which grow well close to the margins of ponds and lakes. Although moisture is required, many of these plants cannot tolerate stagnant conditions.

Border *See* Herbaceous border, this chapter.

Bulbs Plants of this type are often grouped together in categories with corms and tubers for the sake of con-

82 Bog plants. These border the pond which contains aquatic subjects like water lily.

venience. One feature that these plants have in common, is that they contain food reserves in the swollen portion, which enables, some subjects to flower very early in the year. Bulbs, corms and tubers provide some very colourful flowering subjects, which can be used for a variety of purposes. These can provide bedding plants, cut flowers, be grown and naturalised in grass, as well as be used in pots and containers.

Cultivation Bulbs can be successfully grown in ground, prepared as for bedding plants and preferably not too exposed to cold winds. Bulbs for naturalising are planted in groups, in prepared pockets of soil, which should be forked up with some peat and base fertiliser mixed in as for beds. Replace turf over planted areas in grass.

Calcifuge Any plant which dislikes chalk or limestone in soils even in small quantities. The most notable plants of

Table of Bog Garden Plants

Name	Treatment	Colour
Astilbe	HP	Crimson, pink and white.
Caltha	HP	Yellow.
Mimulus	HP	Crimson and yellow.
Myosotis	HB	Blue, pink and white.
Primulas, various	HP	Crimson, orange and yellow.
Ranunculus	HP	Yellow.

Key HP Hardy perennial   HB Hardy biennial

Table of Popular Bulbs, Corms and Tubers

Name	Height (cm)	Planting season	Space apart (cm)	Planting depth (cm)	Flowering season	Colour
Anemone C Windflower	15–45	Aut–Spr	10–15	7	Spr–Aut	Crimson, pink, purple and white.
Begonia × tuberhybrida Tuberous begonia	15–45	Spr	15–30	7	Sum	Orange, pink, red, white and yellow.
Crocosmia C Monbretia	15–120	Spr	5	7	Sum	Orange and yellow.
Crocus N R	10–12	Aut–Win	5	7	Aut–Spr	Purple, white and yellow.
Galanthus N R Snowdrop	15–30	Sum	2	5	Win–Spr	White.
Gladiolus C Sword Lily	30–120	Spr	15	10	Sum–Aut	Orange, pink, red, white and yellow.
Hyacinthus C Hyacinth	15–30	Aut	15	12	Win–Spr	Blue, crimson, pink, white and yellow.
Iris C R	15–60	Sum–Aut	7–15	7	Spr–Sum	Blue, purple, white and yellow.
Lilium C Lily	20–250	Sum–Aut	15–30	10–12	Sum–Aut	Orange, pink, white and yellow.
Narcissus C R Daffodil/narcissus	15–55	Sum–Aut	5–15	10–15	Win–Spr	Orange, white and yellow.
Tulipa C R Tulip	10–70	Aut–Win	15	10	Win–Spr	Pink, purple, red, white and yellow.

Key C Suitable for cutting
     N Suitable for naturalising
     R Suitable for a rock garden

83 Container plants. *Left to right*: rest hanging basket on a pot or bucket; push plant roots through the sides as filling proceeds; completed hanging basket.

the type include heathers, and rhododendrons.

Chalk plants (Calciphiles) A group of subjects which either require or can tolerate chalk or limestone soils. While most plants grow and thrive on slightly acid soils, there are some which only produce the best results under alkaline conditions. Notable members of this group among garden flowers include carnations, dianthus, gypsophila, pinks, stocks, and Sweet William.

Container plants Applied to plants which can be grown successfully in receptacles, such as window boxes, tubs, troughs and hanging baskets. The normal method of treatment is a modified form of pot culture. It includes the provision of some drainage and a good rooting medium or compost. Outdoor containers are usually planted up with bulbs and bedding plants in autumn or spring. Regular watering is necessary and plants should be given an occasional feed with liquid fertiliser. The success of roof and balcony gardening relies on growing plants to a high standard in containers of some kind. Bedding plants, particularly some of the smaller kinds, are outstanding for container cultivation. *See* Bedding Plants this chapter, for lists of spring and summer subjects.

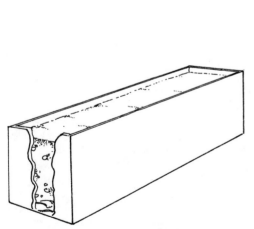

84 Container plants. *Left*: window box, showing coarse crocks for drainage. *Right*: section through filled box, pelargonium centre, with ageratum on each side.

Corms *See* Bulbs, this chapter.

Cottage Garden plants A class of flowering plants which are traditionally associated with old English cottage gardening. These include annuals, biennials and perennials. In the following list HA signifies Hardy Annual; HB, Hardy Biennial and HP, Hardy Perennial. Aquilegia (HP); Calendula (HA); Canterbury Bell (HB); Foxglove (HB); Hollyhock (HP); Old-fashioned Pinks (HP); Primrose (HP); Old English roses (HP); Sweet William (HB).

Dot plants Any plant which is used singly or dotted among a mass of bedding plants. Examples of this type of plant include standard fuchsias and pelargoniums. The addition of only a few of these subjects can alter the character of bedding schemes, frequently to give extra height.

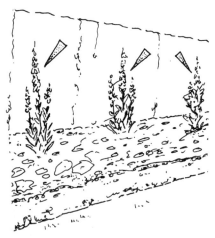

86 Dot plants. Placed among bedding.

85 Dot plants. *Left to right:* grey-leaved Senecio cineraria; standard pelargonium; kochia or Burning bush; pyramid fuchsia.

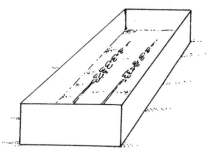

87 Drying flowers. *Top:* foxglove laid on silica gel powder in box. *Below:* covered with more powder and lid placed over.

Dried flowers Flowers which have been preserved by drying for decorative purposes indoors. *See* Everlasting plants, this chapter.

Edging plants These are usually low-growing flowering or foliage subjects which are planted to provide a continuous ribbon of colour and interest around the margins of such as island

beds. Plants which are frequently used for this purpose include French marigold, lobelia and tagetes. *See* Bedding plants, this chapter, for a list of other subjects.

Everlasting plants These form flowers which have petals with straw-like texture. Blooms of this type can be cut when little more than half open and dried by hanging them upside down in a dry, shaded place. Flowers of this group

Table of Popular Everlasting Flowers

Name	Colours	Treatment	Feature
Acroclinium	Pink and white.	HHA	Flower
Anaphalis	White.	HP	Flower
Catananche	Blue.	HP	Flower
Clary	Blue, pink and white.	HA	Flower bracts
Cortaderia	Ivory.	HP	Seed head
Echinops	Blue.	HP	Flower and Seed head
Eryngium	Blue.	HP	Flower and Seed head
Gomphrena	Orange, pink, purple, white and yellow.	HHA	Flower
Helichrysum	Orange, pink, red, white and yellow.	HHA/HA	Flower
Honesty	Purple and white.	HB	Seed head
Molucella	Green.	HHA	Flower
Physalis	White flowers, orange seed head.	HP	Seedhead
Statice	Mauve, orange, pink, white and yellow.	HHA/HHP	Flower

Key	HHA	Half-hardy annual	HA	Hardy Annual
	HHP	Half-hardy perennial	HP	Hardy Perennial

retain their colour well after being treated in this manner, provided they are not exposed to strong sunlight. Other plants included here are various grasses and subjects which produce papery seed heads like Chinese Lanterns.

Ferns These are useful for covering level ground, banks and even walls or rocky slopes, especially in damp shaded situations where few other plants would thrive. The requirements of hardy garden ferns are average medium soils that are moist, and shelter from cold or freezing winds. Useful hardy ferns are *Adiantum pedatum*, Maidenhair fern; *Asplenium trichomanes*, Maidenhair Spleenwort; *Phyllitis scolopendrium*, Hart's Tongue; *Polypodium vulgare*, Polypody.

Florists flowers This is usually applied to double or other blooms which are used mainly for cut flower or pot culture, such as carnations and chrysanthemums.

Foliage plants These are plants which are cultivated for the decorative effect of their leaves. The treatment and methods of propagation of foliage plants vary according to their respective family or class. *See* Table of Foliage Plants for plants useful for flower beds and borders.

Formal Plants Bedding plants provide an example of these, when they are used in regimented or geometrical fashion in flower beds or close to buildings.

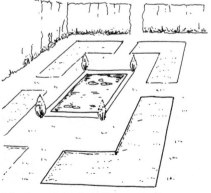

88 Formal garden. Symmetrical arrangement of pool and surrounding beds.

Table of Foliage Plants

Name	Treatment	Feature
Atriplex rubra	HA	Reddish crimson foliage.
Clary	HA	Blue, red and silver leaves/bracts.
Coleus	HHA/HHP	Variegated and self, in red, orange, yellow, brown and green shades.
Kochia	HHA	Green foliage, turning crimson in autumn.
Pelargonium	HHP	Variegated foliage in shades of green, cream, purple, reds and terracotta.
Perilla	HHA	Metallic purplish leaves.
Senecio cineraria	HHP	Grey finely-cut foliage.
Stachys	HP	Grey hairy leaves.
Striped Maize (zea)	HHA	Striped green, yellow and white shades.

Key HA   Hardy Annual   HP   Hardy Perennial
      HHA Half-hardy Annual   HHP Half-hardy Perrennial

Ground cover *See* Chapter 7, Trees and Shrubs.

Hanging basket *See* Chapter 3, Plant Care, for making up, and Bedding plants, this chapter, for list of suitable subjects.

Hardy plants *See* Annuals, *also* Biennials, *also* Perennials, this chapter, for lists of hardy flowers.

Herbaceous Plants which die down each winter and break into growth in spring.

Herbaceous borders rely on hardy herbaceous perennials for their colour and interest. *See* Hardy perennials. Herbaceous subjects are grown on ground prepared as for hardy annuals, but most are set out as plants and not sown *in situ*. Many plants of this type are increased by division and cuttings. *See* Chapter 2, Propagation.

Patch plant *See* Annuals, this chapter.

Perennials The third major group of plants, the other two being annuals and biennials. These are divided into three

Table of Colourful Herbaceous Plants

Name	Height (cm)	Flowering Period	Colour
Achillea	45–150	June–Aug	Yellow or white
Aster	40–150	Jul–Sep	Pink, blue, wine and purple shades
Campanula	45–60	Jun–Jul	Purple and white
Delphinium	75–180	Jun–Jul	Blue, purple, cream, white and pink shades
Dianthus	15–60	Jun–Sep	White, pink, red and purple shades
Doronicum	40–60	Apr–May	Yellow
Erigeron	30–60	May–Jul	White, pink and mauve shades
Gaillardia	45–75	Jun–Oct	Red, yellow, and banded
Kniphofia	60–150	Jun–Sep	Red, yellow and cream shades
Lupin	75–100	May–Jun	Self and bi-colour, pink, blue, purple and yellow
Lychnis	60–90	May–Aug	Crimson, scarlet, and purple shades
Phlox	60–120	Aug–Sep	White, pink, wine and purple shades
Pyrethrum	40–60	Apr–Jun	Pink and scarlet shades
Scabious	60–120	Jun–Sep	Blue and yellow shades
Solidago	45–150	Aug–Oct	Yellow

categories, hardy, half-hardy and tender. Perennials are further subdivided into: herbaceous plants, q.v. this chapter, which die down in winter; and woody subjects which are retained from one year to the next. *See* Chapter 7, Trees and Shrubs for this category.

Hardy herbaceous plants are widely used in flower borders. Perennial bulbs also come within this group of herbaceous subjects.

Half-hardy perennials are similarly sub-divided into herbaceous and woody plants and are overwintered under cover. The most notable garden flowers among half-hardy perennials include begonias, early-flowering chrysanthemums, dahlias, fuchsias and pelargoniums. The cultivation of this class of plant involves raising or starting plants off under cover, hardening off under frames, planting and growing outdoors, lifting plants or stools in autumn and overwintering these indoors.

For details of ground preparation, propagation methods, staking and tying, *see* Chapter 3, Plant Care. The cultural details of overwintering and raising these plants are discussed in Chapter 4, Greenhouses.

Rock plant The art of rock gardening has been developed to a high degree of specialisation by enthusiasts, but the novice can begin with a few reliable plants. As experience is gained, progression to more difficult subjects can be attempted.

Cultivation of easy rock plants. This consists of providing pockets of good soil or compost, such as John Innes, among natural or well-arranged rocks or stones. Planting is normally carried out in autumn and spring, or shortly after flowering in some cases. Outdoor rock plants are categorised into annuals, biennials and perennials.

Roof garden plants *See* Container plants, this chapter.

Scented plants These can be enjoyed especially when grown close to the house where the scent and fragrance can enter open windows. Notable among scented plants are hyacinths, lilies, narcissi and stocks.

Seaside plants Many garden bedding plants grow well close to the sea, provided they are not too exposed to cold winds. The good light conditions suit them and the salt spray troubles this group less than many shrubs.

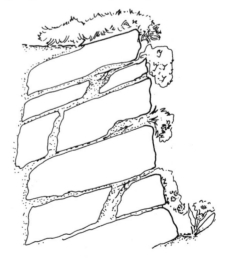

89   Rock garden. The rocks are laid in layers to simulate natural strata.

90   Wall garden. Plants growing in the cracks and crevices of walls can provide a very pleasing garden feature. The rocks should be tilted back as shown, for safety.

Table of Easily Grown Rock Plants, all Hardy Perennials

Name	Height (cm)	Colour	Flowering season
Aethionema	20	Pink.	May–Aug
Alyssum saxatile	25	Yellow.	May–Jun
Arabis	20	Pink and white.	Mar–Jun
Armeria	15–25	Pink, rose-red and white.	May–Jun
Aubretia	10–15	Mauve, pink and purple.	Apr–Jun
Campanula	5–20	Blue and white.	Jun–Aug
Chionodoxa	10–15	Blue, pink and white.	Mar–Apr
Crocus	5–15	Blue, mauve, white and yellow.	Nov–Apr
Dianthus	10–20	Crimson, pink, scarlet and white.	May–Sep
Narcissus, dwarf	7–20	Yellow.	Mar–Apr
Phlox	15–20	Pink and purple.	May–Jun
Saxifrage	5–20	Pink, white and yellow.	Feb–Jul

Variegated plants The attraction of multi-coloured leaves puts these into a prominent place among foliage plants.

Wall plants Many rock plants thrive in conditions provided by walls, such as alyssum, arabis and aubretia.

Chapter 6. Fruit

American blight *See* Chapter 10, Problems.

Apple This is the most widely grown tree fruit in the British Isles for culinary and dessert use.

Cultivation Ideally, a free draining deep, medium loam that is fertile and has a pH of around 6.5, suits this crop. Culinary apples grow well on heavier and wetter ground than is suitable for dessert varieties. Apples normally crop best when sited in open sunny situations with a south or west-facing aspect, protected from east winds. In cold or northern districts dessert apples crop more regularly when grown against a south wall. Plant this fruit tree where it will not outgrow its space

Tree size is affected by several factors including climate, variety or type, kind of root stock, form of tree, methods of pruning, and feeding.

Climate. Mild moist conditions favour strong growth, while warm and dry or cold conditions result in diminished vigour.

Variety. Culinary apples such as Bramleys Seedling are naturally more vigorous than the dessert variety, Cox's Orange Pippin.

Rootstock. Grafting or budding onto dwarfing rootstocks produces small, manageable trees suitable for small, trained forms like cordons.

Tree form. Apples grown as bush, cordon or espalier trees need much less space than those trained as half or full standards.

Pruning and feeding. Hard cutting and generous feeding result in strong growth. However light pruning combined with little or no feeding encourages increased fruitfulness with reduced vigour. In each cluster of immature unthinned apples there is often one fruit larger than the rest. This is referred to as the king apple, which rarely develops satisfactorily and should be removed when thinning.

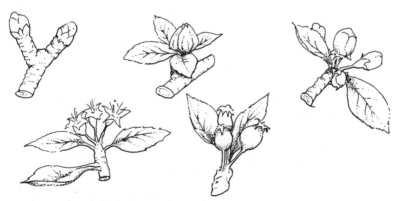

91 Bud development. These are the important bud stages for spraying apples. *Top, left to right*: bud break or burst; green cluster; and pink bud. *Bottom, left to right*: petal fall and fruitlet.

87

Table of Tree Forms of Apple

Tree form	Rootstock	Space needed (m)
Bush	Malling 11	4.5 × 4.5
Cordon	Malling 1X or 1XA	2.5 × 1
Espalier	Malling Merton 106	4.5 × 2.5
Half-standard	Malling Merton 111	7.5 × 7.5
Pyramid	Malling IX or * 1XA	3 × 1.5
Standard	Malling XXV	13.5 × 13.5

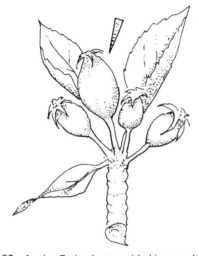

Plant lifted trees during their dormant season in autumn. Those grown in containers can be planted at almost any time of year, provided the ground is not too wet, dry or frozen. But keep them well watered in dry weather.

Set trees out in excavated pits, spreading prepared compost over the roots, firming as filling proceeds and insert stakes before planting. *See* Chapter 3, Plant Care. As a guide, allow trees the amount of space shown in the Table of Tree Forms.

The method of staking will vary slightly, according to the form of tree being grown and its size. Mulch trees each spring after applying $70-100\,\text{g/m}^2$ (2–3 oz/sq yd) of balanced fertiliser.

92 Apple. Fruit cluster with king apple, *arrowed*.

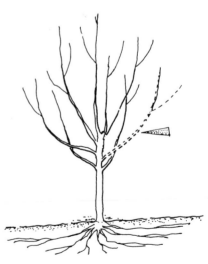

93 Apple. Branches supported by wires attached to centre pole.

94 Apple. Family tree with pollinator variety arrowed.

Table of Apples and Suitable Pollinators

Main variety (M)	Pollinator (P)	Fruiting habit M	P	Season of use
George Cave D	Beauty of Bath D	Spur	Spur	Aug
James Grieve D	Lord Lambourne D	Spur	Spur	Sep–Oct
Lord Lambourne D	Ribston Pippin D	Spur	Spur	Oct–Nov
Cox's Orange Pippin D	James Grieve D	Spur	Spur	Nov–Jan
Bramleys Seedling C	Early Victoria C	Tip	Spur	Nov–Mar
Sunset D	Worcester Pearmain D	Spur	Tip	Nov–Dec

Key D   Dessert variety   C   Culinary variety

Training Most gardeners buy their trees in one of the recognised forms, such as bush or cordon, which have an initial framework of branches at the time of purchase.

Pollination Some varieties produce an abundance of blossom, but fail to set fruit without pollination by another variety. The solution is to plant a suitable pollinator nearby. Alternatively plant a Family tree, which has a branch of a pollinator budded or grafted on as well as the main variety.

Propagation Apple trees are increased by budding a main variety onto a suitable rootstock in July or early August. Similarly this can be carried out by grafting during March. *See* Chapter 2, Propagation.

Bark ringing A practice used to induce flowering in unproductive apple and pear trees. *See* Chapter 3, Plant Care.

Big Bud gall mite A serious pest of blackcurrants. *See* Chapter 10, Problems.

Blackberry A crop grown for the juicy black ripe or very dark red immature fruits which are carried on long canes during September. This crop grows well in deep, moist loams of medium texture, which have been well dug, lightly manured and cultivated.

Cultivation Erect a post and wire frame or fence on which to support the rods or branches, spacing four or five horizontal

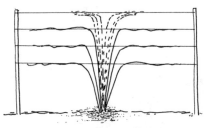

95   Blackberry. Trained on wires, leaving space for new season's shoots to grow vertically, to replace old rods after fruiting.

wires 300 mm (12 in) apart. Planting can be carried out between October and March, but should ideally take place in autumn. Allow each plant 1.8–3 m (6–10 ft) run of wires and where more than one row is grown, leave 1.8 m (6 ft) minimum between rows. Cut back the young plants to within 200 mm (8 in) of the ground. Apply a mulch of manure in spring and keep the ground moist and weedfree.

Training Tie in the rods or growths, one pair for each wire, starting about 75 cm (2½ ft) above soil level, rising to the top support about 1.65 m (5½ ft).

Pruning consists of cutting out the old rods after fruiting in autumn. Tie in the replacement growths and remove any which are surplus to needs at ground level.

Rootstocks are unnecessary for this crop which grows well on its own.

Propagation can easily be achieved by pegging down the tips of young growths into fine soil during July. Keep them moist and weedfree. When well rooted and growing in about September or October lift the young tips, sever them from the parent plant and set them out. *See* Chapter 2, Propagation.

Blackcurrant *See* currants.

Bush fruits A group of fruits which carry their crop on a low framework of branches, such as currants or gooseberries.

Cane fruits A collective name for soft fruits which produce their crop on canes, such as raspberries, or on rods like blackberries and loganberries.

Canker A condition of top fruits, suffering from disease and which occurs among apple trees. *See* Chapter 10, Problems.

Cherry Sweet cherries make excessively large trees due to the absence of dwarf rootstocks, and so are unsuitable for the average garden.

Cob nut *See* Nuts, this chapter.

Cordon A trained form of fruit tree. *See* Chapter 3, Plant Care.

Currants A group of bush fruits, grown for their berries which are highly valued for culinary purposes. Currants consist of three main types: black, red

and white. The black varieties are treated rather differently from the other two.

Blackcurrants These grow best on deep and fertile medium soils, preferably in open or very lightly shaded situations, where there is adequate moisture. The soil should be well dug, manured and cultivated before planting, to break down lumps, improve soil fertility and kill off weeds.

Cultivation. Lime the ground at least 7–10 days after manuring, to raise the pH to 6.5. Where the soil is only moderately fertile, work in 100 g/m^2 (3 oz/sq yd) of balanced, base fertiliser about 10 days before planting and at least a similar minimum interval after any liming.

Planting is normally best carried out in November, but can successfully take place between November and March. Space the bushes about 1.8 m (6 ft) each way. Container-grown blackcurrants can be set out at most times of the year when soil and weather conditions allow. Mulch plants each spring to conserve moisture.

Pruning. Cut back newly-planted bushes to within 50–75 mm (2–3 in) of soil level, to promote strong growth from the base. Blackcurrants produce the best fruits on young wood. Subsequent pruning consists of cutting out about

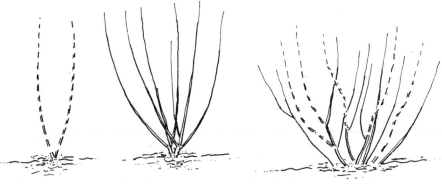

96 Currant, black. *Left to right*: cut new plant to soil level in first year; result of hard pruning; remove about one-third of all branches starting with old wood in fruiting bushes each autumn.

97 Currant, red. *Left to right*: shorten shoots of new plants by one-third after planting; shorten new side growths back to old wood each winter; fruiting bush after pruning.

one-third of all shoots each autumn, removing old or fruited wood first. Aim to form a bowl shaped framework of branches in the process.

Pest and Disease control. *See* Chapter 10, Problems.

Cropping normally commences in the second or third year after planting.

New plants can be raised from 200–300 mm (8–12 in) long hardwood cuttings, taken in autumn. *See* Chapter 2, Propagation.

Suitable varieties include Mendip Cross, Seabrooks Black, Wellington XXX and Baldwin.

Red and White currants

Cultivation. Prepare the ground for these two crops as for black currants, but preferably give them sunny positions.

Set out bush forms as for blackcurrants or plant cordons against a south or west wall about 400 mm (16 in) apart. Mulch plants in the spring following planting and subsequently if possible.

Pruning. After planting, shorten the shoots of bushes by half, but leave cordons stems alone, apart from cutting back any side growths. Subsequent treatment is aimed at providing a permanent bowl-shaped framework of branches for bushes and developing two or three long fruiting stems with cordons. The crop is carried on short spurs from the main branches, and pruning involves shortening back new growths to two or three buds in autumn.

Pest and disease control. *See* Chapter 10, Problems.

Cropping commences usually in the third year after planting and continues for many years once plants are established.

Propagation is by hardwood cuttings as for blackcurrants.

Varieties. Laxton's No 1 and Red Lake are useful types of red currant. White currants are less widely planted than red varieties and White Versailles is one of the main kinds grown.

Espalier A trained form of tree which is grown against a wall or fence and has pairs of horizontal branches. This form is used mainly for apples and pears. *See* Chapter 3, Plant Care.

Family tree A type of fruit tree, which is budded or grafted with two or more varieties, to ensure the setting of gruit by providing adequate pollination. The growing of more than one variety on each tree removes the need to plant more than one tree in small gardens.

Fan A trained form of tree, grown against walls usually, with branches which radiate fan-wise from a short main stem. *See* Chapter 3, Plant Care.

Filbert A type of nut suitable for medium or large-sized gardens. *See* Nuts, this chapter.

Fruit diseases and pests *See* Chapter 10, Problems.

Gages *See* Plums, this chapter.

Gooseberry An easily grown and reliable bush fruit, cultivated for the red, green or yellow berries, some of which can be eaten raw or cooked.

Cultivation This crop grows well on medium loam soils that contain reserves of potash and are free draining, in sunny or part-shaded positions. Dig the soil spade deep, incorporating two buckets-ful 18 litre/m² (3½ gal/sq yd) of manure or compost. Lime the ground if need be to raise the pH level above 6.3, allowing the necessary 10 day intervals between manuring and liming and fertiliser applications. Apply 100 g/m² (3 oz/sq yd) of high potash fertiliser, lightly forking this in before planting. Set gooseberry bushes out at 1.8 m (6 ft) apart each way, and allow 400 mm (16 in) between cordons.

Pruning Treat gooseberry bushes and cordons as for red currants, except that cutting should be carried out in February or March instead of autumn. This helps to reduce bird damage to buds in winter and enable damaged shoots to be cut out after instead of before attack.

98 Gooseberry. *Left*: shorten new side-shoots by half to two-thirds. *Right*: fruiting bush after pruning.

Disease and pest control *See* Chapter 10, Problems.

Propagation This can be by 200–300 mm (8–12 in) hardwood cuttings taken in autumn, like those of red currant, except that all buds and thorns are cut off the bottom two thirds of each shoot. This produces plants with a short

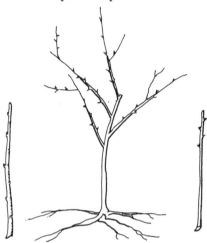

99 Leg. Gooseberry bushes are often grown on a short clear stem or leg to make picking easier. Cuttings are stripped of buds for two-thirds their length as shown *right*, to achieve this, unlike the currant cutting, *left*.

single leg or stem without prickly suckers arising from soil level, making subsequent harvesting easy. *See* Chapter 2, Propagation.

Varieties Leveller, a yellow type, is the finest dessert gooseberry. Other useful kinds include Careless, green; Lancer, green; and Whinhams Industry red.

Grafting *See* Chapter 2, Propagation.

Grapes These can be grown successfully outdoors in very favourable southern districts in warm, sunny situations, but are best grown in greenhouses in most areas.

Guyot A method of training outdoor grapes, which is popular on the continent. It consists of cutting out fruited rods each autumn after cropping and tying in young replacement growths.

Half standard *See* Chapter 3, Plant Care.

Hormone These chemicals are used in gardening to assist rooting in cuttings; to encourage fruit setting and to control weeds and prevent undue dropping of fruit when part grown.

June drop A condition which occurs often among apple trees in summer when considerable numbers of immature fruits fall to the ground. This is more noticeable in years of heavy fruit set than light and is a form of natural thinning. *See* Chapter 10, Problems.

Loganberry A crop which is grown for the delicious dark red berries which ripen in summer and are excellent for dessert and in preserves.
Cultivation The requirements of and preparations for this crop are similar to the blackberry, to which it is related. Plant out healthy, vigorous young loganberries preferably in autumn, but these can also be successfully set out between October and March. Container-grown subjects can be planted out at almost any time of year provided the soil is not too wet, frozen or dry. Allow each plant 2.4–3.6 m (8–12 ft) run of post and wire support or fence. Allow a minimum distance of 2.1 m (7 ft) between each row. Mulch the soil around plants each spring, to smother weeds and conserve moisture.
Pruning Cut the shoots of newly-planted loganberries to within 200 mm (8 in) of the ground. As with blackberries, train and tie in pairs of new growths to horizontal wires, spaced 300 mm (12 in) apart, with the top wire about 1.6 m (5½ ft)above ground. Subsequent treatment consists of cutting out fruited rods each autumn and tying in replacement growths.
Disease and Pest control See Chapter 10, Problems.
Propagation This is achieved by tip layering in July and consists of pegging down the tips of healthy young shoots into hollows in the ground. Cover each tip with 100–150 mm (4–6 in) of fine soil, which should be kept moist and weed-free. When rooting has taken place, sever the young layers from their parents, lift and plant them out into their fruiting positions.
Cropping commences in the second year after planting.
Varieties The variety known as LY59, and The Thornless Loganberry are the most widely grown.

Myrobalan A small fruited type of plum which is sometimes planted to provide a tall hedge. This plum is also used as a rootstock for other varieties, making fairly large trees eventually.

Nicking and notching *See* Chapter 3, Plant Care.

Nuts Trees or shrubs grown for their hard, but edible nuts or fruits, which are eaten raw or used for culinary purposes.
Cultivation These can be grown on most well-drained soils of average fertility, but need considerable space and are slow to come into bearing. Select a warm sunny position that is protected from cold north or east winds for best results. Hazel nuts, also known as cobnut and Filbert, are more widely grown than other types. On well prepared ground, plant out the young hazels, preferably in autumn, spacing them 2.1 m (7 ft) apart for hedge cultivation or double that distance for individual specimens. Apply a mulch around the plants each spring.
Pruning This consists of shortening new shoots by half each autumn until flowering starts, about five or six years after planting, to promote branching and develop a strong framework of stems. Subsequently cut out old fruited spurs in autumn, to encourage new replacement spurs or shoots.
Disease and Pest control See Chapter 10, Problems.

Table of Tree Forms of Pear

Tree form	Rootstock	Space needed (m)
Bush	Malling Quince A	4.5 × 4.5
Cordon	Malling Quince C on good soils	2.5 × 1
	Malling Quince A on poor soils	2.5 × 1
Espalier	Malling Quince A	4.5 × 2.5
Pyramid	As for cordon	3 × 1.5
Half-standard	Malling Quince A	6 × 6

Propagation is normally by means of layering in autumn. Layers should be ready to lift and sever from the parent one year later and then be planted in a nursery bed for a further couple of years. *Variety* Kentish Cob is one of the best varieties, producing nuts of good size and appearance.

Pear A crop grown for the distinctive fruits which are harvested during summer and early autumn for eating raw and for culinary purposes.

Cultivation This fruit grows and crops best on deep, medium loams that are fertile, only slightly acid with a pH level of 6.5. The site should ideally be sheltered, warm and sunny. Prepare and manure the land as for apples, making sure that the soil is free draining. Select trees of the right type and variety so that they do not outgrow their space and are fruitful. Tree size is affected by similar factors to those controlling apples. Planting is best carried out during November, but can be carried out from November to March for lifted trees. However, container-grown stock can be planted at almost any time provided the soil is not too wet, frozen or dry.

Erect a suitable framework of wire supports before planting cordon, espalier, pyramid or other trained forms. Excavate tree pits at the correct spacing, *see* Table of Pear Trees, and of sufficient size, hammering in posts for such as half-standards, before placing trees in position. Cover the roots with good topsoil or prepared mixture, working this in and around them. Firm the soil as filling proceeds and make sure the trees are at the same depth after planting as before the move. Mulch the trees during the first spring. And subsequently, apply 100 g/m² (3 oz/sq yd) of balanced fertiliser before mulching.

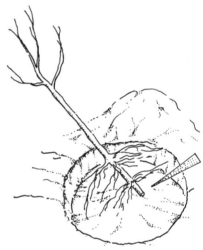

100 Planting. Shorten excessively vigorous tap roots *as arrowed*.

Pruning Assuming that trees with a ready-made initial framework of branches have been planted then normal spur pruning can be carried out successfully on most varieties in autumn or winter. Cordon, espalier and pyramid forms will also need summer pruning. This involves shortening the new growths to four or five buds in July, but leaving the main leaders of each cordon alone until the desired height is reached,

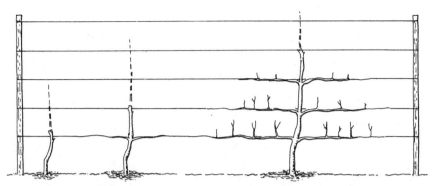

101 Pear. Training as espalier. *Left to right*: cut back young maiden stem to bottom wire in first winter; train one resulting shoot on each side of stem in following summer, and cut main stem just above next wire in winter; repeat the process each year, this tree is three years older than that shown on the left.

when these are shortened. *See* Chapter 3, Plant Care.

Pollination This presents more of a problem with pears than with apples, requiring the use of pollinator varieties. This involves either planting another suitable variety near the tree of one's choice, or using a family tree in confined spaces.

With the exception of Bristol Cross, which is no good as a pollinator, all the varieties in the table are interchangeable as pollinators. All those kinds listed are suitable for eating raw as dessert when ripe.

Propagation Pears are increased by budding and grafting in the same manner as for apples, except that different rootstocks are used.

Planting Most kinds of outdoor fruit are best planted in autumn, but this operation can successfully take place at other times of year where soil conditions are satisfactory. *See* Chapter 3, Plant Care.

Plum and gages A group of crops, grown for their usually juicy fruits, each of which contains a large stone. Harvesting takes place during summer and the fruits are eaten raw or cooked as well as used in jams and preserves.

Cultivation Plums grow well in deep, rich fertile soils that do not dry out completely, but are free draining. Cooking varieties tolerate cooler and wetter conditions than dessert plums and gages, which produce the best fruit in warm sunny positions, sheltered from cold north or east winds. Dig the ground spade deep, manuring generously and break down lumps by cultivation. Lime the soil to bring the pH up to 6.8, but

Table of Pear Trees and Suitable Pollinators

Main variety	Pollinator	Season of use
Gorham	Beurre Hardy	Sep
Williams Bon Chrétien	Conference	Sep
Bristol Cross	Laxtons Superb	Sep–Oct
Conference	Fertility	Oct–Nov
Doyenne du Comice	Laxtons Superb	Nov
Winter Nelis	Clapps Favourite	Nov–Jan

Table of Fruit Planting Seasons

Fruit	Planting season Lifted stock	Planting season Container stock
Apple	Nov–Mar	Sep–May
Blackberry*	Oct–Nov	Sep–Apr*
Blackcurrant	Nov–Mar	Sep–May
Gooseberry	Nov–Feb	Sep–May
Loganberry*	Oct–Feb	Sep–May*
Nuts	Nov–Feb	Sep–May
Pear	Nov–Feb	Sep–May
Plums and grapes	Nov–Feb	Sep–May
Raspberry*	Oct–Feb	Oct–Apr*
Red and white currant	Nov–Mar	Sep–May
Strawberry*	Aug–Nov	Aug–May*
Walnut	Nov–Dec	Sep–Apr

* Plants set out after December may take a year longer to reach fruiting than those which are planted in autumn.

leave a minimum 7–10 day interval between manuring and liming. Leave a similar period before working in $100 \, \text{g/m}^2$ (3 oz/sq yd) of a balanced fertiliser. Plums are usually trained and grown as fans against walls or as free-standing bush or half-standard forms.

Plant these fruits in tree pits, hammering stakes into place for such as half-standard trees before covering the roots with topsoil or prepared mixture. Give trees the space shown in the Table of Plums and Suitable Pollinators. However, the area needed finally does depend on climate, variety, rootstock, soil, pruning and feeding. Firm the soil

103 Plums. Thin, to leave one fruit per cluster.

102 Plums. Propping up heavy cropping trees to prevent breakages.

as filling proceeds and ensure that trees are at the same depth as before the move, otherwise scion rooting can occur with budded or grafted trees losing the benefit of the rootstocks.

Pruning Apart from fan-trained trees, the less pruning of healthy plants that is carried out the better the results are likely to be. This is based on the assumption that plums with a basic

Table of Plum Trees and Suitable Pollinators

Main variety	Pollinator	Cropping season	Space (m)
Cambridge Gage D	Early Transparent Gage D	Aug	Standard 7.5 × 7.5
Laxton's Gage D	Czar C	Aug	
Victoria C	Pershore C	Aug	Half standard 5 × 5
Severn Cross D	Victoria C	Sep	Fan 4.5 × 2.5
Coe's Golden Drop D	Denniston's Superb D	Sep–Oct	Bush 4.5 × 4

Key   C   Culinary varieties
     D   Dessert varieties

branch framework have been purchased. Cut out dead, overcrowded or crossing branches during late spring or summer. With fan-trained forms, tie in short new shoots in late summer to replace those which have recently carried fruit.

Pollination This aspect of plum growing also presents problems because many varieties cannot set fruit without pollen from another tree.

The rootstocks for plums and gages are various and are selected by the nurseryman to suit the variety as well as the form.

Pests and diseases. See Chapter 10, Problems.

Propagation Plums and gages are usually increased by budding in July or grafting in March onto selected rootstocks. A few varieties can be raised from semi-ripe and hardwood cuttings taken in July/August and September/October respectively.

Varieties See the Table of Plum Trees and Suitable Pollinators.

Propagation The methods of increasing top and soft fruits are discussed in Chapter 2, Propagation.

Table of Methods of Fruit Propagation

Fruit	Method	Time of operation
Apples	Budding	Jul–Aug
Apples	Grafting	Mar
Blackberry	Tip layering	Jul
Blackcurrant	Half ripe cuttings	Jun–Jul
Blackcurrant	Hardwood cuttings	Sep–Nov
Gooseberry	as for blackcurrant	
Loganberry	as for blackberry	
Nut, Hazel	Layering	Oct–Nov
Pear	as for apple	
Raspberry	Suckers	Oct–Nov
Red and white currant	as for blackcurrant	
Rhubarb	Division	Oct–Nov
Strawberry	Runners	Jul–Aug
Walnut	Budding	Jul–Aug
Walnut	Grafting	Apr–May

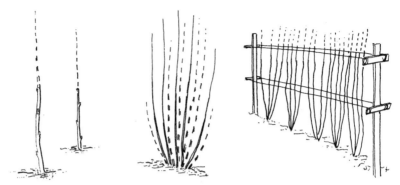

104 Raspberries. *Left to right*: cut down the stems to 15–20 cm (6–8 in) high after planting; remove old canes after fruiting; method of training.

Raspberry A popular cane fruit, grown for the berries which are produced in summer and autumn and are eaten raw or cooked and preserved.

Cultivation This crop grows well on light or medium fertile soils that are free draining, but which do not dry out. While open sunny situations are excellent, raspberries can produce good yields in shaded positions when healthy and well cared for. Well-dug and manured ground should if necessary be limed, to bring the pH to 6.5 allowing a 10-day interval after manuring and before liming.

Erect supporting posts with pairs of horizontal wires at 900 mm (3 ft) and 1.5 m (5 ft) over the area where each row is to be planted.

Work in 100 g/m^2 (3 oz/sq yd) of base fertiliser 7–10 days before planting, but preferably not before a similar minimum interval has elapsed since liming. Plant out healthy ministry certified raspberry canes between October and February, spacing them about 450 mm (18 in) apart with 1.5 m between rows. Mulch new plants in the folling spring and subsequently.

Pruning Cut down the canes to 150–200 mm (6–8 in) above ground immediately after planting. In subsequent seasons, remove fruited canes as soon as cropping finishes and limit the number of young shoots per crown to four or five. Autumn-fruiting varieties are cut to soil level in January or February each year.

Diseases and pests See Chapter 10, Problems.

Propagation Raspberries are increased by digging up healthy disease-free stock, removing the 'spawn' or suckers and planting these out in fruiting beds. It is unwise to propagate from other than ministry certified stock.

Cropping commences in the second season after planting.

Varieties Glen Clova, Malling Jewel and Malling Promise are excellent for the summer crop. Autumn-fruiting types include Norfolk Giant, September and Zeva.

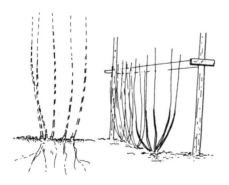

105 Raspberries. *Left*: cut autumn-fruiting varieties down to soil level in February. *Right*: method of support.

Rhubarb A crop grown for its leaf stalks which although cooked and eaten as a sweet, are not fruits.
Cultivation This is a gross feeder and needs generous treatment. Plant up beds between October and December, spacing plants 750–900 mm (2½–3 ft) apart on well dug, heavily manured ground which has also received 140 g/m² (4 oz/sq yd) of base fertiliser. Mulch the beds in spring and keep plants watered and weedfree. Hard cropping should not take place for two seasons after planting, with picking ceasing in late May each year.

When grown for the outdoor crop, picking should cease about mid-June each year to give the crowns time to build up for the following season. Rhubarb can be forced when the crowns have grown for three years or more without disturbance. Natural forcing consists of inverting a straw-filled bucket or box over selected crowns during January or early February. This keeps the buds dark and warmer than otherwise, producing blanched stems and earlier than the uncovered crop. Feed the crowns each spring with 100 –140 g/m² (3–4 oz/sq yd) of balanced fertiliser.

Three-year-old roots for forcing are carefully lifted out of the soil in October and are left lying on the ground until ready to take into a warm greenhouse in December or January. For details of forcing *see* Chapter 4, Greenhouses.

106 Rhubarb. *Left to right*: ground level buds; cover with straw and bucket; young stems ready for use.

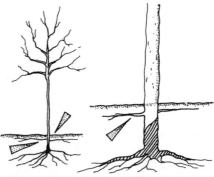

107 Scion-rooting. *Left*: a grafted tree, planted too deeply, showing the roots growing from the scion or top part, *arrowed*. *Right*: a close-up, where the rootstock hatched can be seen to be buried, allowing the scion to form roots.

Scion rooting This occurs when the scion – top variety of budded or grafted plants – forms roots of its own in addition to those of the rootstock. It usually occurs where the soil level is too high and covers part of the scion, and is caused by planting excessively deeply. The consequence of this condition, if prolonged, is the loss of part or all of the beneficial influence of the rootstock.

Strawberry This fruit crop is grown for the delicious, usually red or scarlet berries which are produced in summer, but which can be available in late summer and autumn.
Cultivation This crop grows well on light or medium, slightly-acid soils that are well supplied with phosphate and potash. The site for strawberries should be sheltered, but open and sunny, though some light shade is tolerated without undue ill effects. Dig and cultivate the ground, incorporating two bucketsful 18 litre/m² (3 gal/sq yd) of manure or equivalent plus 70 g/m² (2 oz/sq yd) of balanced fertiliser. Plant out Ministry Certified stock between July and November. Allow 450 mm (18 in) between plants, in rows 750 mm (2½ ft) apart, where beds are to be cropped for two or three years as is usual

108 Strawberries. Keep berries clean by placing straw or mats beneath them.

109 Strawberries. Burn off old straw and leaves after cropping to prevent carrying disease over into next season.

for open-air culture. The earliest crops are obtained from plants set out during late July and August.

Deblossom strawberries where planting is delayed until after December. This consists of picking off the flowers as they form at least until mid-summer of the year of planting. Where plants are allowed to set fruit within a few weeks of being set out, crops are usually almost worthless in later years. Protect ripening fruit with nets against birds. Remove runners from fruiting beds as they develop, to conserve the energies of established plants and not interrupt air circulation. Very early or very late crops benefit from cloche protection.

Disease and pest control See Chapter 10, Problems.

Propagation Standard or conventional varieties are increased by pegging runners, up to four or five from one parent, into small pots of potting compost or into fine soil. Keep the soil moist and weedfree. Cut off the shoot, growing from the pegged runner to prevent others developing at the expense of the first plant. As soon as rooting has taken place, sever each runner from its parent, and set out the new plants in their final positions, in prepared beds immediately.

Varieties Gorella and Tamella are good for early crops. Cambridge Favourite and Royal Sovereign are well established and popular second earlies. Domanil and Cambridge Late Pine are excellent for later crops. Gento and Hampshire Maid are perpetual fruiting varieties, which crop more or less continuously through summer and into autumn, to extend the season.

Top fruits Applied to tree fruits, such as apples, pears and plums as distinct from bush and cane fruits.

Walnut A tree grown in part for the nuts, as well as for appearance and shade qualities.

Cultivation This tree is slow growing, taking twenty or more years to mature and it requires more space than many present day gardens can provide. Walnuts grow well on deep, fertile loams that are free draining and in warm, sheltered positions where damaging late spring frosts rarely occur.

Pruning is minimal once the branch framework is formed and consists of removing the odd crossing branch in autumn. Avoid cutting trees in spring because these bleed profusely at this time of year.

Cropping The nuts are gathered, either when green and immature for pickling, or are left until fully ripe.

Diseases and pests See Chapter 10, Problems.

Propagation This is by means of seed sown in spring and by grafting named varieties onto seedling rootstocks, in March and April.

Varieties The Common Walnut is more suitable for nut production than the Black variety.

Chapter 7. Trees, Shrubs and Climbers

Acid soil Trees and shrubs are seemingly more sensitive than other groups of garden plants to acidity or alkalinity of the soil. Heathers and rhododendrons thrive on acid ground with a pH level less than 7, but often look sickly on chalk or alkaline land where the pH is above 7. Some plants including climbers, such as clematis, dislike acid conditions at the roots. *See* Table of Climbers, Shrubs and Trees for soil preferences.

Adult Some trees and shrubs form leaves of different shapes as they grow. Various plants such as junipers, develop adult foliage once they reach a certain age and stage of growth. The needle-like juvenile leaves give way to adult awl-shaped scales which are frequently adpressed to the shoots. Plants of this type are sometimes referred to as dimor-

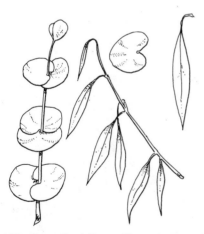

110 Juvenile foliage. Many trees and shrubs produce two types of leaves. *Left*, the juvenile form of *Eucalyptus gunnii*, with adult foliage, *right*. *Top*: the difference in leaf shape is very distinct.

phic. This changing of the foliage often causes confusion, particularly for people buying young plants after seeing adult specimens.

Alkaline soil *See* Acid soil, this chapter.

Aspect With garden plants and climbers in particular, it is necessary to consider at planting time which direction they eventually face. Sunny, south-facing walls or slopes are much warmer than those which face north, advancing or retarding flowering dates. The effects of aspect can. sometimes make a difference between success and failure.

Balled; balled-and-wrapped; Bare root. *See* Chapter 3, Plant Care.

Boundary plants *See* Hedges, this chapter.

Classification In addition to the botanical systems of grouping plants into genera and species, these are also classed into other categories according to their use in the garden. Shrubs, trees and most climbers are perennials, but these can also be grouped according to size, habit and flowering season. *See* Tables in this chapter for details.

Broad-leaf Applied to trees other than conifers. Most Broad-leaved trees are deciduous, but some, such as the evergreen oak, are not. The most colourful flowering and fruiting small garden trees belong to this group and to the genera, Acer, Crataegus, Prunus and Sorbus. The habit of growth of members of this group can be placed into the few basic types of columnar, globose or round, pyramidal, upright spreading, and weeping. Broad-leaved trees, unlike many conifers, do not as a rule produce diminutive, dwarf forms, but are nonetheless useful for providing shelter, screening, colour and interest.

Cultivation When obtaining trees, particularly for small or average-sized gardens, the choice of variety is important. Select those which are unlikely to outgrow their space; hardy; well suited to the available site, and soil; as well as being healthy. Trees of this type are usually obtained as, or trained into, one of various forms, such as bush, half-standard and standard. *See* Chapter 3, Plant Care. Buying trees which have an established basic framework of branches should result in saving a year or two in waiting for flowers and fruits than planting and training 'whips' or nursery trees. Broad-leaved trees are prepared and sold as bare-root, balled, balled-and-wrapped and container-grown. *See* Chapter 3, Plant Care.

Planting season Trees are normally best set out in autumn, but can be safely planted between November and February during mild weather. Container-grown trees can be set out at

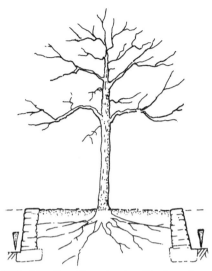

112 Planting. Changing level by lowering surrounding soil.

almost any time of year. Avoid planting any trees during drought, on waterlogged land or in freezing conditions. Where leafless trees are received in severe weather, as in winter, either store

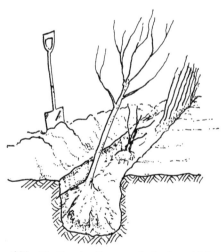

111 Heeling in. Trees and shrubs which cannot be planted in their final positions immediately can be kept in good condition by covering their roots with soil.

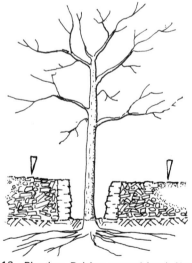

113 Planting. Raising ground level. Note coarse material, rubble over root area to allow roots to breathe.

them under cover, placing straw or sacking over the roots, or heel them temporarily into the ground. Then plant out these trees as soon as circumstances allow, soaking dry roots overnight in clean water before setting them out.

Soil preparation The ground should be free draining, well dug, manured and cultivated. Trees, other than small nursery stock or whips, are planted in pits or holes of sufficient size to comfortably accommodate the roots at a similar depth as before the move. Allow each tree plenty of space to grow and avoid planting too close to buildings, leaving a distance equal to the final width. The stakes should be hammered into position in the excavated pits before the trees are set out. Cover the roots with prepared soil, firming as filling proceeds, working the soil into position and leaving no large air spaces. Secure each tree firmly to a stake, using plastic ties, making sure that there is a space between stem and stake to avoid chafing. Where cord is used instead of plastic tree ties, place a piece of hessian around each stem first to avoid bark damage. After planting, water the

Table of Some Hardy Broad-leaved Trees Suitable for the Average Garden

Name	Ht × Width (m)	Feature	Colour	Season of colour	Soil pH
Acer palmatum Japanese Maple	5 × 3	Lvs	Green and purple	May–Oct	5.5–6.8
Betula pendula Silver Birch	10 × 4	Lvs and stem	Green leaves and silvery stem	May–Oct	6–7
Crataegus oxyacantha 'Pauls Scarlet' Scarlet Thorn	6 × 5	Fls	Scarlet	May	6–7.5
Crataegus oxyacantha 'Rosea Flore Pleno' Double Pink Thorn	6 × 5	Fls	Pink	May	6–7.5
Laburnum × watereri Laburnum	7.5 × 4	Fls	Yellow	May	6–7.3
Malus 'John Downie' Crab Apple	8 × 6	Fls and Frts	Fls white, Frts red/yellow	May and Sep	6–6.8
Malus × purpurea Purple Crab	7.5 × 5	Lvs and Frts	Purple	May–Sep	6–6.8
Populus alba White Poplar	12 × 7	Lvs	Grey white	May–Oct	6.5–7.5
Prunus cerasifera 'Pissardii' Purple-leaved plum	7 × 6	Lvs	Lvs purple, Fls white	May–Sep	6.5–7.5
Prunus 'Kanzan' Japanese Flowering Cherry	8 × 6	Fls	Pink	Apr–May	6.5–7.5
Sorbus aria Whitebeam	8 × 4	Lvs and Frts	Lvs grey, Frts scarlet	May–Oct	6–7.5
Sorbus ancuparia Mountain Ash Rowan	9 × 4	Lvs and Frts	Lvs aut tints red/yellow, Frts scarlet	Oct–Nov Aug–Nov	5.5–7

Key   Lvs   Leaves
       Fls   Flowers   Frts   Fruits

103

ground as necessary and provide a mulch during spring in the first and succeeding years. Keep the soil weedfree within a 60 cm (2 ft) diameter of each stem and hoe occasionally.

Pruning This is normally best carried out in autumn for deciduous trees or late spring and summer for evergreens. Routine pruning consists mainly of cutting out crossing and badly-placed branches, thinning as necessary, to let in light and air, as well as removing any dead or diseased wood. For details of formative and remedial pruning, *see* Chapter 3, Plant Care.

Disease and Pest control See Chapter 10, Problems.

Climbers Plants of ascending habit, with long stems, which need some form of vertical support. These may be one of two types: self clinging, and those wall plants which require tying. Self-clinging climbers obtain their support either by twining stems, tendrils, aerial roots, or by suction pads. Clematis and vines are examples of the first type. Ivy obtains a hold on walls by means of roots which form up the stems, and grow into cracks in the masonry, causing damage in some cases. Virginia Creeper develops small pads, which can be similarly destructive to buildings.

Climbing roses need tying and are here termed wall plants.

Climbers with tendrils and twiners, as well as those which need tying present few serious problems. But others, such as ivies and Virginia Creeper, need to be kept severely under control. Where climbers and wall plants are to be grown against the side of a building, it is wise to first fix a timber or wire mesh trellis about 50 mm (2 in) away from the wall. This allows air to circulate between climber and wall, preventing dampness, and enables easier control of the plants. The cultivation of climbing plants closely follows that outlined for shrubs, *see* this chapter. The essential difference is the training and tying where necessary. The climbers are best cut back as needed after flowering. Trim the wall plants after flowering, shortening vigorous new shoots of such as chaenomeles back to the older fruiting wood. Pyracantha is given a light pruning to keep plants in shape during May and June. Tie in long shoots as needed in August and September. Climbing Hybrid Tea roses can have the side growths shortened back to within two or three buds of the main stem in autumn or early spring. Remove the flowered stems in the case of rambler roses, tying in new growths before winter.

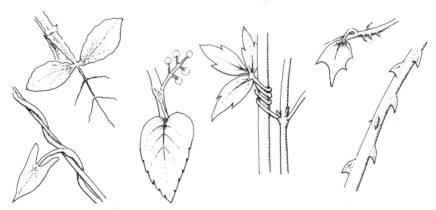

114　Climbers. Methods of attachment. *Left to right*: twining stems; tendril; adhesive pads; coiling leaf stalk; aerial or stem rooting; hooks or thorns.

Table of Decorative and Reliable Climbers

Name	Height (m)	Season	Soil pH	Site	Colour
Clematis, species and large-flowered hybrids	2–6	May–Oct Flowers	6.8–7.5	Sun	Crimson, mauve, pink, purple and white.
Hedera, various Ivy	2–4	Year round Leaves	6–7.5	Sun/ shade	Green, variegated with gold or silver.
Lonicera, various Honeysuckle	1.5–4.5	Jul–Sep Flowers/ scent	6.5–7.5	Sun/ shade	Pale yellow, pink and purple.
Polygonum Russian Vine	3–7.5	Jul–Sep Flowers	6–7.5	Sun	White.
Wistaria floribunda Japanese Wistaria	3–6	May–Jun Flowers/ scent	6.5–7.5	Sun	Pink, violet-blue and white.

Table of Wall Plants

Name	Height (m)	Season	Soil pH	Site	Colour
Ceanothus, various Ceanothus	2.5–5	May–Oct Flowers	6.5–7.5	Sun	Blue.
Chaenomeles speciosa Cydonia or Japonica	2–3	Mar–Apr Flowers	6–7.5	Sun	Pink, scarlet and white.
Cotoneaster, various Cotoneaster	1–2.5	Sep–Nov Berries	6–7.5	Sun	White flowers, red berries.
Garrya elliptica Garrya	2–4	Jan–Feb Flowers	6.5–7.5	Sun/ shade	Grey-green catkins
Jasminum nudiflorum Winter-flowering jasmine	2–4	Nov–Mar Flowers	6–7.5	Sun/ shade	Yellow.
Pyracantha, various Fire Bush	3–4.5	Sep–Dec Berries	6.5–7.5	Sun	White, with red and yellow berries.
Rosa, climbing Roses	2.5–4.5	Jun–Oct Flowers/ scent	6.5–7.5	Sun	Crimson, orange, pink, red and yellow.

Conifer A cone bearing plant. Conifers form a large group of mainly evergreen trees and shrubs, many of which are garden-worthy subjects. Although many conifers produce seeds in cones, one large genus, Juniperus, produces berries instead. Other important genera include Abies, Cedrus, Chamaecyparis, Picea, Pinus, Thuja and Taxus. Conifers occur in numerous varieties which vary greatly in size, shape and colour.

Size The range varies from tall forest trees down to dwarf conifers and procumbent shrubs.

Shape Conifers are obtainable in the following shapes: columnar, pyramidal, procumbent, weeping and globose or rounded. There are many variations of these basic forms.

Colour Conifers do not as a rule produce conspicuous, brightly-coloured flowers. However, the foliage of many varieties provides year-round interest, in shades of blue, gold, grey-green, copper and bronze.

Use To provide a main feature as a single specimen or group of two or more trees in lawns, in shrubberies or beds for year round interest, of particular value in winter, as hedging and as background for flowering plants. Dwarf conifers are invaluable for confined spaces, and to provide height and interest when placed among heathers and rock plants.

Cultivation When buying or obtaining conifers, there are a few points to observe to avoid disappointment later. Check that the variety is suitable for your purpose; to have the correct species may not be sufficient: the difference in height between two varieties after 15 years can, for example, be as much as 6 m (20 ft). Avoid plants with bare stems or patches of dead foliage, because new growth is unlikely to hide these blemishes. Well-furnished plants – those that are well covered with foliage, are healthy and of good shape – should be selected. The root systems should be well developed in proportion to the height and size of the branch framework of each specimen. If the aim is to transplant many conifers they should be undercut about a year in advance to encourage a good root system. When planting, position each conifer so that the best side is shown to maximum effect – many plants develop better foliage on one side than another. Site each conifer in the sun or shade as best suits the individual variety. Gold, blue, va-

riegated or coloured kinds grow well and are seen to advantage when planted in sunny situations. The ground should be free draining, fertile and well prepared. *See* Chapter 1, Site and Soil.

Conifers are best planted out during October/November and March/April, preferably when small and between 15 cm and 90 cm (6 in to 3 ft) in height, depending on variety. Allow adequate space for the subsequent growth of each conifer. Large specimens need tying to stakes to provide support until well established and root firm. Subsequent

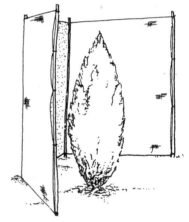

115 Tree. Wind protection of newly planted conifer, provided by simple hessian screen.

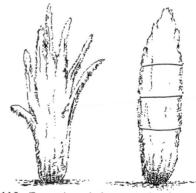

116 Tree tying. A few strands of green plastic wire, nearly tied, keeps trees in shape.

Table of Conifers Suitable for the Average Garden

Name	Height (m)	Colour	Soil pH	Shape
Chamaecyparis lawsoniana 'Allumii'	5–6	Blue grey	6–7.5	Pyramidal
Chamaecyparis lawsoniana 'Ellwoodii'	3–5	Grey green	6–7.5	Columnar
Chamaecyparis lawsoniana 'Lutea'	7–9	Golden	6–7.5	Pyramidal
Chamaecyparis otusa 'Nana'	0.6	Green	6.5–7.5	Globose
Chamaecyparis otusa 'Nana Aurea'	0.6	Golden	6.5–7.5	Globose
Chamaecyparis pisifera 'Boulevard'	4–5	Blue, silver and green	6.5–7.5	Pyramidal
Juniperus communis 'Compressa'	0.6	Green	6–7.5	Columnar
Juniperus communis 'Hibernica'	3–5	Grey blue	6–7.5	Columnar
Juniperus horizontalis 'Bar Harbor'	0.2	Blue	6.5–7	Procumbent
Juniperus squamata 'Meyeri'	1.5–2	Blue	6.5–7.5	Globose
Pinus mugo 'Gnom'	1.5–2	Green	6–7.5	Globose
Thuja occidentalis 'Rheingold'	1–1.5	Gold	6–7.5	Pyramidal

treatment consists of keeping plants well watered and weedfree for a minimum 45 cm (18 in) diameter from each stem. Mulch the soil around each conifer in the spring of, or after, planting, and for the following few years. Protect newly-planted conifers in exposed sites with a temporary shelter of hessian or similar material placed on supports.

Pruning Little treatment is usually necessary, consisting of limiting tall varieties to a single upright stem. Remove or shorten crossing, diseased or badly-placed shoots, including untidy growths. Prune conifers and evergreens between early May and late July.

Crown lifting *See* Chapter 3, Plant Care.

Crown thinning *See* Chapter 3, Plant Care.

Deadheading *See* Chapter 3, Plant Care.

Deciduous Applied to woody plants which shed their leaves each autumn. Many garden subjects are deciduous, which results in their having a bare appearance during winter. To overcome this naked effect, deciduous plants should be mixed with evergreens when planting beds and borders for year-round interest.

Diseases of trees, shrubs and climbers. *See* Chapter 10, Problems.

Evergreen Applied to plants which carry leaves all year round. Members of this group do shed their leaves, but not all at the same time.

Ground cover While any vegetation covers soil to some extent, the most satisfactory ground-cover plants are usually low-growing shrubs. When well managed, these form a dense mat which crowds out and smothers weed seedlings. This form of treatment can provide an attractive, labour-saving treatment, needing little subsequent attention. The necessary requirements for success with ground-cover plants are good soil preparation, the correct use of suitable plants, and good cultivation.

Ground preparation This consists of ensuring that the soil is free draining, fertile and weedfree. The ground should be well worked, and be devoid of hard lumps of earth, and be manured, limed and have fertiliser added as needed.

Table of Ground-cover Plants for Gardens

Name	Ht × width (cm)	Season of colour	Feature	Soil pH
Calluna vulgaris, various Heather	60 × 45	Jul–Sep	E. Fls various colours	5.5–6.5
Caryopteris × clandonensis Caryopteris or Blue Spiraea	60 × 45	Aug–Sep	Fls blue	6.5–7.5
Cotoneaster dammeri Cotoneaster	15 × 150	Aug–Oct	E. Frts red	6–7.5
Daboecia St Daboec's Heath	45 × 45	Jul–Aug	E. Fls purple/white	5.5–6.5
Erica, various Heather	45 × 40	Nov–Oct	E. Fls various colours	5.5–7
Euonymus fortunei radicans Creeping Euonymus	60 × 120	Year round	E. Lvs green, purple and cream	6–7.5
Hebe armstrongii Hebe or Veronica	40 × 75	Year round	E. Lvs gold	6–7
Hypericum calycinum Rose of Sharon	40 × 40	Jun–Sep	E. Fls yellow	6–7.5
Mahonia aquifolium Mahonia	75 × 90	Feb–Apr	E. Fls yellow	6–7
Pernettya mucronata Pernettya	75 × 75	Sep–Dec	E. Frts various colours	5.5–6.5

Key Fls Flowers   Frts Fruits
　　　 Lvs Leaves   E   Evergreen

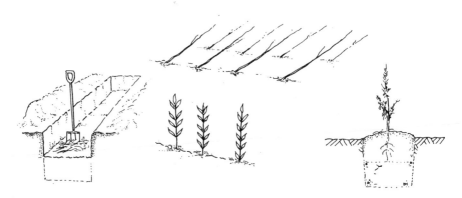

117　Hedge planting. *Left*: fork manure or compost into bottom of the trench. *Top*: double row of thorn planted obliquely to provide dense hedge. *Centre*: single row planting. *Right*: section to show new hedge and trench.

The cultivation required for ground cover plants is similar to shrubs.

Hedge A living wall or screen of plants used to provide a physical barrier; conceal ugly views; protect and screen areas from prevailing winds and to give privacy and seclusion. The ground for hedges should be well prepared and free draining. Dig a trench at least 60 cm (2 ft) wide and a spade deep. Fork manure in and work in fertiliser at 70 g/m (2 oz/yd) run of trench. Mix peat or manure in with the topsoil as it is returned. Planting is best carried out in November and December for deciduous subjects, but set evergreens out in October and April to May.

With young hedges, trim the plants lightly after each 15–20 cm (6–8 in) of growth, to encourage plants to bush out and thicken. Keep the soil moist and weedfree for the first two or three years, until the plants become well established.

Lopping *See* Chapter 3, Plant Care.

Pest control *See* Chapter 10, Problems.

Table of Hedging Plants for Use in Gardens

Name	Planting distance (cm)	Feature	Season of interest Lvs	Season of interest Fls and Frts	Cut
Berberis thunbergii atropurpurea	45	Lvs. Fls and Frts	May–Sep	Apr and Sep	Jul–Aug
Chamaecyparis lawsoniana E	45	Lvs	All year	—	Jun and Sep
Cotoneaster simonsii	40	Lvs Frts	May–Sep	Aug–Oct	Jun and Sep
Crataegus monogyna	30	Lvs	May–Sep	—	Jun–Aug
Escallonia E	45	Lvs Fls	All year	Jul–Oct	Jun
Fagus sylvatica	45	Lvs	May–Feb	—	Jul–Aug
Fagus sylvatica purpurea	45	Lvs	May–Feb	—	Jul–Aug
Ilex aquifolium E	60	Lvs Frts	All year	Oct–Jan	Jul
Ligustrum ovalifolium	35	Lvs	May–Sep	—	May–Aug
Lonicera nitida E	25	Lvs	All year	—	Apr–Sep
Olearis haastii E	40	Lvs Fls	All year	Jul–Aug	Jun–Jul
Prunus 'Cistena'	45	Lvs Fls	May–Sep	Mar–Apr	Jun–Jul
Rosmarinus officinalis E	35	Lvs Fls	All year	Apr–May	Jul–Aug
Taxus baccata E	45	Lvs	All year	—	Jun–Jul

Key	E	Evergreen		Fls	Flowers
	Lvs	Leaves		Frs	Fruits

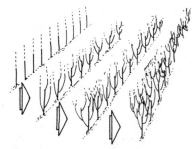

118 Hedge trimming. *Left*: correct. *Right*: wrong, resulting in bare lower branches and loose top.

119 Hedge trimming. *Left to right*: shorten new plants; remove tips of new shoots resulting from first; subsequent trimming and thickening of hedge.

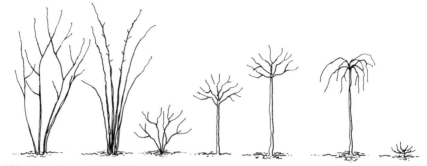

120   Rose forms. *Left to right*: climber; rambler; bush; half-standard; standard; weeping standard and miniature.

Rose

Classification The rose is one of the oldest of cultivated flowers and has been altered greatly due to the work of plant breeders. To list all the various types which have appeared over the centuries would be almost impossible. However the main types which are currently available and grown in gardens at present are outlined below.

For practical garden purposes, and disregarding the finer botanical division, roses can be broadly categorised into six major groups as follows.

Species roses. This group consists of wild species, many of which form single flowers with only one circle of petals. Included are *Rosa canina*, *Rosa gallica*, *Rosa moyesii*, *Rosa rubiginosa*, *Rosa rugosa* and *Rosa spinosissima*, the Scotch or Burnet rose.

The Old Roses. This group comprises the following divisions: Albas; Bourbons; Damasks; Dwarf Polyanthas; Gallicas; Hybrid Musks; Hybrid Perpetuals; Hybrid Sweet briars; Moss Roses; Portland Roses; Provence or cabbage; and Scotch Roses.

The Hybrid Tea roses, H.T., which are almost continuous flowering, produce large blooms with high centres and are double. Many are exquisitely scented. This group is now the most widely planted and grown of all.

Floribunda roses. This group runs closely behind the H.T. roses for popularity. Double and semi-double blooms are produced in clusters on vigorous plants. The individual flowers are smaller than H.T. roses, but with some varieties the blooms resemble small H.T. roses. Floribundas are often slightly more vigorous than H.T. varieties.

Modern Shrub roses. These consist of hybrids between the species of the Old Roses. Many of this type produce single and semi-double flowers. These varieties range in height from 90 cm–1.8 cm (3–6 ft).

Climbers and Ramblers. These consist of very vigorous plants, growing to 9 m (30 ft) or more in the case of climbers and to 7.5 m (25 ft) with some kinds of

121   Rose types. *Left*: Hybrid Tea. *Right*: Floribunda, double and single flowered.

Ramblers. The latter have more pliable stems than climbers.

Cultivation The soil preparation, manuring, fertilising and planting are broadly similar to those used for shrubs in general. Roses produce the best results on medium or heavy, fertile loams, situated in sheltered, sunny positions. Planting is normally carried out from November to February for lifted stock. Container-grown plants can be set out between September and May in suitable conditions. The space needed between plants depends on variety, rootstock and soil, but 60–90 cm (2–3 ft) is usually adequate for most bush varieties. Vigorous shrub varieties need about 1.2 m (4 ft). Allow 90 cm (3 ft) between standards and between half-standards. Mulch plants with manure or peat each spring to conserve moisture and smother weeds.

Pruning

Species and Old Roses. Cut out dead wood, and remove one-third to one-quarter of the old wood stems, shortening them to soil level. Cut out weak and spindly shoots, but leave some sturdy replacements growths.

H.T. and Floribunda roses. Cut back all growths in spring to two or three buds with H.T., and to three, four or five with floribundas.

New species roses. These should be pruned in a broadly similar manner to the Species and Old Roses.

Climbing roses. Shorten the laterals to within two or three buds of the main stems, removing weak shoots and spindly growths. Train in strong new replacement wood as this arises and cut out old wood which becomes bare of new growths.

Ramblers. Cut out flowered stems to soil level and tie in the new wood to supports.

Prune miniature roses as for H.T., cutting them back to two or three buds. Treat standard and half-standard H.T. and floribunda roses as for their respective bush forms.

Disease and pest control See Chapter 10, Problems.

Shrubs The successful cultivation of this group of plants consists of creating the right conditions for each plant. Obtain healthy, well-grown plants which are informatively labelled. Select varieties which are suited to your soil, site and climate.

Cultivation The ground should be well prepared, free-draining and fertile. Dig the ground spade deep, manuring and liming as necessary. Cultivate the ground to break up any hard lumps and

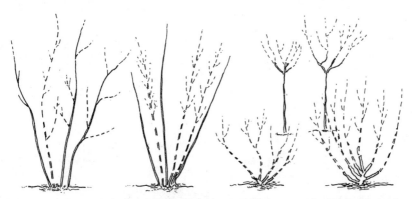

122 Rose pruning. *Left to right*: climber, shorten side shoots and remove worn out rod; rambler, cut out flowered stems; Hybrid Tea bush and standard, cut shoots back to 2–4 buds; Floribunda bush and standard, cut shoots back to 3–6 buds.

Table of Shrubs Suitable for Gardens

Name	Colour	Ht × width (m)	Feature and season of colour	Site needs	Soil pH
Berberis darwinii E Berberis	Orange	2.5 × 1.2	Fls Apr–May	Sun/shade	6.5–7.5
Buddleia davidii Buddleia	Pink, purple and white	3 × 3	Fls Jul–Sep	Sun	6.5–7.5
Ceratostigma willmottianum Ceratostigma	Blue	0.6 × 0.6	Fls Aug–Sep	Sun	6–7
Chaenomeles speciosa Japonica	Pink, scarlet and white	2.5 × 2	Fls Mar–Apr	Sun	6.5–7.5
Cotoneaster franchetii E Cotoneaster	White, with red berries	2.5 × 2.5	Frts Aug–Oct	Sun/shade	6.5–7.5
Cytisus scoparius Broom	Yellow	1.8 × 1.5	Fls May	Sun	6.5–7
Daphne mezereon Mezereum	Pink and white	0.6 × 0.6	Fls Feb–Mar	Sun/shade	6.5–7.5
Erica carnea E Winter-flowering heather	Carmine, pink and white	0.3 × 0.4	Fls Dec–Mar	Sun	6–7.5
Forsythia suspensa Forsythia	Yellow	2 × 2	Fls Mar–Apr	Sun	6.5–7.5
Ilex, various E Holly	White with red and yellow berries	2–12 × 2–5	Frts Oct–Feb	Sun/shade	6–7.5
Mahonia aquifolium E Oregon Grape	Yellow	1.2 × 1.5	Fls Mar–May	Sun/shade	6.5–7.5
Potentilla fruticosa Potentilla	White and yellow	1 × 1	Fls May–Sep	Sun	6.5–7.5
Rhododendron, various E Rhododendron	Crimson, pink, purple, white and yellow	0.3–6 × 0.3–5	Fls Mar–Jun	Shade	5.5–6.5
Ribes sanguineum Flowering currant	Pink	2.5 × 2	Fls Mar–Apr	Sun/shade	6.5–7.5
Senecio laxifolius E Senecio	Yellow, grey foliage	1.2 × 1.5	Fls Jul–Sep	Sun	6.5–7.5
Syringa Lilac	Lilac, pink, purple and white	4 × 3	Fls May–Jun	Sun	6.5–7.5
Weigela, Hybrids Diervilla	Crimson, pink and white	2 × 2	Fls May–Jun	Sun	6.5–7.5

Key   E   Evergreen   Fls   Flowers   Frts   Fruits or berries

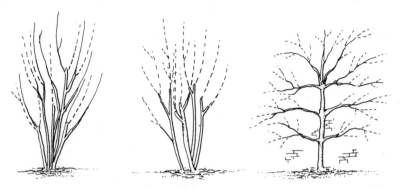

123 Shrub pruning. *Left to right*: early-flowering type, Forsythia, remove year old shoots after flowering in spring; summer blooming on new growth, Buddelia, cut down all flowered shoots to older wood in spring; wall-trained flowering shrubs, shorten laterals back to main branches after flowering.

rake in 100 g/m² (3 oz/sq yd) of balanced base fertiliser 10–14 days before planting. Plant out lifted deciduous shrubs in November and December, although this can be carried out successfully up to early March. Evergreens are normally planted in late September/October and during April/May. Allow each plant space according to its habit of growth.

Roses and some small plants can be moved with bare-roots, but shrubs with balled and balled-and-wrapped roots receive less check to growth than those moved without soil around the roots. Container-grown plants can be moved to their final positions at almost any time of year when conditions allow. Plant shrubs to the same depth as they were previously, in holes of adequate size. Cover the roots with good topsoil, working and firming this around them as planting proceeds. Water the shrubs in as necessary and mulch with peat in spring. Keep the ground weedfree and hoe regularly.

Pruning This is usually best kept to a minimum and is carried out after flowering. Cut out any dead wood, and encourage the production of sufficient new growth to replace worn out branches. Trim plants as necessary to keep them in good shape.

Propagation Most shrubs can be increased from semi-ripe wood cuttings, taken during summer and rooted under shaded frames or in greenhouses. Many plants of this type can be raised from hardwood cuttings taken in autumn and placed in sandy soil in a sheltered position outdoors or under frames.

Topiary This consists of trimming close-growing hedging plants such as privet, box and yew, into the shape of animals and birds, for example.

In early times when labour was cheap this practice was often used. Now, without the aid of electric or powered hedge trimmers, topiary is not a practical proposition. Frequent cutting is necessary or the outlines soon become obscure.

Tree cement This can consist of sand and cement, or be a bitumen preparation. These materials are used for filling large cavities in old trees trunks, to keep out rainwater and slow down or prevent decay. Cut out as much of the dead and rotten wood as possible and paint the exposed surfaces with bitumen or lead preparation before cementing.

Chapter 8. Turf Care

Aeration All garden plants need a circulation of air for their oxygen needs and the methods of providing this vary according to the crop. With established lawns this can be achieved by raking or scarifying, to remove old leaves and rubbish and by slitting or spiking to relieve compacted turf.

Alpine lawn This consists of short, fine-leaved grasses, among which are planted or sown small spring-flowering plants. The turf mixture is left uncut for most of the year. Small-flowered bulbs and corms, such as crocus, galanthus and dwarf narcissi are suitable. Plants such as ajuga or Bugle, crepis or Hawksbeard, and dwarf ranunculus, do not look out of place in this type of turf. Alpine lawns of this type are in character with wild or natural gardens.

Annual dressing Grasses, like other plants which occupy the ground for many years, need to have their food

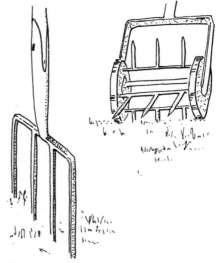

125 Aeration of turf. A solid-tine garden fork or small spiker provide useful means of improving aeration.

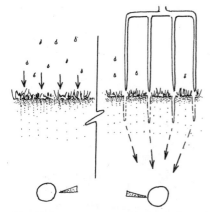

124 Aeration. Water lies on the surface of hard packed soil. Relieving the compaction improves percolation and drainage.

126 Top-dressing. A fine compost mixture can be easily and evenly applied by using a sieve to scatter the top dressing as required.

supply replenished to ensure continued good growth. On lawns, an annual top-dressing of compost consisting of soil, peat and sand, or any one or more of these ingredients, plus balanced ferti-liser, can be applied to sustain the grasses. John Innes potting compost No 2 or similar is excellent for this purpose. Spread a 3 mm ($\frac{1}{8}$ in) layer of the mixture over the lawn in late September or early October.

Chamomile lawn As an alternative to grass, common Chamomile, *Anthemis nobilis*, can be planted 15 cm (6 in) square, to form a low-growing mat of scented foliage. The non-flowering va-riety 'Treneague' is most suitable for this purpose, growing to height of about 15 cm (6 in). This should be cut once or twice per year to remove any hard stems and encourage new growth. This type of lawn is unsuitable where heavy use is required.

Chitting A practice of germinating seeds in damp sand or moist peat before sowing. In districts where birds are particularly troublesome, or on sandy soils, chitting can assist by shortening the period between sowing and the appearance of grass.

Thoroughly mix two parts by bulk of dry sand, to one of seed. Gradually add water, stirring the mixture in a plastic bucket until it is uniformly moist. Place a piece of damp sacking over the mix-ture, and keep it moist in a cool place at 10°C (50°F) for three to five days. Stir the mixture at least once per day and sow the seeds as soon as the white root radicles appear. Any delay at this stage can result in seeds and roots becoming a mass which cannot be separated without damage, and waste results.

Cylinder mower *See* Chapter 11, Tools and Equipment, Mower.

Disease *See* Chapter 10, Problems.

Divot A small irregularly-shaped piece of turf, which has become dis-placed, such as frequently occurs on golf courses. These should be replaced im-mediately, firmed in and kept moist until re-established.

Earthworm *See* Chapter 10, Problems.

Edging A piece of timber boarding or metal strip, which is placed at the edge of lawns or turf areas beside paths. These help to prevent the edges being broken when walked on inadvertantly. The surface level of these pieces of timber or metal should be about 3–6 mm ($\frac{1}{8}$–$\frac{1}{4}$ in) below the surface of the turf.

Also the process of straightening and trimming the edges of a lawn.

Also refers to some kinds of bedding plants.

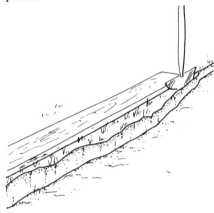

127 Edging. Sawn timber and half-moon enable straight edges to be cut.

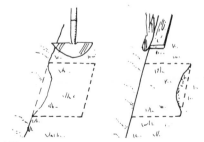

128 Damaged Edges. Damaged edges, *left*, can be remedied by cutting and turning turf around as *right*.

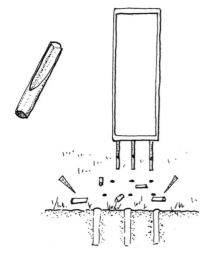

129 Hollow-tine forking. The removal of small cores or plugs of earth allows top dressings to be worked into turf, and improves root growth.

Forking This consists of spiking turf by means of forks, to improve aeration and as a preliminary operation to top dressing. Forking involves piercing the soil about 15–20 cm (6–8 in) deep preferably in autumn, with a solid or hollow tined fork. Working backwards, the fork is dug in at 20–30 cm (8–12 in) intervals, gradually covering the whole area. An ordinary solid-tined fork will serve for average purposes. Where, however, turf

is liable to very heavy wear, hollow-tined forks are more effective, and will remove small cores of soil. The small cores should be swept up, and a top or annual dressing applied.

Grasses Varieties suitable for turf are very different from those used in agriculture, being finer and are able to withstand regular mowing.

Hollow-tine *See* Forking, this chapter.

Hydro seeding A technique of sowing grass seeds in a stream of water. While this method is used mainly for large-scale operations, it can be used on steep banks where conventional methods are not practical or are difficult. The seeds are mixed with water in a tank. The mixture is then pumped out through a hosepipe, in a fairly coarse spray, onto the area being seeded.

Lawns These can be made in various ways, but in practice two main methods are used: by sowing seeds on well prepared soil and by laying turves, usually termed turfing. The preliminary operations are similar for both methods. Lawns are also classed according to their nature and purpose, such as fine lawns, general purpose or hard wearing. The different types can be achieved by using a variety of grasses in differing proportions.

Table of Common Lawn Grasses

Name	Common name	Use
Agrostis tenuis	Bent Grass	F G/P H/W S W
Cynosurus cristatus	Crested Dogs-tail	D F
Deschampsia flexuosa	Wavy-Hair Grass	S
Festuca durior	Hard Fescue	D
Festuca rubra	Red Fescue	F G/P H/W S W
Lolium perenne	Perennial Ryegrass	H/W
Pleum pratense	Timothy	D
Poa nemoralis	Wood Meadow Grass	S W
Poa pratensis	Smooth-stalked Meadow Grass	D G/P H/W
Poa trivialis	Rough-stalked Meadow Grass	S W

Key | D | Used in turf mixtures for dry conditions | H/W | Hard-wearing turf
| F | Fine bowling-green-type turf | W | Used in mixtures for wet soils
| G/P | General purpose turf | S | Used in mixtures for shaded sites

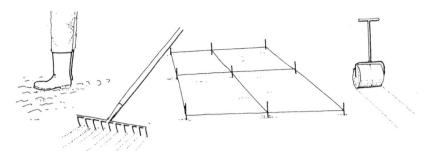

130   Lawn from seed. *Left to right*: firm the ground by treading; rake and provide fine level surface; divide the area into equal sized plots for ease of even sowing; lightly roll sandy soils.

Lawns can be laid in various sites, such as on dry or wet soils and in sunny or shaded situations, for which special mixtures of grass seeds should be used. *See* Table of Grasses. The sequence and details of the various operations are given below.

Clearing and levelling When starting on a new site clear away all rubbish, unwanted vegetation and weeds. Grade out the top and subsoil to the required levels, removing or importing materials as necessary.

Where levelling and grading are carried out, remove the topsoil to one side and keep it separate. This is necessary where changes of level of more than 50–75 mm (2–3 in) are intended. Level and grade the subsoil, using a spirit level, pegs and straight edge as described in Chapter 1, Site and Soil. Carry out

soil drainage by means of a sump or by laying drain pipes.

Cultivation Fork up any badly compacted subsoil before returning the topsoil. Cultivate the top soil to break up any lumps and rake in 100 g/m² (3 oz/sq yd) of balanced fertiliser, 10 days before sowing or turfing.

Liming is not normally carried out because the best turf is produced on acid soils as a rule. Never cultivate or work the ground when it is very wet or waterlogged otherwise the soil will form a slurry and set like concrete into a solid mass. When the land is fairly dry, firm it by walking heel-to-toe fashion and rake level. Mark out the area to be seeded or turfed. This can be carried out by using pegs and line, or by marking out the boundary in sand.

Seed sowing April and May, as well as

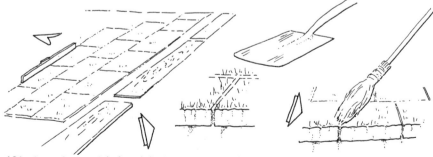

131   Lawn from turf. *Left to right*: lay turves from planks, placing them level and coursed like brickwork, working towards the area being laid; firm turves gently in position with back of spade; brush fine sifted compost into the spaces between turves.

September and October are good months for this operation.

In mild districts, sowing can successfully take place during winter also. Germination is slower and frosty spells should be avoided. Divide the plot to be sown into convenient squares or areas of equal size to simplify sowing. Measure out sufficient seed to sow, one or a number of areas, at the rate of 50 g/m² (1½ oz/sq yd). Sow the seeds broadcast, preferably sowing first one way and then across the line of direction. Carefully rake the seeds in and then firm by lightly rolling. Use seed that has been treated with bird repellent and have bird scarers in position.

Turfing The ground preparation is similar to that used for seed sowing up to and including marking out. When buying turf, specify fine or general purpose. Make sure that the turves are weedfree, of uniform size and thickness and not discoloured, or broken.

Two sizes are commonly used: turves 30 cm (12 in) square by 30–36 mm (1¼–1½ in) thick, and turves 30 × 90 cm (12 × 36 in) of similar thickness. The smaller size is more convenient to handle. Turfing can be carried out at most times of the year, when soil conditions are suitable, but should preferably be carried out during late September and October. Trim each turf

to uniform thickness by placing in a shallow box and paring off surplus soil with an old scythe blade or a large knife, for example. When turfing, start by laying the turves at the outside edge and work forwards over the unturfed area. Pull each turf firmly into the next to avoid leaving gaps. And lay them coursed, like bricks so that there are not continuous lines between turves in two directions. Work from planks, placed over the new-laid turves, to firm evenly and avoid damage. On steep banks, peg each turf with two or more short sticks pushed through into the soil below, to prevent slippage. When the lawn has been laid, scatter fine soil, John Innes No 1 compost along the joints between the turves, and brush this in to fill any gaps. Water the turves during dry weather and as necessary.

Lifting In terms of lawn care, this operation consists of cutting turf into squares or rectangles and then levering out the cut turves. Commercially this is carried out by machine. Cut the turves vertically with a half-moon cutter, using a straight-edged plank as a guide. Then undercut each turf about 36 mm (1½ in) deep and lift out as required. Lifting is necessary when naturalising bulbs, patching and in repair work.

Luting The filling of hollows in turf

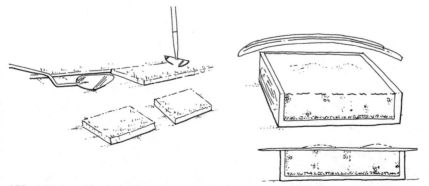

132 Lifting and boxing. Cut turf into squares or rectangles with a half-moon edging iron, and use a turfing spade for undercutting and lifting. Turves can be boxed and trimmed to a uniform thickness, using an old scythe blade to remove surplus soil.

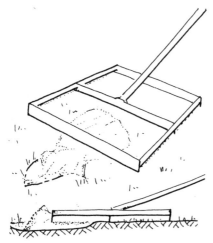

133 Repairs to hollows. Fill them with fine compost mixture using a lute to provide a level finish before sowing. The side view shows surplus compost being pushed forward.

areas by pushing fine loose soil into place with a lute. Surplus material is removed to raise other areas.

Matting In private gardens, the use of metal drag mats for working in top dressings is less common than the use of a stiff broom, which works well for average purposes.

Mowing Grass cutting is an important aspect of lawn care and is carried out in various ways. The two chief factors

which influence mowing are the regularity or intervals between cuts and height. *See* Turf Care Calendar, this chapter.

Regular mowing at short intervals of seven days is much less harmful to lawn turf than infrequent mowing. For average garden purposes a height of cut of 9–12 mm ($\frac{3}{8}$–$\frac{1}{2}$ in) is about right for cylinder mowing.

Nursery Very few gardens today are large enough to accommodate an area for growing turf to repair worn-out areas. This practice can only be fully justified where high-quality turf is needed for patching, such as croquet lawns. However, where only a few turves are needed to repair the edges of a lawn, these can be lifted from an inconspicuous spot. The hole can be filled with good top soil or prepared compost, and then sown with an appropriate grass seed mixture.

Pegging This consists of hammering two or more pieces of wood, about 10 cm (4 in) long by 13 mm ($\frac{1}{2}$ in) thick into each turf, leaving the top of each level with the surface of the turf. This practice is used on steep banks, to prevent slippage of turves until new roots grow into the soil below.

Pests *See* Chapter 10, Problems.

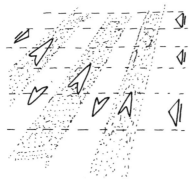

134 Mowing. Cut grass areas back and forth, first up and down, then across.

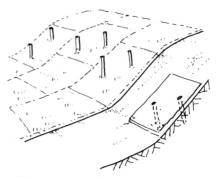

135 Pegging. Turf can be prevented from slipping on banks by hammering small pegs level with the surface and through into the soil below.

Propagation While various grass species, such as some fescues can be increased by division, the most practical method of propagation is by means of seed. The time required to lift, divide and replant clumps of grass is considerable, and lawns consisting of single species are usually less satisfactory than those with two or more species in the sward.

Rhizome Some grasses, such as Smooth-stalked Meadow Grass spread and increase by rhizomes or underground stems. This habit of growth enables some kinds of grasses to tolerate dry conditions better than others.

Rolling The excessive use of the roller does more harm than good to lawns, compacting the soil and suffocating plant roots. The greatest benefit from rolling, which should not be carried out when the soil is waterlogged, is to firm lawns in spring after winter frost, before mowing starts in earnest. The rolling, which occurs during normal mowing with a roller-type mower, is adequate for most lawns.

Where side-wheel mowers or rotary cutters are used, an occasional rolling, two or three times each spring is beneficial. Roll once before the start of cutting and again if the ground feels soft and spongy.

Scarifying This consists of vigorously raking turf with a spring-tine wire rake, pulling out dead, matted grasses and also scattering worm casts. This is usually carried out in autumn or spring. Scarifying improves aeration and increases the resistance of turf to fungal diseases. On large areas of grass, this operation is carried out mechanically, with the use of a rotorake.

Sea-washed turf A high-quality fine turf which is obtained in certain coastal districts, in Cumbria for example, where sea water washes the grass at high tide. This type of turf is less used than formerly, and then was mainly for

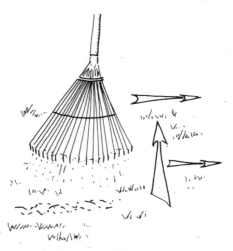

136 Scarifying. Remove dead and matted remains of grass by using a wire rake, working first one way and then across.

bowling greens and golf courses. Cultivated inland turf is often better than the sea-washed variety for lawns that are sited well away from coastal areas.

Slitting This involves cutting turf, usually mechanically with knife-like solid tines, to relieve compacted turf and improve aeration. Autumn and spring are the usual best times for slitting, which should not be carried out in mid-summer, otherwise severe drying out can occur. This operation is an alternative to forking and spiking.

Spiking *See* Forking, this chapter.

Stolon Some grasses, such as Rough-stalked Meadow variety spread by means of over-ground or surface stems. Grasses of this type are better suited to wet soils and shaded areas than those having a rhizome-forming habit.

Sward An area of ground covered with mown turf.

Switching This consists of scattering wormcasts and dew with a long, supple switch or cane, before mowing.

121

Turf Care Calendar

Task		Spring	Summer	Autumn	Winter
Raking		✓	✓	✓ ✓	✓
Switching		✓ ✓	✓	✓ ✓	✓
Scarifying		✓ ✓	—	✓ ✓	✓
Forking Solid tine	a	✓ ✓	—	✓ ✓	✓
Forking Hollow tine	b	✓	—	✓ ✓	—
Slitting mechanical	c	✓	—	✓ ✓	✓ ✓
Lifting		✓	—	✓ ✓	✓
Patching		✓	—	✓ ✓	✓
Top dressing		✓ ✓	—	✓ ✓	—
Rolling		✓ ✓	✓	—	—
Mowing		✓	✓ ✓	✓	—
Edging grass cutting		✓ ✓	✓ ✓	✓ ✓	✓
Watering		✓	✓ ✓	✓	—
Feeding		✓ ✓	✓ ✓	✓	—

Key ✓ ✓ main season(s) for the operation
✓   task can be safely carried out

N.B. Never work on frozen or waterlogged turf, or damage may occur.
a) Solid-tine forking is most used in gardens and can be carried out annually.
b) Hollow-tine forking is usually only necessary once every second or third year as an alternative to (a).
c) Slitting is usually carried out as an alternative to (a) and (b).

Switching enables grass cutting to be carried out more conveniently and with less mess than otherwise.

Watering This should be carried out before feeding if the ground is dry and also before drought conditions take effect. During the summer months lawns in open, sunny positions in mild climates need about $20 \, \text{l/m}^2$ (4 gal/sq yd) of water each week, to keep them in good condition. Applications should start before lawns lose their colour. Lawns can be watered by hosepipe, sprinkler or watering can. Ideally, water should be applied gradually as a fine spray, to ensure thorough wetting of the soil. Most soils cannot absorb large quantities of water quickly; in consequence, wastage can be high due to water running off the surface and away into drains. Oscillating sprinklers which deliver a gentle, but steady fall of water backwards and forwards over the ground are particularly useful. The square area which is covered ensures an even distribution of water.

Rotary sprinklers are handy, convenient and provide a wetting spray, but usually cover a small area, necessitating frequent moves. Pulse-jet sprinklers enable large areas to be watered at a time without moving the equipment, but the pattern of distribution is circular. This results in some overlapping of the watered areas, but otherwise this type of equipment serves its purpose well. Watering cans are really only suitable for watering small areas, but are excellent for applying chemicals and liquid fertilisers.

Chapter 9. Vegetables and Herbs

Asparagus A choice vegetable grown for the succulent shoots, which occur from May to early June and are cooked or frozen.
Cultivation Plants are raised from seeds sown outdoors about April on well prepared beds in drills 12 mm ($\frac{1}{2}$ in) deep and 300 mm (12 in) apart. Subsequently thin the rows to 150 mm (6 in) apart and grow on for two or three years. Transplant two or three-year old seedlings to final position, in heavily manured 600 mm or 1.2 m (2 or 4 ft) wide trenches. Space the crowns 450 mm–600 mm (1$\frac{1}{2}$–2 ft) apart, and 100–125 mm (4–5 in) deep. Apply 140 g/m^2 (4 oz/sq yd) of balanced fertiliser before planting and subsequently in each spring before growth starts. Cutting commences lightly in the first year after planting, increasing in later years. But this should stop by mid-June each summer, to enable the crowns to build up reserves for the next year. Keep beds weedfree at all times. Asparagus beds last for many years when well made and cared for.

Beans, broad A crop grown for the beans which can be gathered from June to August, eaten cooked or frozen for later use.
Cultivation Sow the seeds, in autumn or early spring for open air or cloche crops, 50 mm (2 in) deep in two rows, 200 mm (8 in) between seeds and rows, over well manured trenches. Before sowing, apply 100 g/m^2 (3 oz/sq yd) of balanced fertiliser to the trenches. Where two or more pairs of rows are grown together, allow 600 mm (2 ft) minimum between each pair. Keep the ground weedfree. Support the rows of plants with canes and strings, especially in exposed situations. Remove the growing point of each plant, when four or five flower clusters have developed, to encourage

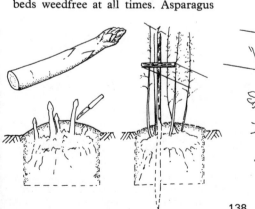

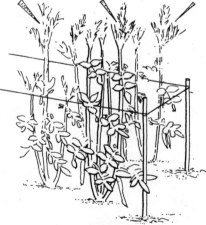

137 Asparagus. A cut stem. A section through bed, showing shoots. Method of support for the foliage in summer.

138 Broad beans. Use canes and string to keep beans tidy. Remove growing points, *arrowed*, when plants are 90–120 cm (3–4 ft) tall for tall standard varieties.

early cropping and prevent the build up of blackfly. Pick the pods before the seeds become hard and tough. Two types of broad bean are grown, namely Longpod and Windsor. Longpod varieties, which are very hardy, can be used for autumn sowings. Beans of the Windsor type are larger and broader than the former.

Beans, French or dwarf This type of bean is grown for the tender pods which are cooked when freshly gathered, or can be frozen for later use. These are normally ready for picking from July to October.

Cultivation The ground for this crop should be fertile, free draining, and well limed, preferably during the winter. Apply 100 g/m² (3 oz/sq yd) of balanced fertiliser before sowing. Sow the seeds 200 mm (8 in) apart and 40–50 mm (1½–2 in) deep, with 450 mm (18 in) between rows. This can be carried out in open ground from mid-April to late June. Keep them well watered and weedfree. There are climbing varieties of French beans, which are similar in other respects, but they are grown like

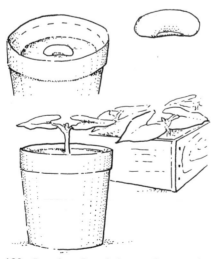

139 Dwarf or French beans. Sow seeds 13 mm (½ in) deep in pots or boxes of compost for early outdoor crops.

runner beans. Gather the crop while young and tender.

Beans, runner Also known as stick beans, these are cultivated for the edible pods, which can be cooked when gathered, or frozen for subsequent consumption. This crop is more tender and slightly later than French beans, being grown in warmer districts for picking from late July to September.

Cultivation The earliest crops are grown from sowings made in greenhouses and planted outside, or sown under cloches in April. Seeds can also be successfully sown in the open from mid-May to early June. Prepare well-manured 600 mm (2 ft) wide trenches in autumn and apply 140 g/m² (4 oz/sq yd) of balanced fertiliser a few days before sowing or planting. Sow seeds 300 mm (12 in) apart and 50 mm (2 in) deep, in two rows with 300 mm (12 in) between each, sowing a few extra for replacements. Before sowing, place bean poles in position 300 mm (12 in) apart, in two rows with similar distance between. Tie the tops to horizontal poles. Plants, if used, can be set out at the base of each pole instead of seeds. Keep the ground weedfree and well watered, syringing plants in warm weather to encourage pods to form. An occasional liquid feed is beneficial to heavy-cropping plants. Pick pods regularly when large enough, but before they become tough, freezing any which are surplus to immediate needs.

Beetroot A crop which is valued as a vegetable when cooked and eaten hot, or used as a salad when cold. Valuable for pickling. Fresh roots can be available for lifting from July to October, but can be used all year round if stored.

Cultivation Avoid freshly manured land, but preparations should be thorough, breaking the ground down and producing a good tilth. Apply and rake in 100 g/m² (3 oz/sq yd) of balanced fertiliser. Sow the seeds 12 mm (½ in) deep in drills 300 mm (12 in) apart,

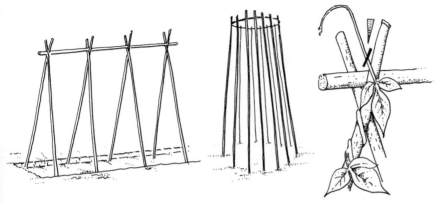

140 Runner beans. Methods of supporting this crop. Remove the growing point, *arrowed*, when plants reach the top of the posts.

watering the drills before sowing in dry weather.

Keep the ground weedfree and moist. Subsequently thin the seedlings to 50 mm (2 in) apart when large enough to handle, repeating this process, to leave individual seedlings 100–150 mm (4–6 in) apart for round or long varieties. Lift round varieties of beetroot when the roots are 50–60 mm (2–2½ in) in diameter, and are most tender.

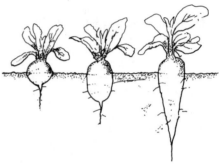

142 Tankard. *Centre*: intermediate or cylindrical beetroot known also as Tankard varieties. *Left*: round beet. *Right*: long type.

141 Beetroot. Remove the foliage by twisting the leaf stalks, and store roots for winter use in layers with sand between them.

When lifting roots for storing, take care not to damage them, or bleeding and loss of condition and colour can occur. Twist off the leaves, about 12–25 mm (½–1 in) above the root top. Do not cut, or bleeding and discolouring can arise. There are three main types of beetroot: round, tankard or intermediate and long. Round varieties are globe shaped, tankard types are more oval, and the long are large and taper gradually to the tips.

Blanching This consists of excluding light from stems and leaves to improve the quality, flavour and colour of crops, such as celery, endive and leeks.

125

Bleeding *See* Chapter 10, Problems.

Borecole *See* Kale, this chapter.

Brassica The group name for cabbage and allied crops like Brussels sprouts and cauliflower.

Broadcasting *See* Chapter 2, Propagation.

Broccoli A group of vegetables which are grown for the heads, curds or shoots of unopened clusters of flower heads.

The large white-headed types are a form of cauliflower.

Most kinds of broccoli are cooked when gathered, or frozen for later use, or used in chutneys and pickles.

Green broccoli, also known as calabrese and Italian sprouting, produce 'spears' of leaves and green bud clusters in summer and autumn.

Purple and white-sprouting varieties are hardy, start cropping in spring and provide spears of leaves and bud clusters in their respective colours.

Winter cauliflower produce large cauliflower-type curds from December to June in southern districts, or March to June in northern areas.

Cultivation The land for broccoli should be fertile, free draining and limed, with a pH of 7 or slightly above, to reduce the chance of attack by Club

144 Spear. *Top*: this shoot of sprouting broccoli has a curd of buds and tender leaves. *Below*: mature plant with several spears which are ready to use.

Root disease. Dig or cultivate the ground deeply, well in advance of cropping, allowing the land to settle and provide a firm bed. In May or early June, sow the seeds in a well prepared seed bed about 12 mm ($\frac{1}{2}$ in) deep in moist drills, spaced about 250 mm (10 in) apart. Cover the seeds lightly with fine soil and firm gently. Water the seedlings as necessary and keep the ground weedfree. When the seedlings are 100–125 mm (4–5 in) tall, carefully lift and transplant them. Rake in 100 g/m^2 (3 oz/sq yd) of a balanced fertiliser a few days before planting. When planting with a dibber, make sure the hole is large enough. Set the plants out 450 mm (18 in) apart with 600 mm (2 ft) between rows, planting firmly. Hoe frequently and keep the ground moist. Protect crops from birds, pests and disease. In February, top dress the latest maturing varieties with 35 g/m^2 (1 oz/sq yd) of Nitro-chalk. Protect winter cauliflower by bending a leaf or two over developing curds, to

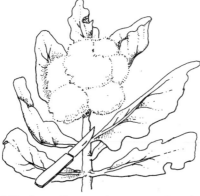

143 Broccoli, sprouting green. Cut the centre curd early to allow side sprouts or spears to develop.

prevent discoloration from sun or frost. Cut the spears or heads before the tight buds start to swell, freezing any that are surplus to immediate requirements.

Brussels sprouts A green crop grown for the edible buttons or buds which develop on the main stem and sometimes the large terminal cabbage-like bud. Sprouts are cooked when gathered or frozen until needed for use.

Cultivation Depending on variety, sowing date, climate and season, sprouts can be available for gathering from September to March. Sowings are best made outdoors in March and April, but can also be carried out in warmth in February for the early crops. On a well prepared and level bed, sow seeds 12 mm (½ in) deep, in moist drills, spaced 250 mm (10 in) apart. Prepare the ground as for broccoli, making sure that the pH level is not below 7. When the ground is moist, plant out 100–150 mm (4–6 in) high seedlings, spacing them 750 mm (2 ft) apart, with a similar distance between rows. Water the plants as necessary, and hoe regularly to keep the ground weedfree. Protect the plants from pigeons with bird scarers. Picking commences at the base of plant stems, breaking off firm, solid buttons with a

146   Brussels sprouts. Start picking at the base, removing old, yellowing leaves. The crown bud, *arrowed*, is left to grow in later crops for use as 'tops'.

downward pull. Regular gathering helps to ensure that the buttons at the top of the stems have a chance to develop. When selecting varieties it is advisable to include early and late varieties to provide a succession.

Cabbage A group of plants which are grown for the large terminal bud or head, surrounded by leaves, all of which can be cooked and eaten. The heart or bud in some tender varieties can be used raw in salads.

There are three main groups of cabbage which are commonly grown in

145   Brussels sprouts. The earliest crops are obtained by removing the growing point, *arrowed*, before the buttons develop. The leaves have been removed here to show the crop.

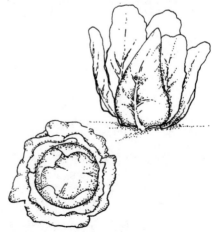

147   Cabbage types. Pointed or ox-heart and round.

127

gardens: spring-sown varieties, autumn-sown type and Savoy or crinkled.

Cultivation Prepare the seed bed as for broccoli. Sow seeds under frames in February for June cutting, outdoors in April and May for harvesting, according to variety, from July to March, including Savoy types. Sowing in July and early August can provide 'greens' or heads from March to May or June. Sow the seeds 12 mm (½ in) deep in moist drills, spaced 250 mm (10 in) apart. Keep the ground weedfree and moist and transplant the seedlings when 100–125 mm (4–5 in) high into their final positions. Allow 450 mm (18 in) between plants and rows for spring sown, with Savoys slightly wider at 600 mm (2 ft) square. The ground for Savoys and spring-sown crops can be prepared as for broccoli. With autumn-sown cabbage, especially where they follow early potatoes, apply only 70 g/m² (2 oz/sq yd) of balanced fertiliser, to avoid producing soft, sappy plants in winter. Keep the ground weedfree, and hoe regularly. Top dress autumn-sown plants in February with 35 g/m² (1 oz/sq yd) of Nitro-chalk to promote good growth and solid hearts. Keep pigeons and other birds away with scarers or nets. Cut the heads of all kinds when firm and solid, except for early spring greens which are harvested before becoming so. The three groups of cabbages are further sub-divided into pointed or ox-heart and round varieties.

Calabrese *See* Broccoli, this chapter.

Carrot An important crop, grown for the vitamin-rich roots which can be eaten cooked as a vegetable, or raw in salads. These can be stored in a frost-free place, and tender young roots can be quick frozen. Carrots can be used fresh from July to November and stored for year-round use.

Cultivation Ideally the ground should be a deep, sandy, fertile and free-draining loam, but avoid large quantities of freshly-applied manure, which can cause the roots to be forked and mis-shapen. Cultivate the ground deeply, finally forking and raking to produce a fine tilth and seed bed. Work in 100 g/m² (3 oz/sq yd) of a balanced or high potash base fertiliser a few days before sowing. Sow quick maturing varieties from March to June, or maincrop types in April and May, in moist drills, spaced 300 mm (12 in) apart and 12 mm (½ in) deep. Keep the ground well watered and weedfree and hoe regularly. When the seedlings are 25–50 mm (1–2 in) high, thin the quick-maturing types if necessary, to 25–50 mm (1–2 in) apart when the soil is moist. Maincrop varieties are thinned again to remove alternate plants, leaving a final spacing of double the first. Burn, bury or use all thinnings to avoid attracting Carrotfly. Harvest quick-maturing varieties as soon as they are large enough to use. Maincrop types can be used when ready or left in the soil until October or November and be lifted all together and stored. But first, cut off the foliage about 12 mm (½ in) above the roots.

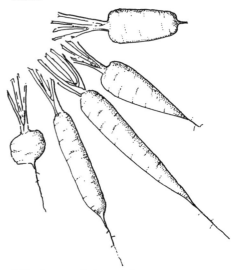

148 Carrots. *Left to right:* round; stump rooted; long; intermediate; stump-rooted intermediate.

Four types of carrot are commonly grown, which are classed according to root shape into small round, stump-rooted, intermediate and long. The quickest maturing are the small, round varieties and the long kinds provide the maincrop, needing a deep soil and a long growing season. The intermediate types are similar to long varieties but are shorter and taper more sharply. In the stump-rooted class are both early and maincrop varieties.

Catch crop Any quick-growing crop which can be taken between harvesting one main crop and sowing or planting another. Radish is a common example. This practice, unlike inter-cropping, does not involve growing a maincrop simultaneously with an inter-planted quick growing crop.

Cauliflower A group of plants grown for their cream and white curds or heads of unopened flowers. They are cooked as a vegetable, used in chutneys and pickles, or quick frozen for future use. Cauliflowers can be ready for harvesting from June to November, depending on sowing date and variety. For winter cauliflower *see* broccoli, this chapter.
Cultivation Sow under glass in September or January and February for planting outdoors in April, for cutting in June and July. Seeds are sown in boxes of seed compost and pricked out into 90 mm ($3\frac{1}{2}$ in) pots of potting compost or into peat pots. Harden off seedlings in readiness for planting out on well-limed and prepared ground, as for broccoli. Sow autumn-maturing varieties during April and May on seed-beds prepared as for broccoli, sowing in 12 mm ($\frac{1}{2}$ in) deep drills, spaced 250 mm (10 in) apart. Transplant the outdoor-sown seedlings at the same spacing as the pot-grown, indoor-sown, allowing 450 mm (18 in) between plants in rows 600 mm (2 ft) apart, on ground prepared as for broccoli. Keep plants well watered, weedfree and hoe regularly. Take precautions against pigeons and pests. *See* Chapter 10, Problems.

Celeriac Also known as Turnip-rooted celery, which is grown for the bulb as well as the leaf stalks, both being cooked before eating. Harvesting is normally carried out in autumn, when the tops can be used like celery, and the bulbs eaten or stored.
Cultivation Sow seeds in warmth under cover during March as for celery. Prick

149 Cauliflower. Protect developing curd from sun or frost by bending one or two leaves, *arrowed*, or placing a leaf over it.

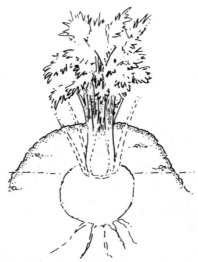

150 Celeriac. Remove one or two outer circles of leaves before earthing up.

out the seedlings, 40 mm (1½ in) apart, into boxes of potting compost and harden off in frames. Plant out the seedlings into fertile soil, prepared as for self-blanching celery, spacing them about 300 mm (12 in) apart each way. Keep the plants well watered and weed-free. Feed the plants occasionally with liquid fertilisers. Remove the two outer rings of leaves, once in late August and again in September, also taking off any side growths as they arise. Earth up the stems in August, to blanch them ready for lifting from late September to early December.

Celery A stem crop that can be cooked and eaten as a vegetable or used raw in salads. Two types are grown: self-blanching, normally harvested between July and September, and trench varieties, which are lifted between October and early January.

Cultivation Sow self-blanching varieties in pans or boxes in gentle warmth about mid-April, but no earlier, or plants go to seed prematurely. Prick out the seedlings, about 40 mm (1½ in) apart, into boxes of potting mixture, such as John Innes potting compost No 2 or equivalent. Harden off these plants in frames, before planting them out, about 250 mm (10 in) apart each way, on flat beds in June. The ground for this crop should be dug spade deep, incorporating plenty of well-rotted manure, compost

or similar. Rake in 140 g/m² (4 oz/sq yd) of balanced fertiliser about a week before planting. Keep the plants well watered, and weedfree, feeding them occasionally with liquid fertiliser when about 150 mm (6 in) high and over. Lift roots of self-blanching celery before the arrival of frost. The stems of this type are less hardy and not so well protected as those of trench varieties with their covering of earth. Raise plants of trench celery as for self blanching, but sow seeds during March because a long growing season is needed. Deeply dig and manure 450 mm (18 in) wide trenches in autumn for preference. Apply and rake in 60 g/m (2 oz/yd) run of trench a few days before planting, leaving the soil level about 150 mm (6 in) below the surrounding ground. Set out the young plants, 225 mm (9 in) apart in two rows with a similar distance between seedlings. Keep these plants well watered and weedfree. Loosely tie the stems together when plants are 200–250 mm (8–10 in) tall, removing any side shoots at the same time and earth up the stems. Subsequently, gradually add more soil as plants grow.

Pests and Diseases Spray the leaves with malathion insecticide or benomyl fungicide where leaf mining maggot, or leaf spot respectively, are troublesome.

Chard Also known as leaf beet and Silver or Sea kale. This is grown for the

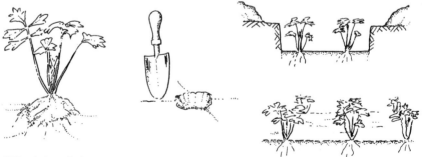

151   Celery. *Left*: a well developed seedling. *Centre*: set plants out, using a trowel. *Top right*: newly planted trench celery. *Below right*: set self-blanching varieties in blocks on the flat.

leaves which are cooked and eaten like spinach. The leaf stalks or mid-ribs can be used as an excellent substitute for sea kale, but edible roots are not formed. It is sown and grown like Summer spinach to which it is related.

Chervil *See* Herbs, this chapter.

Chicory A crop grown for the 'Chicons' or buds, used in salads. Is usually produced in warmth under cover during winter. The best variety for this purpose is Witloof or Brussels Chicory. *See* Chapter 4, Greenhouses.

Chinese cabbage A crop grown for the slender, solid heads or buds in the same way as conventional cabbage. Sow seeds 12 mm ($\frac{1}{2}$ in) deep in moist drills, spaced 375 mm (15 in) apart on land prepared as for cabbage during June and July. Thin the resultant seedlings to 300 mm (12 in) apart in the rows, subsequently treating the crop as for summer cabbage.

Chive *See* Herbs, this chapter.

Clamp An open air form of storage for root vegetables, such as beetroot, carrots and potatoes. This consists of placing roots on a 100–150 mm (4–6 in) layer of straw, placed on bare earth. Cover them with a similar thickness of straw, followed by a 150–200 mm (6–8 in) layer of

soil, leaving a small hole near the top for ventilation. Avoid siting clamps on low-lying land that is liable to flooding.

Composting *See* Chapter 1, Site and Soil.

Courgette A type of marrow which is cut while still small and tender when about 100–150 mm (4–6 in) long. This is very popular on the continent. *See* Marrow, this chapter, for details of cultivation.

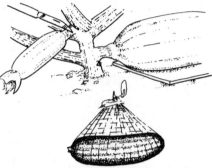

152 Courgette. These are ready for cutting when 10–15 cm (4–6 in) long. Store large end-of-season marrows in nets suspended in air.

Cucumbers A crop grown for the cool, refreshing fruits which are used in salads. Small fruited varieties are used in

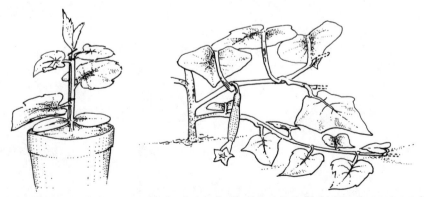

153 Cucumber. *Left*: stop outdoor varieties after the fourth leaf. *Right*: laterals are stopped after the second leaf beyond the first fruit, and sub-laterals after one leaf.

pickles and chutneys. These are best grown under cover. *See* Chapter 4, Greenhouses.

Dandelion A winter salad vegetable; the young leaves are eaten green or blanched.

Cultivation In April or May sow seeds 6 mm ($\frac{1}{4}$ in) deep in moist drills, spaced 300 mm (12 in) apart on a well prepared seed bed. Thin the seedlings to 75–100 mm (3–4 in) apart. Blanch the leaves under inverted pots in autumn. Fresh young leaves appear again in spring, which can be used green or blanched.

Endive A salad crop which is grown for the leaves.

Cultivation The method of cultivation is similar to that of lettuce. Dig the ground spade deep, incorporating well-rotted manure or compost in autumn. After a 14–day minimum period, lime the ground as necessary to raise the pH level to 7 in winter. Fork and rake the ground level, breaking down lumps and working in 100 g/m^2 (3 oz/sq yd) of balanced fertiliser about one week before sowing. Sow summer varieties from March to July and winter types from July to Autumn 6 mm ($\frac{1}{4}$ in) deep, in

moist drills, spaced 375 mm (15 in) apart. Thin the seedlings to 300 mm (12 in) apart, when about 25–50 mm (1–2 in) high. Keep the seedlings moist and weedfree, and hoe regularly. Cover each plant with an inverted pot or box about 10–21 days before required for use. The shorter period is appropriate to summer conditions, unlike the 21 or more days needed in winter. Protect plants from severe frost in late autumn by covering with cloches, or lifting and placing plants in frames and covering with frame lights.

Fennel *See* Herbs, this chapter.

Fluid sowing A modern technique which has been developed for raising plants, mainly outdoors, consisting of sowing chitted seed in a clear, gelatinous paste. This mixture is placed in moist drills, rather like tooth paste from a tube, and is covered with fine soil as in normal sowing. The method of applying this paste can be by means of a special dispenser kit, delivering the mixture from a thin tube, fed from a bottle. A simple approach is to use a plastic bag, cutting off one corner and forcing the jelly out like icing on a cake. The advantages of this system are quick germination, low loss of seed, and less rapid drying out on sandy soils.

Globe artichoke A luxury crop, grown for the edible buds which are

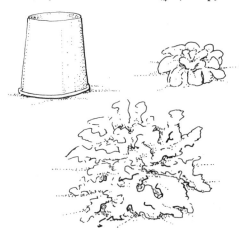

154 Endive. Blanch each head before use. *Top*: Batavian type. *Below*: Exquisite Curled variety.

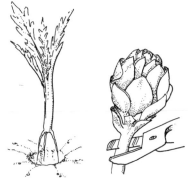

155 Globe artichoke. An off-shoot ready for planting. Harvesting the crop.

picked while unopened in summer and cooked as a vegetable.

Cultivation Plants are raised from off-shoots or suckers that are removed in autumn, overwintered in frames and planted out in permanent beds, about 750 mm (2½ ft) apart, in April.

The beds should be deeply worked, moderately well manured and free draining. Replanting is normally carried out every fourth year.

Herbs A group of plants, the shoots of which are mainly used for flavouring and seasoning a wide range of foods and drinks. These can be grown successfully in confined spaces, in beds, boxes or even pots, preferably close to the kitchen for convenience. The herbs which are most frequently found in small gardens include chives, mint, parsley, sage and thyme. The reasons for the popularity of this group are ease of cultivation – once planted they last for a few years – easiness of propagation and their general usefulness. Where space is available a wider range of plants can be grown, details of which are given in the Table of Herbs.

Cultivation Herbs need a free-draining soil that is neither too fertile nor too wet and many succeed best in sheltered sunny situations to develop their maximum flavour and scent. The soil should be well worked, friable and have a good tilth.

Hydroponic cultivation The growing of crops in or on a rooting medium other than soil.

Intercrop The practice of growing plants of one or more crops among those of another, such as a row of radish between two rows of lettuce. This technique is more commonly used under cover than with outdoor cultivation. *cf.* Catch crop, this chapter.

Jerusalem artichoke A crop grown for the tubers which are dug up in autumn, and can be cooked and eaten as a vegetable.

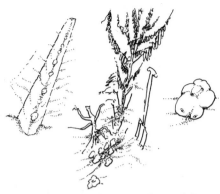

156 Jerusalem artichoke. *Left to right*: planting; cut down tops and lift; tuber.

Cultivation In March, plant the tubers 300 mm (12 in) apart in fertile, well worked soil, 125 mm (5 in) deep, with 900 mm (3 ft) between rows. A sunny or partly-shaded position is suitable for this crop. Manure and fertiliser are not applied unless the soil is poor; then give a light dressing of manure and rake in 100 g/m² (3 oz/sq yd) of a balanced fertiliser. Earth up the young shoots when about 150 mm (6 in) high like potatoes, drawing crumbly, loose earth into ridges around them. When the foliage dies down in autumn, cut the stems down to about 450 mm (18 in) and lift the tubers as required. In December, lift all the roots and store only the best tubers in sand, dry soil or peat, in a frost-free place.

Kale Also known as borecole, an extremely hardy crop, producing valuable green leaves during winter and spring which are cooked and eaten as a vegetable.

Cultivation The ground should be dug spade deep in autumn. Work in a light dressing of manure unless kale follows early potatoes, when the residue from that crop should suffice.

Lime the soil if need be, in winter or after the early potato crop, to raise the pH level to 7. Allow a minimum gap of 7–10 days between manuring and liming. After at least a similar period apply

133

Table of Herbs

Name + Height (cm)	Propagation	Situation	Season
Angelica archangelica Angelica 150	Seed Sow outdoors, Mar	Deep moist soil and shaded site Allow 30 cm between plants	Gather leaves, stems and roots in summer
Melissa officinalis Balm 60—90	Seed Sow outdoors, Apr—May Division in autumn	Light sandy soil and warm sunny positions Allow 30 cm between plants	Foliage gathered in summer
Ocimum basilicum Basil, sweet 30	Seed Sow in warmth, Feb—Mar	Sandy loam soil and sunny warm site or in semi-shade Allow 30 cm between plants	Gather in summer
Borago officinalis Borage 45	Seed Sow outdoors, Mar—Apr	Light sandy soils in sheltered sunny site Allow 30 cm between plants	Pick in summer
Carum carvi Caraway 60	Seed Sow outdoors autumn or Mar—Apr	Medium soil in open sunny position Space plants 30 cm apart	Gather seeds in late summer
Anthriscus cerefolium Chervil 40	Seed Sow in open ground, late spring and summer	Light or medium soil in open or part shaded site Allow 30 cm between plants	Pick 6—8 weeks after sowing
Allium schoenoprasum Chives 15—25	Seed Sow outdoors, Apr Division in autumn	Medium soil and semi-shaded or sunny site Allow 30 cm between clumps	Gather leaves all year round
Coriandrum sativum Coriander 60—90	Seed Sow outdoors, Apr	Warm, medium soil and sunny, sheltered site Allow 30 cm between plants	Harvest seeds in August
Peucedanum graveolens Dill 60—90	Seed Sow in open ground, Apr—Jun	Light or warm medium soil and sunny sheltered position Allow 25 cm between plants	Gather seeds in summer

Florence Fennel 75	Sow outdoors, Mar	site Space plants 45 cm between rows and 15 cm in the row	and autumn as required
Origanum onites Marjoram, Pot 30	Seed Sow outdoors, Mar–Apr Division, Mar–Apr	Light or medium soil in sunny position Allow 30 cm between plants	Cut foliage in summer
Origanum marjorana Marjoram, Sweet 60	Seed Sow in warmth, Mar or outdooors, May–Jun	Medium to rich warm soil in sun Allow 20 cm between plants	Gather foliage in summer
Mentha rotundifolia Mint, apple	Seed Sow outdoors, Apr Division, Mar–Apr Cuttings in summer	Light, rich moist soil in partly shaded position Allow 20 cm between plants	Pick shoots in late spring and summer
Carum petroselinum Parsley 20–30	Seed Sow under cover or outdoors, Apr–Jul	Medium, rich moist soil and semi-shaded site Allow 20 cm between plants	Pick all year round
Salvia officinalis Sage 60–75	Seed Sow in warmth, Mar Cuttings, Apr in frames	Light, rich soil and sunny position Space plants 40 cm apart	Pick mainly in summer
Rumex scutatus Sorrel 30–60	Seed Sow outdoors, Mar–Apr Division, Mar	Medium, rich, moist soil in open position Space plants 30 cm apart	Gather leaves during summer
Thymus vulgaris Thyme 15	Seed Sow outdoors, Apr. Cuttings, summer Division, Apr	Light, fertile soil in warm, sunny position Allow 15 cm between plants	Harvest mainly in summer

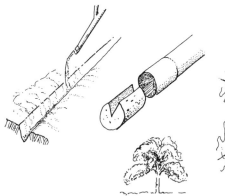

157 Kale. Water seed drills in dry weather before sowing. A piece of cork, cut as shown, and pushed firmly into the spout of a watering can cuts down the flow of water.

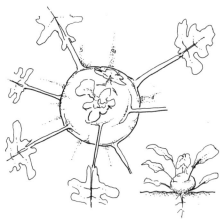

158 Kohl-rabi. Harvest and use these when about the size of a tennis ball.

and rake in 100 g/m² (3 oz/sq yd) of balanced fertiliser. Sow kale on a well prepared seedbed during April and May in 12 mm (½ in) deep, well moistened drills, spaced 250 mm (10 in) apart. Cover the seeds with fine soil and gently firm. Keep the ground well watered and weedfree. When the seedlings are 100–150 mm (4–6 in) tall, set them out in their final positions, 600 mm (2 ft) apart, with a similar spacing between rows. Harvesting involves picking tender young leaves from the crowns and subsequent young growth.

Varieties Four types of kale are grown in gardens: curly or Scotch varieties with very frilled foliage, are hardy and popular; the smooth or plain-leaf varieties are hardy, but less attractive; the rape-kale varieties such as Hungry Gap are sown and thinned, but not transplanted; the leaf-and-spear type is proving to be very hardy and productive and is represented by the variety Pentland Brig.

Kohl rabi This vegetable, also known as the Cabbage-turnip, is grown for the edible turnip-like roots which develop above ground and are harvested during summer and autumn.

Cultivation Sow the seeds on well prepared ground, where they are required to grow, about 12 mm (½ in) deep in well-moistened drills, spaced about 375 mm (15 in) apart. Sowings made from April to late June can produce root globes in 10–14 weeks from sowing. The land for this crop should be well worked, lightly manured and limed if necessary to raise the pH to 7. But leave a minimum interval of 7–10 days between manuring and liming. Allow a similar period after liming and before applying 70–100 g/m² (2–3 oz/sq yd) of balanced fertiliser before sowing. Keep the ground moist, weedfree and hoe regularly. Thin the seedlings when 25–50 mm (1–2 in) high, spacing them about 150–200 mm (6–8 in) apart. Harvest the globes when they are small and tender, about the size of a tennis ball.

Leaf crops Vegetables having similar soil requirements are grouped together for the purposes of crop rotation, usually into three classes. The aim is to ensure that the same or closely related crops are not grown on the same piece of ground for two or more years in succession. This is to prevent the build up of pests and diseases. Leaf crops, for this purpose,

136

consist mainly of members of the brassica tribe or cabbage family. These include broccoli of green, purple and white-sprouting varieties, Brussels sprouts, cabbages of all kinds, cauliflowers and cauliflower broccoli, kale and Savoy.

Although not strictly classed as leaf crops, kohl rabi, radish, swedes, and turnips are members of the cabbage family, but are usually grouped with root crops.

Leek A very hardy crop grown for the edible stems, which are harvested during autumn and winter, for use as a cooked vegetable.

Cultivation Early crops are sown in boxes of seed compost, in warmth during January and February, pricked out into boxes, hardened off and planted outdoors. Sowings can also be made in March and April on well-prepared seed beds under frames and cloches, or outdoors for later crops. Sow the seeds thinly, 12 mm ($\frac{1}{2}$ in) deep, in moist drills, spaced 200 mm (8 in) apart, covering them with fine soil and firming gently. The ground for leeks should be deep, rich, fertile and free draining. Deeply dig the ground, incorporating a generous dressing of manure. Apply lime if necessary, to raise the pH level to around 6.5, after a minimum of 7–10 days following manuring. Allow at least a similar period before raking in 140 g/m² (4 oz/sq yd) of balanced fertiliser a few days before planting. Set leek seedlings out when 100–125 mm (4–5 in) tall, placing them about 200 mm (8 in) apart, into half their height in dibber holes which are not firmed, but watered. Space the rows about 300 mm (12 in) apart. Keep the plants well watered, weedfree and hoe regularly during the growing season. Earth up the crop two or three times as it grows to blanch the stems for culinary pruposes, during late summer and autumn. Leeks for show purposes are often blanched by using a short length of drainpipe or using

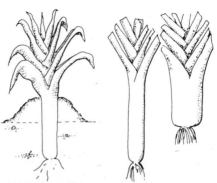

159 Leeks. *Left*: earthing up provides well blanched stems. *Centre*: trench or long varieties. *Right*: pot leek.

corrugated paper for a collar. This crop requires generous feeding and benefits from the occasional liquid feed during summer. Lift and use the crop as required.

Varieties Three main types of leek are grown: the long type; intermediate and pot leek. The long type produce tall stems of medium thickness, compared to the short, broad pot leeks. Intermediate varieties, as the name implies, produces crops of medium height and thickness.

Legume A term applied to plants and crops of the pea and bean family.

Lettuce A group of salad crops, of varying texture, habit and shape, which are grown for their tender leaves. Members of this group are grown under cover and in the open air for harvesting all the year round.

Cultivation Lettuce grow best on light, rich, fertile loams that are free draining and well supplied with lime, having a pH level of 6.8 or near. Plants are raised from seeds: they are either sown in containers under cover, pricked out and subsequently planted out, sown in beds and transplanted or sown *in situ* and later thinned. *See* Table of Outdoor Lettuce. The soil should be well dug, forked and cultivated, supplied with organic matter and limed if need be. Allow a minimum interval of 7–10 days between manuring

160 Lettuce. Seeds can be sown outdoors and thinned where they are to mature. Open-air crops can also be raised from indoor sowings, subsequently priced out in boxes, and then planted out.

and liming, and a similar gap before applying and raking in fertiliser at the rate of $100 \, g/m^2$ (3 oz/sq yd). The transplanted crop can also be sown about 6 mm ($\frac{1}{4}$ in) deep in well-moistened drills, spaced 200 mm (8 in) apart and moved to their cropping positions when about 25 mm (1 in) high. The *in situ* crop, sown where it is grown to maturity, is started off as for the transplanted crop, but the row width is increased to 300 mm (12 in). The distance between plants for both transplanted and thinned crops, depends on the type of lettuce being grown. *See* Table of Outdoor Lettuce. Transplant seedlings into moist soil, preferably in dull or showery conditions. Thinning is carried out in two or three stages, starting when

161 Lettuce. Excellent plants are also produced by sowing or pricking out small seedlings in soil blocks.

seedlings are small and subsequently at weekly intervals. Thin the seedlings at first to about 50 mm (2 in) apart, then remove alternate plants, finally thinning to the required distance. Lettuce are best when quickly grown, and should be kept well watered and weedfree. Take precautions against pests such as slugs, and make use of bird scarers or netting. Start cutting before plants are fully mature to spread out the cropping period. Regular successive sowings ensure a continuity of supply.

Varieties Several types of lettuce are grown. Butterhead: these are hearted cabbage varieties, with soft leaves and are quick maturing. Cos: tall narrow semi-hearted varieties mainly for summer use. Crisphead: these form medium to large cabbage-type hearts of crisp brittle leaves which, in common with Cos varieties, stand warm summer conditions well. Curly: non-hearting varieties which are very popular on the continent, producing attractively curled leaves.

Marjoram *See* Herbs, this chapter.

Marrow Grown for the fruits, which are produced during summer and are cooked before eating.

Courgettes are small-fruited types of marrow, cut when less than 150 mm

Table of Outdoor Lettuce

Type	Sow	Harvest	Space between plants (mm)
Butterhead	Sep	Apr–May	250
Butterhead	Mar–Jun	Jun–Oct	250
Cos	Mar–May	Jun–Sep	200
Crisphead	Mar–May	Jun–Sep	300
Curly	Mar–Jun	Jun–Oct	300

(6 in) long. Many varieties, if left, would form large marrows.

Cultivation Seeds are sown during April, in warmth, singly in pots of seed compost for best results. Harden off these seedlings and plant out under cloches or frames in May or outdoors in June into well-prepared beds, in a warm sunny position. Marrows can also be sown 25 mm (1 in) deep, and 600–900 mm (2–3 ft) apart under cover where they are to mature, in prepared fruiting beds, which are made up as follows. Dig out a hole, spade deep and at least 450 mm (18 in) square. Fill the holes with a prepared mixture of equal parts of loam and well-rotted manure, adding sand if the soil is heavy. Mix in 90 g (3 oz) of balanced fertiliser with the mixture. Raise the level of the mixture in each hole to at least 100 mm (4 in) above the surrounding soil. Plant out hardened-off marrows, 600 mm (2 ft) apart for bush varieties or 900 mm (3 ft) for trailing varieties. Training consists mainly of removing the growing points of trailing varieties when the stems are about 500 mm (20 in) long, to encourage the production of female flowers and early fruiting. Pollinate female flowers, those with small fruits below the petals, using a piece of cotton wool. Dab this into open male flowers, those without fruits below, and transfer the yellow dust or pollen into the centres of open female flowers. This helps to ensure fruit setting early in the season. Later in the season pollination is carried out naturally by insects. Feed plants weekly with dilute liquid fertiliser once the

fruits start to swell and keep them well watered. Cut the fruits regularly as soon as they are large enough to use, to encourage continuous cropping.

Mint *See* Herbs, this chapter.

Mustard A quick-growing plant which has two main uses: as a salad when in the seedling stage; or for green manuring. *See* Chapter 4, Greenhouses, for salad. *See* Manuring, Part Two.

Onion A group of crops grown for the edible seedling stems and leaves as with salad onions; also for the swollen bulbs which are eaten cooked as a vegetable or

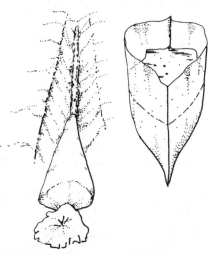

162 Onion. A recent technique referred to as fluid sowing, and often used for onions, consists of mixing seeds in a clear gel, and placing the seeds and gel, like toothpaste, in a line in drills.

in stews and other dishes. The small bulbs are used in pickles and chutneys. *Cultivation* Onions grow best on rich, fertile loams. Large bulb-type onions can be sown indoors in containers of seed compost, and then pricked out 40 mm (1½ in) apart in boxes, before hardening off and planting outdoors. Maincrop bulb onions can be sown in frames for transplanting, or outdoors for thinning. Seedlings, raised in beds for transplanting, are sown in rows 200 mm (8 in) apart, increasing this to 300 mm (12 in) for crops which are thinned. Prepare the ground as for leeks for average purposes. Sow the seeds 12 mm (½ in) deep in moist drills, subsequently thinning bulb onions to 150 mm (6 in) apart in two stages, but salad onions are left unthinned as are small pickling varieties. Crops of bulb onions can be easily grown from sets, planted on well prepared ground in spring. Allow 150 mm (6 in) between sets, same distance for transplanted seedlings in the rows. Keep the plants well watered, feed swelling bulb onions occasionally and hoe regularly. When bulb onions start to change colour in summer, bend over the tops to assist ripening. Lift and dry the bulbs before storing, placing them on slatted or wire bottomed trays. When dry, place them in a frostfree room or shed. Lift salad onions as required. Avoid leaving onion thinnings or remains around at any time, to lessen the

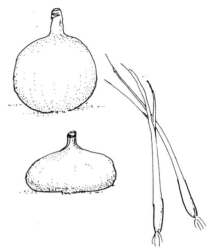

163   Onion. Onion types. Round, flat and salad varieties.

risk of onion fly. Two main types of bulb onions are grown, based on shape, namely flat and round. Flat types have a short swollen axis compared with the longer and often larger round varieties.

Parsley   *See* Herbs, this chapter.

Parsnip   A hardy crop, grown for the edible roots which are harvested in autumn or winter and used as a vegetable after cooking. *Cultivation* The ground for this crop is prepared as for carrots. Sow the seeds 12 mm (½ in) deep in moist drills, spaced

Table of Onion Crops

Type/crop	Sow/plant	Harvest	Space between plants (mm)
Bulbing onions			
Sets	Feb–Apr	Aug	150
Pickling	Mar–Jun	Jun–Sep	unthinned
Thinned	Mar–Apr	Aug–Sep	150
Thinned	Aug	Jun–Jul	150
Transplanted	Dec–Feb	Jul–Sep	150
Transplanted	Feb–Mar	Aug–Sep	150
Salad onions			
Salad onion	Mar–Jul	Jun–Oct	unthinned
Salad onion	Aug–Sep	Apr–Jun	unthinned

140

400 mm (16 in) apart, from February to May. Thin the subsequent seedlings when 25 mm (1 in) high, spacing them 75 mm (3 in) apart. Remove alternate plants when the seedlings are 50–100 mm (2–4 in) high. Keep the ground weedfree and hoe regularly. Roots are normally lifted in autumn and winter and used as required. The flavour and quality is better if they are left in the ground until required, rather than stored. In cold districts lift a few at a time in mild spells, and store in damp peat.

Varieties Two types are commonly grown: short and long rooted varieties. The short kinds are particularly well suited for growing on shallow soils. It is advisable to use Canker-resistant varieties such as Avonresister.

Peas A group of plants grown for the seeds, which are harvested during summer. These are used cooked, hot as a vegetable, or cold in salad and ideal to deep freeze.

Cultivation This crop is normally sown where it is to grow to maturity. Sow peas in autumn, spring or summer 40–50 mm (1½–2 in) deep, in moist 150 mm (6 in) wide flat-based drills, over trenched ground, prepared as for broad beans.

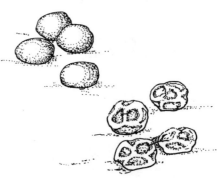

165 Marrowfat-pea. Garden peas are either smooth and round seeded, or Marrowfat, the wrinkled variety. The latter are less hardy but have finer flavour than the round kind which are often sown in autumn.

Scatter the seeds 50–75 mm (2–3 in) apart. Cover them with fine soil and gently firm with the teeth of a rake. Place netting or bird scarers over each row. Allow 600–900 mm (2–3 ft) spacing between rows, according to variety. Support the crop with brushwood, pushed into the ground as the seedlings appear. Trim the tops of the twigs to a uniform height for neatness. Water the plants if dry and keep them weedfree. Pick the pods regularly to ensure continuous cropping.

Varieties Two main types of conventional garden peas are cultivated. The very hardy round-seeded varieties are suitable for outdoor sowing in autumn and winter. Wrinkle seeded varieties, which are rated highly for flavour, are best sown during spring and summer.

Potato A crop cultivated for the underground tubers, which are cooked and used in many ways.

Cultivation Yields can be increased by chitting – spreading out seed potatoes in shallow trays in a light, airy, frost-free place to produce sturdy shoots. This is carried out about two months before planting. Deeply dig the ground, preferably in autumn, incorporating a good dressing of well-rotted manure. Apply 175 g/m² (5 oz/sq yd) of balanced ferti-

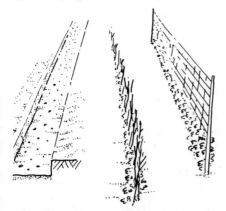

164 Peas. These are sown in flat drills 50–75 mm deep and a similar distance between seeds. Sticks or netting provide useful support.

141

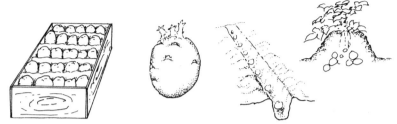

166 Potatoes. In spring, place tubers in single layers in boxes in a light, ventilated, frost-free place to form sprouts before planting. Earth up roots to give protection and prevent tubers from greening.

liser and lightly fork this dressing in a few days before planting. Potatoes crop best on acid soils, so liming for this crop is not necessary. Allow 300 mm (12 in) between tubers of early varieties placing them 125 mm (5 in) deep in drills, spaced 600 mm (2 ft) apart. Planting is carried out during late March in mild districts or early April in cold areas. Plant late varieties at the same depth as early kinds, but slightly further apart, at a spacing of 400 mm (16 in), with 700 mm (2 ft) between rows. Protect early kinds against late spring frosts, with straw if necessary. When shoots are 100–150 mm (4–6 in) high, earth them up with loose soil from between the rows. Keep the ground weedfree, and give the final earthing up before the leaves of plants in adjoining rows touch each other. Spray late kinds with a copper or other fungicide against blight disease during July. Lift early varieties when they start flowering and have produced sufficient weight of tubers. When the foliage of late varieties starts to die off, then lifting should commence without delay. Potatoes are grouped into classes according to the shape of the tubers as round, oval and kidney-shaped. The first two terms are fairly descriptive, and the kidney-shaped type are more long and straight in outline. Store sound potatoes either in clamps or in a dark frost free place, until required for use.

Pumpkin Also known as squash, this is

grown for the fruits which are produced in summer. These can be stored in a frost-free room for several weeks or cooked when freshly cut and used like marrow. The fruits can reach a considerable size. The method of cultivation is very similar to that used for growing marrows.

Radish A crop grown for the crisp, tender and often attractive edible roots which are pulled, washed and eaten raw, during late spring and summer.
Cultivation These are often grown as a catch crop *q.v.* this chapter, or on ground prepared for another crop, raked finely and levelled. Sow the seeds outdoors between March and August, placing them thinly 12 mm ($\frac{1}{2}$ in) deep in well-moistened drills, spaced 250 mm (10 in) apart. Cover them with fine soil, and gently firm. Grow this crop quickly, never allowing it to dry out and keep it weedfree. Pull the radish about three weeks after sowing as soon as they are large enough to use. Make repeated sowings at 14–21 day intervals for a succession of roots. Winter radish, which are larger than summer varieties, are sown in July, and mature 8–12 weeks later. Rake in 100 g/m² (3 oz/sq yd) of balanced fertiliser on well worked ground, making a crumbly, level seed bed. Sow as for summer radish, but increase the distance between rows to 300 mm (12 in). Thin the resultant seedlings, first to 100 mm (4 in) apart, when about 25 mm (1 in) high and again

142

7–10 days later removing alternate plants. Lift roots as required, but protect from frost.

Root crop Applied to any vegetable which has swollen or enlarged roots which are grown for culinary purposes. Included in the group are beetroot, carrots, Kohl rabi, potatoes, parsnip, salsify, swede and turnips. This is another important group of vegetables which are grown together for crop rotation purposes.

Rotation The successful cultivation of vegetables involves preventing the serious build up of pests and diseases, and avoiding soil sickness. One of the best ways to achieve this is to rotate the crops, growing them on a different part of the vegetable plot each year. Vegetables are grouped into three categories: green crops; pod and stem crops; and root crops. In practice this involves dividing any vegetable garden into three plots of equal size, one for each group of vegetables. Each year, every group of vegetables moves onto another plot. The aim is that no piece of ground carries the same type of crop or similar for more than one year in three.

Sage *See* Herbs, this chapter.

Salsify Also known as Vegetable Oyster, grown for the roots which are harvested in winter and are cooked and eaten. The roots resemble long, thin parsnips and the cultivation of salsify is very similar to that crop.

Shallots An easily grown crop which is cultivated for the bulbous off-sets that are cooked and used like onions.
Cultivation Treat shallots like onion sets. Plant them on well prepared land during February and March. Allow 150 mm (6 in) between bulbs, in rows 300 mm (12 in) apart. Harvest the bulbs in July or early August when the stems die down. Lift, divide and dry the shallots before storing them in an airy, frost-free place.

Spinach A crop grown for the leaves which are cooked and eaten as a vegetable during summer and autumn.
Cultivation Dig the ground spade deep, incorporating a medium dressing of manure of about one bucketful (18 litre/m² or 3 gal/sq yd). Lime the ground, if need be, to raise the pH level to 6.5, but allow 7–10 days minimum interval after manuring and the same gap before adding fertiliser. Apply 100 g/m² (3 oz/sq yd) of balanced fertiliser several days before sowing. Rake the soil, breaking down lumps, to create a fine crumb-like tilth and level surface. Sow summer spinach from February to July, 12 mm ($\frac{1}{2}$ in) deep in well-moistened drills, spaced 300 mm (12 in) apart. Winter kinds can be sown during August and September in the same manner as the summer type. Thin the seedlings to 150–200 mm (6–8 in) apart when about 25 mm (1 in) high. Keep the ground well watered and weedfree. Pick the leaves regularly as soon as they are large enough to use, to ensure continuous cropping.
Varieties There are several types of spinach: summer varieties, such as Long-standing Round; winter varieties like Long-standing Prickly and Perpetual spinach to provide continuous picking during autumn and winter.

Swede A hardy crop grown for the roots, which are lifted, cooked and eaten as a vegetable in winter.
Cultivation On well-worked ground, allow a minimum period of 7–10 days

167 Swede. Sow and grow this crop on ridges in wet areas. Remove the tops and tail-like roots before storing in winter.

between manuring and liming. Leave a similar gap before applying $100 \, g/m^2$ (3 oz/sq yd) of balanced fertiliser. Rake this in, forming a firm, level seed bed except in wet districts where seeds are sown on low, potato-type ridges. In May, sow the seeds 12 mm ($\frac{1}{2}$ in) deep in moist drills, spaced 450 mm (18 in) apart. Cover them with fine soil and firm. Thin the resultant seedlings in two or three stages, to stand finally 250 mm (10 in) apart, starting when the plants are large enough to handle. Keep the crop well watered and weedfree. Lift the roots as required during winter and early spring.

Tomato *See* Chapter 4, Greenhouses.

Turnip A crop grown for the edible roots, which are cooked and eaten as a vegetable during summer and early autumn.
Cultivation The preparation of the land is similar to that needed for swedes, but sowing can be carried out from March to August. Turnips are less hardy than swedes, but quicker growing. Sow the seeds 12 mm ($\frac{1}{2}$ in) deep in moist drills, spaced 300 mm (12 in) apart.

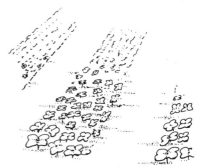

168 Turnips. Small tender roots are obtained from sowing and growing in bands instead of single rows.

Subsequently thin the seedlings in two stages, to a final spacing of 100–150 mm (4–6 in) apart. *See also* fig. 168. Grow the crop quickly, keeping the ground well watered and weedfree, and hoe regularly. The roots should be ready for lifting 10–12 weeks from sowing.
Varieties There are several types of turnip: white, golden, and red skinned. Another variation is shape, which ranges from globe to flattened.

Vegetable diseases and pests *See* Chapter 10, Problems.

Chapter 10. Problems

Introduction
In this chapter some common ailments of garden plants are outlined, together with details of the appropriate remedies. The main causes of unthrifty plants are diseases, pests and weeds. Other disorders, for example bud drop in Sweet peas, or tip burn in lettuce, are caused by unbalanced growing conditions. These ailments are not infectious, but still result in poor crops.

The measures for disease, pest and weed control fall into two main categories, namely prevention and eradication. In most cases, preventing an outbreak is more likely to be successful than its control and cure.

Preventive measures These consist of providing a good standard of cultivation and the correct use of protective materials. The modes of action of these protective substances vary: some are effective only where they are applied by direct contact with, or leaving a protective covering to check disease or pest. Others, known as systemics, can be absorbed by plant roots and are carried in the sap to the leaves to give protection.

Eradication and remedy This involves cutting out and removing affected parts or whole plants, and burning, together with the use of chemicals. Certain pests such as Whitefly, can be brought under control by using a natural parasite, Encarsia, which feeds on the pest.

Materials and Application

Dusts and granules. Chemicals can be applied in dry form from a simple bellows-type puffer or canister dispensers. This method obviates the need to mix water and material, but should not be applied in high winds. Granular materials are sometimes scattered over,

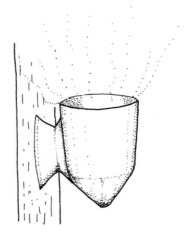

169 Fumigator. Electrically operated model providing continuous protection.

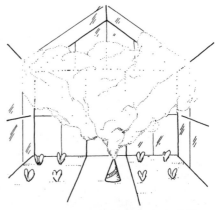

170 Smoke generator. A simple, but effective, means of pest and disease control.

or mixed with, soil, as with some fumigants.

Liquid materials. These can be applied as fine sprays to cover plant foliage, or as drenches to saturate soils and composts.

Fumigants. Some materials, such as

171 Soil sterilisation. Chemical disinfection with formaldehyde. Cover the soil with plastic or similar material to keep the fumes in after the application for several days.

sulphur, when heated, give off fumes or vapours, which provide effective control of diseases and pests. Special electrically heated holders are available which, when topped up with chemicals, provide continuous protection.
Fogs and smokes. Liquids which are released from special canisters under high pressure produce penetrating fog-like clouds of aerosols – minute droplets which float on air. Smoke cones which resemble a firework release clouds of the active ingredient in smoke form.
Fumigants, fogs and smokes can be very effective, but are mainly suitable for greenhouse use because their efficiency is reduced by wind or air current.
Sterilisers. Wet or dry, these materials are used for disinfecting soils, containers, greenhouses and frames. Commercial soil sterilisation is also carried out by heating, usually with steam, but small electrically heated sterilisers are available.
Poison baits, or sticky traps are also used to kill slugs, and snails and catch insects.
The substances which are commonly used to safeguard garden plants can be grouped into four main categories: fungicides; herbicides; insecticides and miscellaneous. Fungicides are applied to control diseases of mainly fungal origin;

herbicides to kill weeds; insecticides to kill insect pests; and miscellaneous for a variety of purposes, including baits to control pests, tree bands to trap insects, sterilisers to disinfect soil, greenhouses, etc, and selective eradicators such as moss killers. Protective paints and trace element nutrients are also considered.

In the interests of safety, two points should be made. (1) use materials which are ministry approved products and can be relied on. (2) observe the safety code of use of chemicals.

a) Read the label carefully BEFORE USE.

b) Use the product as recommended.

c) Avoid spraying, or spilling, chemicals where people, pets, animals and other crops can be contaminated.

d) Never transfer chemicals into other storage containers, such as beer or soft drinks bottles.

e) Seal and store chemicals safely, out of reach of children and animals.

f) Wash hands, face and any protective clothing after using chemicals.

g) Safely dispose of used receptacles.

h) Never use chemical containers for other purposes.

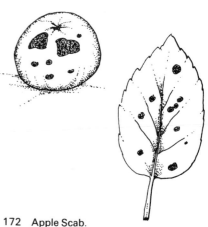

172 Apple Scab.

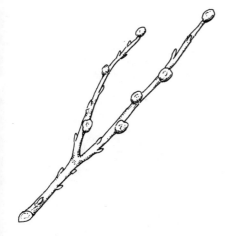

173   Big Bud mite.

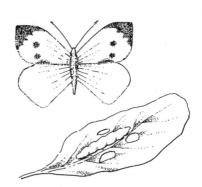

175   Cabbage White Butterfly.

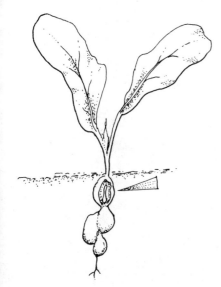

174   Cabbage Rootfly. The galls contain larvae or grubs, *arrowed*.

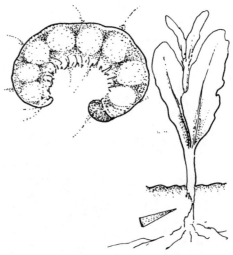

176   Chafer larva. *Left*: grub. *Right*: typical damage to stem, *arrowed*.

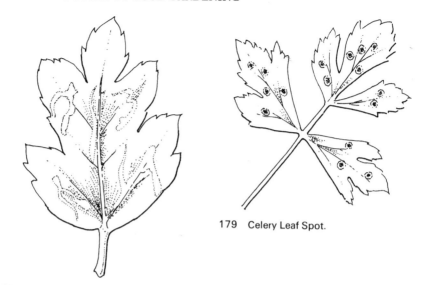

179 Celery Leaf Spot.

177 Chrysanthemum Leaf Miner. The leaf mines.

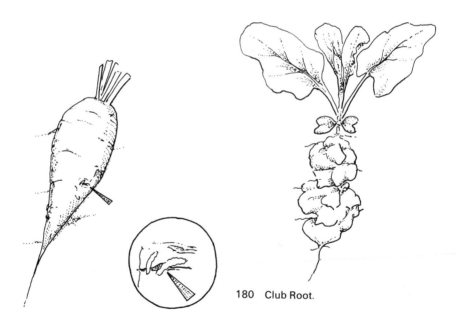

180 Club Root.

178 Carrot Fly. *Left*: outer signs. *Right*: section showing damage.

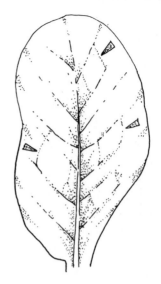

181   Earwig. *Left*: dahlia shoot damaged by earwig. *Right*: adult earwig.

183   Lettuce   Mildew.   Affected   areas *arrowed*.

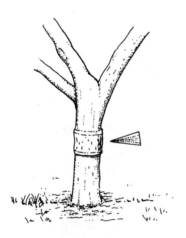

182   Grease-banding.

184   Peach Leaf Curl.

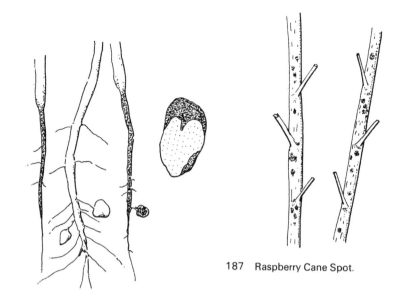

187   Raspberry Cane Spot.

185   Potato Blackleg. Healthy root *centre*.

186   Potato Blight. Affected leaf and root.

188   Rose Black Spot.

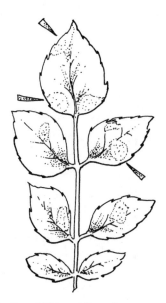

191 Tomato Greenback. Above the horizontal line will not ripen.

189 Rose Mildew. Affected areas *arrowed*.

192 Tomato Leaf Mould.

190 Foot Rot or Damping-off.

193 Turnip Flea Beetle.

The following tables are concerned with common garden problems: listed in the first table are some materials which are commonly used to protect garden plants from harm. Following is a table of general ailments which can affect plants in two or more specialist groups. Succeeding lists refer to problems of specific types of plants: vegetables; fruit; flowers; trees, greenhouse crops and turf.

Table of Materials Used to Protect Garden Plants

Fungicide	Place used	Control
Benomyl	Indoors and open air	Fungal
Captan	Indoors and open air	Fungal
Cheshunt Compound	Indoors and open air	Fungal
Copper	Indoors and open air	Bacterial and fungal
Dinocap	Indoors and open air	Fungal and insecticidal
Thiram	Indoors and open air	Fungal
Lime sulphur	Outdoors	Bacterial and fungal
Calomel	Outdoors	Bacterial and fungal
Dodine	Outdoors	Fungal
Sulphur	Indoors and open air	Fungal

Herbicide	Type	Use
CMPP	Selective	Lawns
Dalapon	Grasskiller	Vacant land
Paraquat	Total	Vacant land and paths
2–4 D	Selective	Lawns
Simazine	Total	Vacant land, paths and inter row spaces
Sodium chlorate	Total	Vacant land and paths

Insecticide	Place used	Pests controlled
Bromophos	Open air, soil	Cutworms and soil pests
Calomel	Open air, soil	Club Root and onion fly
Chlordane	Lawns	Leather jackets and worms
Dimethoate	Open air	Leaf and stem pests
Derris	Indoors and open air	Leaf and stem pests
Fenitrothion	Indoors and open air	Biting pests
HCH	Indoors and open air	* Leaf, stem and soil pests
Lime sulphur	Open air	Leaf and stem pests and diseases
Malathion	Indoors and open air	Leaf, stem and soil pests

Chemical	Placed use	Purpose
Dazomet	Indoors and open air, soil	Soil sterilization
Formaldehyde	Indoors and open air, soil	Soil sterilisation
Hormone fruit set	Mainly indoors	Fruit setting
Lawn sand	Lawns	Moss killer and fungicide
Lead paint	Trees and shrubs	Seal cut surfaces
Meta	Indoors and open air	Bait for slubs
Sequestrene, iron	Indoors and open air	Supply soluble iron
Tar oil	Open air	Disinfect trees and shrubs

Table of General Ailments

Cause	Effect	Control
Ants	Spreading and encouraging the increase of aphids. Damaging small plants	Apply HCH dust to nests and runs.
Aphid, greenfly and blackfly	Sap sucking insects feeding on many kinds of plants, weakening them and spreading virus diseases	Insecticide sprays of derris or malathion
Armillaria	Sickly and dying trees and shrubs. These can develop honey-coloured toadstools above ground and black or dark rhizomes in the soil	Remove and burn affected plants and roots. Sterilise affected soil with formaldehyde
Bark wound	A cut surface left after cutting off a branch or limb, providing an entry for disease	Apply a layer of lead or bitumen paint
Birds	Seeds, seedlings and buds as well as fruits and vegetables eaten or damaged	Brushwood or netting covers. Bird scarers and deterrent anthoquinene sprays.
Blackfly	*See* Aphid, above	
Black-leg *See* fig 185	Cuttings and various plants, such as pelargoniums and potatoes turn black at soil level, rot and die	Burn affected plants. Use sterilised soil for cuttings and seedlings
Bleeding	Excessive loss of sap from cut stems after pruning, or loss of colour from beetroot	Avoid pruning deciduous trees in spring. Twist the leaves off beetroot before storing
Bootlace fungus	*See* Armillaria, above	
Botrytis	*See* Grey mould below	
Canker	Sunken or dead patches on branches or trunks, often on fruit trees, sometimes killing them	Cut out affected areas and paint cut surfaces with lead paint
Capsid bug	*See* Common green capsid, below	
Caterpillar *see* fig 175	Eaten or defoliated plants with caterpillars of various colours occurring indoor and in open air	Spray with derris or fenitrothion
Chafer beetle *See* fig 176	Damaged and eaten buds and flowers by large black beetles. Roots of many plants eaten by fat cream coloured grubs with brown heads	Control weeds and use HCH dusts. Treat soil with bromophos before planting
Cherry blackfly	Ornamental and culinary varieties affected. *See* Aphids, above	
Chlorosis	Yellowing leaves on such as camellias, rhododendrons and hydrangeas on chalk soils	Spray or water affected plants with sequestrene of iron
Click beetle	*See* Wireworm, below	
Cockchafer	*See* Chafer Beetle, above	
Common froghopper	Small, yellowish-green insects, enveloped in frothy bubbles, feeding on and weakening plants	Spray with malathion

Table of General Ailments—*continued*

Cause	Effect	Control
Common green capsid	Bright green winged insects, which cause distortion and malformation of leaves, flowers and fruits. Small brown spots appear where feeding has taken place. Apple fruits develop swollen areas	Spray with fenitrothion or malathion
Coral spot disease	Pink or reddish pinhead cushions first occur on dead branches, spreading to and killing new wood.	Cut out and burn affected areas
Couch grass	Troublesome weed, spreading by whitish underground runners, smothering small plants above and below soil level	Apply dalapon to vacant ground before planting
Crown gall	Woody swellings occur on roots, shoots and stems, often near soil level. Not usually serious	Cut out affected areas
Cuckoo spit	*See* Common froghopper, above	
Cutworms	Dark coloured grubs which eat and sever the stems of small plants at soil level, usually at night	Sterilise soil or treat with dazomet or bromophos
Daddy longlegs	*See* Leatherjacket, below	
Damping-off *See* fig 190	Seedlings become constricted at soil level, topple over and die. Caused by a number of diseases, but all with similar effect	Use sterilised soil. Treat seeds with thiram or water seed containers with Cheshunt compound before sowing
Die-back	Shoots of various kinds wither at the tips and die back progressively towards the main stem	Cut out affected areas. Spray with benomyl
Docks	A persistent perennial weed. Spreads rapidly, smothering small plants	Dig out and burn the roots. Apply Sodium chlorate to vacant land, avoiding trees and shrubs
Earthworms	Form casts or small mud piles on lawns, resulting in bare patches and weeds. When in pots of compost, roots are disturbed and drainage is impeded	Apply chlordane to lawns. Avoid standing boxes or pots on bare earth
Earwigs *See* fig 181	Flower petals and young leaves are eaten, usually at night. Brown creatures with pincer-like tail ends	Dust around plants with HCH
Eelworms	Microscopic worms feeding on and in plants, resulting in weak, sickly growth. Most crops can be affected by one type or another	Crop rotation. Sterilise soil with dazomet. Burn affected plants. Avoid using infected stock

Table of General Ailments—*continued*

Cause	Effect	Control
Foot rot	*See* Damping off, above	
Grubs	*See* Chafter beetles, Cutworms and Caterpillars, above	
Grey mould	Affected leaves and plants rot and develop a grey mould	Spray with benomyl or thiram
Honeydew	Shiny, sticky secretion left by aphids, resulting in the growth of sooty moulds and weakened plants	Spray with derris or malathion against aphids
Honey fungus	*See* Armillaria, above	
Infertility	Flowers failing to set fruit, occurring with soft-stemmed and woody plants	Apply fruit-setting spray. Pollinate flowers or plant pollinator variety nearby
Infertility	Few or no blooms produced on trees or bushes which flower freely	Root prune deciduous trees in autumn
Leatherjacket	Dark, leathery grubs which feed on the roots of lawn grasses and other plants, weakening them	Apply chlordane on lawns. Dress soil with bromophos or HCH
Mildew	Browny or powdery whitish covering on leaves and stems, also buds	Spray with benomyl. Avoid overcrowding.
Mustard beetle	Leaves and stems of plants and seedlings of cabbage family holed and eaten, spoiling and weakening them	Dust or spray with derris or malathion
Nitrogen deficiency	Small, hard pale plants, highly coloured small fruits	Apply nitrogenous top dressing to trees or shrubs. Apply balanced base fertiliser before sowing or planting crops
Peach leaf curl *See* fig 184	Affected leaves are crinkled, distorted and reddish crimson, followed by premature leaf fall	Spray with benomyl or copper fungicides in spring and autumn
Peach scale	Brownish spots or patches on the surface of leaves and stems. These feed on and weaken ornamental and fruiting varieties	Cut out and burn badly affected areas. Spray with malathion
Phosphorous deficiency	Delayed flowering and poor root system	Apply balanced base fertiliser before sowing or planting, and give balanced feed to growing plants
Red spider mite	Attacks wide range of plants, causing mottling, bronzing and stunting of leaves and growth. Numerous reddish or yellowish creatures on leaf undersides	Spray with derris or malathion. Damp down in greenhouses in summer to create unfavourable conditions for this pest
Root knot eelworm	*See* Eelworm, above	

Table of General Ailments—continued

Cause	Effect	Control
Scion rooting	Trees and bushes which have been budded or grafted become very vigorous and/or unfruitful. The scion forms roots in addition to the stock	Avoid excessively deep planting. Remove soil round existing trees to the level of the graft union
Slugs and snails	Leaves, flowers, fruits, stems and underground bulbs or tubers eaten. Silvery slime trails	Place meta bait near seedlings and young plants
Spittle bug	*See* Common froghopper, above	
Stem and bulb eelworm	*See* Eelworm, above	
Symphilid	Weak or poorly developed root system and small white insects in the soil	Apply HCH dust to the soil
Tarnished plant bug	Distorted or deformed flowers and blind buds in such as chrysanthemums, dahlias and zinnias. Yellowish green, winged bugs with mottled markings are also present	Spray with HCH or malathion
Vapourer moth	*See* Caterpillars, above	
Verticillium wilt	*See* Wilt, below	
Virus diseases	Distortion of all plant parts, mottling of foliage and stunting. Severe malformation and death are a few of the symptoms of these diseases	Burn affected plants. Spray to control aphids which can spread these diseases from plant to plant
Watersprouts	Very vigorous vertical shoots arising from branches of trees, usually after cutting off large limbs	Remove the shoots and avoid severe pruning
Weeds	Unwanted plants on paths, drives and vacant ground	Cut off the surface vegetation and apply sodium chlorate or simazine
Weeds	Unwanted plants in turf	Apply selective weedkillers, such as CMPP and 2-4D
Weeds	Seedling weeds between rows or around trees and bushes on otherwise bare ground	Water the seedlings with paraquat
Wilt	Sickly, stunted pale plants which wilt, even when well moistened, and collapse	Burn affected plants and sterilise the soil
Wire stem	*See* Damping off, above	
Wireworm	Shiny, tough yellowish wormlike grubs, which eat and burrow into underground roots, stems and tubers	Treat soil with bromophos before sowing or planting on newly dug grass land
Woodlice	Seedlings and young plants eaten at or near soil level, and grey creatures which roll into a ball when touched	Dust the soil with HCH

Table of Ailments Affecting Vegetables

Cause	Effect	Control
Anbury	*See* Club root, below	
Anthracnose	Dwarf or French beans develop dark, sunken patches with pale edges on the pods which can rot completely in wet seasons	Pull up badly affected plants. Spray with copper fungicide at the first sign of the disease
Black bean aphid	Broad beans are subject to attack by blackfly. *See* Aphid, General list	Remove the growing point of plants when the bottom pods are set
Botrytis	*See* Grey mould, General list	
Cabbage aphid	*See* Aphid, General list	
Cabbage caterpillars	*See* Caterpillars, General list	
Cabbage rootfly *See* fig 174	Stunted and wilting young plants of the cabbage tribe, which have the stems tunnelled by whitish maggots	Crop rotation. Treat the soil with bromophos at or before planting time
Cabbage White Butterfly	*See* Caterpillars	
Carrot fly *See* fig 178	Yellowish white maggots feeding and tunnelling into the stems, spoiling and weakening the crop	Crop rotation. Treat soil with bromophos before sowing. Remove all thinnings
Celery fly	The leaves develop blisters or blotches which contain small grubs, weakening and disfiguring plants	Spray affected plants with derris, HCH or malathion
Celery leaf spot *See* fig 179	A disease causing leaf spotting which if left unchecked can ruin crops of celery	Spray with benomyl or copper fungicide two or three times at 14 day intervals at the first sign of the disease
Club root *See* fig 180	The most serious disease affecting members of the cabbage family. Swollen, rotting and bad smelling roots which result in severe stunting and death of plants	Crop rotation. Use healthy plants only. Dip roots into calomel paste at planting. Burn affected old roots
Dry rot of Potatoes	Potatoes in store, or set out for 'seed' become shrivelled and rot	Plant sound tubers only. Store undamaged potatoes
Greening of Potatoes	Tubers are green when lifted or become so after lifting	Earth up growing crops. Store tubers in darkness
Halo blight	A disease affecting French and runner beans, causing dark sunken spots with light coloured circle around. The pods are ruined in severe attacks.	Sow clean seed. Remove and burn infected plants. Crop rotation
Lettuce aphid	*See* Aphid, General list	
Lettuce brown spot	Seedling stems develop brown spots, the disease eventually killing the plants	As for Damping-off. *See* General list

Table of Ailments Affecting Vegetables—*continued*

Cause	Effect	Control
Lettuce downy mildew *See* fig 183	Leaves coated with whitish, downy covering weakening and stunting plants	Crop rotation. Spray with thiram at 10-day intervals
Lettuce mosaic	*See* Virus, General list	
Lettuce root aphid	Stunted small plants with whitish or greyish aphids with mealy coating, feeding on the roots, causing yellowing and death	Crop rotation. Treat soil with bromophos before sowing or planting
Lettuce tip-burn	The leaf margins wither and turn brown. A non-infectious complaint caused by faulty cultivation	Careful watering
Onion fly	Whitish grubs feeding on and damaging the stems or bulbs, weakening the plants and increasing the risk of other diseases	Crop rotation. Treat the soil with bromophos before sowing or planting. Remove all thinnings
Onion white rot	Yellowing and wilting of bulbs of onions and related crops like shallots. Rotting and a white fluffy mould appears at the base	Crop rotation. Calomel root dip for transplanted crop
Parsnip canker	Brown or dark patches develop on the surface of the roots, which can rot in bad attacks	Crop rotation. Use resistant varieties
Pea aphid	*See* Aphids, General list	
Pea and bean weevils	The leaf margins of peas and broad beans are damaged and eaten, weakening young plants especially	Spray or dust affected plants with derris or fenitrothion
Pea moth	The peas inside the pods are infested with yellowish, dark-headed maggots and are useless	Crop rotation. Spray or dust plants at flowering time and 14 days later with fenitrothion
Pea thrips	Plants and pods become speckled, stunted and weakened by attacks of numerous minute dark insects	Spray affected crops with malathion. Sow resistant varieties like Kelvedon Wonder
Potato aphid	*See* Aphid, General list	
Potato blackleg	*See* Blackleg, General list	
Potato blight *See* fig 186	Potatoes and outdoor tomatoes can be affected, resulting in blackened and rotting foliage, tubers and fruits	Spray with copper fungicide about mid-July and again 14 days later
Potato eelworm	*See* Eelworm, General list	
Potato scab	Black or dark spots and blotches on the surface of the tubers	Crop rotation. Avoid planting on heavily-limed land
Swede midge	Attacks various members of cabbage tribe, resulting in crinkled leaves, blind or many-stemmed stunted plants	Dust or spray seedlings with HCH. Crop rotation

Table of Ailments Affecting Vegetables—*continued*

Cause	Effect	Control
Turnip flea beetle *See* fig 193	Seedlings of turnips and other members of the cabbage family develop numerous small round holes in the leaves. In bad cases plants are weakened and severely damaged	Crop rotation. Dust the seeds or seed beds with HCH before sowing, also dust affected plants
Turnip gall weevil	Roots and stems of cabbage and turnip are swollen, galled and hollow or with grubs inside. Unlike Club Root the stems are not usually slimy and bad smelling	Crop rotation. Treat the soil before sowing with bromophos or HCH. Burn affected plants
Turnip moth	*See* Cutworm, General list	
Wart disease	A serious potato problem, resulting in swollen, wartlike masses which develop on tubers and stems of susceptible varieties	Crop rotation. Grow immune varieties such as Foremost. Burn affected plants and tubers

Table of Ailments Affecting Fruit Bushes and Trees

Cause	Effect	Control
American blight	*See* Woolly aphid, below	
American gooseberry mildew	Leaves, stems and fruits become coated with a brownish felt-like covering. If left unchecked, bushes can become severely stunted or die	Cut out and burn affected parts. Spray with lime sulphur at flowering stage and again when fruitlets are formed
Apple aphid	*See* Aphids, General list	Tar oil winter spray to dormant trees. Dimethoate or malathion sprays when aphids present
Apple blossom weevil	Unopened flower buds which turn brown and die. When opened, buds reveal small larvae inside	Apply derris or HCH spray at bud-burst stage
Apple capsid	Leaves and shoots distorted and with brown spotting. Fruits become marked, cracked or mis-shapen. Affects other bush and tree fruits also	Spray at green or pink bud stage with fenitrothion. Apply tar oil winter wash when dormant
Apple mildew	Powdery whitish covering of leaves, shoots, buds and fruits, weakening trees	Apply dodine or sulphur sprays in late spring and summer. Cut out badly affected parts. Tar oil winter wash when dormant
Apple sawfly	Fruits develop ribbon-like scars due to grubs tunnelling below the skin	Apply dimethoate or fenitrothion spray 7–10 days after petal fall stage

Table of Ailments Affecting Fruit Bushes and Trees—*continued*

Cause	Effect	Control
Apple scab *See* fig 172	Fruits and leaves develop dark circular spots which enlarge and coalesce. This spoils the appearance of fruits and weakens trees. Pears are also attacked	Spray with captan or lime sulphur at green and pink bud (or white with pear) petal-fall and fruitlet stages
Big Bud mite *See* fig 173	Enlarged buds which fail to open on blackcurrant bushes. Weakening plants, making them unfruitful and spreading reversion virus	Cut off and burn badly affected branches. Spray with lime sulphur about April
Blackcurrant eelworm	*See* Eelworm, General list	
Blackcurrant gall mite	*See* Big Bud mite, above	
Blackcurrant leaf spot	Brown spots, which if unchecked results in premature defoliation, weakening plants	Benomyl or copper sprays at 10–14 day intervals from bud burst to fruitlet stage
Cherry bacterial canker	Dead and gnarled branches with shoots dying back. Trees dying when girdled by cankered areas	Spray with copper fungicide. Cut out affected areas
Cherry blackfly	*See* Aphid, General list	Spray affected trees with malathion. Apply tar oil spray when dormant
Codlin moth	Apples eaten in the centres by whitish grubs leaving them holed	Spray in mid-June with derris or malathion
Currant powdery mildew	The foliage becomes coated with a fine powdery covering, puckering the leaves and weakening the bushes	Spray with benomyl at 14–21 day intervals in the growing season
European gooseberry mildew	Greyish coating on the leaves. Fruits not usually affected	Spray severely affected bushes with lime sulphur in spring and summer
Fruit tree red spider mite	*See* Red spider mite, General list	Spray affected crops with derris or malathion. Apply tar oil winter spray to dormant bushes and trees
Fruit tree tortrix	*See* Caterpillars, General list	Spray apples and pears at green bud stage with fenitrothion
Gooseberry aphid	*See* Aphid, General list	Spray with derris or malathion. Apply tar oil winter wash to dormant bushes
Gooseberry moth	*See* Caterpillars, General list	
Gooseberry sawfly	Gooseberry and currant foliage holed and eaten, or removed completely in severe attacks by green caterpillars with black markings	Spray bushes with fenitrothion at the first signs of caterpillars
Peach chlorosis	*See* Chlorosis, General list	

Table of Ailments Affecting Fruit Bushes and Trees—*continued*

Cause	Effect	Control
Peach leaf curl	*See* General list	
Pear midge	Affected fruitlets fall off or blacken when about marble size	Spray with HCH at white bud stage
Pear scab	*See* Apple scab, Fruit list	
Plum aphid	*See* Aphid, General list	As for cherry blackfly
Plum rust	Yellowish or rusty brown leaf spotting in wet seasons	Apply copper or thiram spray
Plum sawfly	Small fruits, which are eaten by small caterpillars, fall prematurely to the ground	Spray trees at the petal-fall stage with dimethoate or fenitrothion
Raspberry aphid	*See* Aphid, General list	
Raspberry beetle	The ripe fruits are eaten by and contain whitish maggots, ruining the crop in severe attacks	Apply two fenitrothion sprays one 10 days after flowering and again 10 days later
Raspberry cane spot *See* fig 187	Affected canes of raspberry and loganberry develop dark spots, causing, in severe cases withering and death	Cut out and burn badly diseased canes. Apply copper or thiram sprays in spring
Raspberry mosaic	Stunted plants with leaves mottled with yellow markings. Plants become unfruitful	Burn affected plants. Spray to control aphids which spread virus diseases
Raspberry moth	The growing tips wither and die. In the stems, reddish or brownish larvae are present	Remove and burn dead tips. Apply tar oil winter spray to dormant canes
Reversion	A virus disease of blackcurrants causing unfruitfulness and nettle effect on leaves	Burn affected bushes
Shy cropping	*See* Infertility, General list	
Silver leaf	Silvering of the foliage, mainly affecting plums and cherries, but other fruits also, resulting in the death of limbs and sometimes trees. The heartwood of badly diseased trees develop a dark-coloured core	Cut down and burn affected branches and trees. Apply tar oil winter wash to dormant trees
Strawberry aphid	*See* Aphid, General list	
Strawberry blossom weevil	The flowers are severed from their stalks, usually to reveal small grubs in the dying remains	Dust around the plants with HCH before the buds show colour
Strawberry eelworm	*See* Eelworm, General list	
Strawberry leaf spot	The leaves develop various spots which increase in size, weakening the plants and reducing yields	Apply copper fungicide sprays before flowering. Cut or burn off leaves after fruiting
Watersprouts	*See* General list	
Winter moths	*See* Caterpillars, General list. Attacks tree fruits and nuts	Greaseband tree stems in autumn, *see* fig 182. Apply tar oil winter wash

Table of Ailments Affecting Fruit Bushes and Trees—*continued*

Cause	Effect	Control
Woolly aphid	Cotton wool-like tufts surrounding colonies of small insects feeding on stems, roots and trunks of apple and pear trees. These pests reduce vigour and spread disease	Spray or paint affected areas with dimethoate or malathion

Table of Ailments Affecting Flowers

Cause	Effect	Control
Antirrhinum rust	Brown spots occurring on leaves and stems, weakening, stunting and disfiguring plants	Spray plants with copper fungicide
Aphids	*See* General list	
Aster wilt	Stems and basal leaves of plants blacken, wilt and are stunted or die	Avoid planting on infected land for several years. Burn diseased asters
Auricula root aphid	Sickly yellow and unthrifty plants with small greyish aphids, covered with a meal-like coating, feeding on the roots	Water affected plants with malathion
Chrysanthemum problems	*See* Greenhouse list	
Earwig	*See* General list	
Eelworm	*See* General list	
Gladiolus scab	The corms of gladioli and crocus develop dark areas which rot. Affected foliage has brown spots around the base which coalesce in severe attacks, resulting in stems breaking off	Before planting dip bulbs in benomyl solution, prepared as for spraying. Avoid planting on infected land for at least two or three years.
Gladiolus thrips	The foliage, flowers and buds become speckled and stunted. In severe attacks the top flower buds fail to open	Dust corms with derris when planting. Spray affected flowers and foliage with HCH or malathion
Hollyhock rust	Orange, yellow or brown patches on leaf undersides, stunting and weakening plants	Apply copper or thiram sprays to affected plants and repeat 10 days later
Lily problems	*See* Greenhouse list	
Mildew	*See* General list	
Narcissus base rot	The bulbs become soft, rotten and die	Plant or store firm healthy bulbs only, burning any that are soft or diseased

Table of Ailments Affecting Flowers—*continued*

Cause	Effect	Control
Narcissus flies	Affected bulbs are holed and eaten by small grubs, resulting in poor plant growth and death. Damaged bulbs are soon infected by disease organisms	Apply HCH dust to soil around bulbs between late April to late June. Plant healthy bulbs only
Narcissus stripe	A virus disease, causing lines of lighter markings on the leaves and abnormal flower colouring	Plant healthy bulbs only. Burn affected plants
Pansy sickness	Affected plants turn yellow, often wilt and die, rarely if ever recovering. This problem affects violas as well as pansies	Sprinkle calomel dust into the planting holes. Avoid setting out plants on soils which have carried diseased pansies within previous two years
Slugs and snails	*See* General list	
Solomon's Seal sawfly	Greyish-blue caterpillar larvae feed on and, in bad cases, defoliate the plants	Spray or dust with HCH at the first sign of attack
Sweet William rust	Brown patches occur on the leaves, growing and enlarging. In warm, wet seasons outbreaks are more severe and can result in killing Sweet William. But other dianthus can be affected also	Spray with copper fungicide. Burn badly diseased plants
Tulip fire	All parts of the plant can be affected, usually the leaf tips and flowers are covered with a greyish mould	Plant only healthy firm bulbs. Spray emerging shoots with thiram three or four times at 7–10 day intervals
Virus diseases	*See* General list	
Wilt	*See* General list	

Table of Ailments Affecting Trees, Shrubs and Climbers

Cause	Effect	Control
Aphid	*See* General list	
Armillaria	*See* General list	
Bleeding	*See* General list	
Canker	*See* General list	
Clematis wilt	Plants wilt and die for no apparent reason	Remove and burn affected plants. When starting afresh, set healthy new plants in pockets of fresh soil or compost
Coral spot	*See* General list	
Honey fungus	*See* Armillaria, General list	

Table of Ailments Affecting Trees, Shrubs and Climbers—*continued*

Cause	Effect	Control
Leaf rolling rose sawfly	This pest rolls the leaves lengthwise and feeds from inside killing the leaves and weakening the plants. Roses of various kinds are affected	Spray with malathion in May to prevent egg laying, and in June to kill the young nymphs on the leaves
Lilac blight	Dark spots occur on the leaves and growing tips become blackened and blind	Spray with copper fungicide
Lilac leaf miner	The leaves of affected plants are blistered and blotched with ribbon like lines with small insects feeding inside	Spray attacked plants with HCH or malathion
Lime-induced Chlorosis	*See* Chlorosis, General list	
Peach leaf curl	*See* General list	
Rhododendron bud blast	A disease which results in the terminal buds turning brown and dying	Spray in spring summer and autumn with copper fungicide, to control the disease and check Rhododendron leaf hopper which aids the spread of this ailment
Rhododendron bug	The leaves become mottled with brownish spots caused by the feeding of this pest, weakening plants in heavy attacks. The adults are black and shiny but the nymphs are greenish	Spray with HCH at 21 day intervals from mid-June to the first frosts of the season
Rhododendron leaf hopper	By feeding on and damaging buds this pest is thought to encourage the spread of Rhododendron bud blast (q.v. above)	Spray with HCH or malathion in spring and summer
Rhododendron whitefly	White, winged insects with yellowish young feeding on the leaves causing honeydew and weakening plants	Spray with HCH when noticed
Rose aphid	*See* Aphid, General list	
Rose black spot *See* fig 188	The leaves develop dark or black spots, weakening and stunting plants	Sprays affected plants with captan at 10–14 day intervals. Gather and burn fallen leaves in autumn
Rose chafer	*See* Chafer, General list	
Rose die-back	Leaves and shoots wither and die and if left unchecked can kill the plants	Remove affected shoots and spray with benomyl when seen
Rose powdery mildew *See* fig 189	A white powdery coating on leaves, buds and shoots, weakening plants and preventing flowering	Remove badly affected shoots. Spray at 14–21 day intervals with benomyl, dinocap or sulphur fungicides during the growing season

Table of Ailments Affecting Trees, Shrubs and Climbers—*continued*

Cause	Effect	Control
Rose rust	Yellowish spots which turn brown, affecting leaves and young shoots, resulting in weakening plants and sometimes defoliation	Spray affected plants with copper fungicide
Rose sawfly	Small brownish-yellow grubs skeletonising the leaves causing them to dry and wither	Spray affected plants with derris or HCH
Suckering	Shoots arising from near or below soil level of root-stocks, as briars on roses	Cut these out as close to the stem as possible

Table of Ailments Affecting Greenhouse, Frame and Cloche Crops

Cause	Effect	Control
Algae	Green film or growth on benching, walls, floors and on glass or plastic	Fumigate empty greenhouses between crops and wash down
Aphids	*See* General list	
Azalea gall	Reddish swellings occurring on the leaves and later forming a white growth	Spray with copper fungicide
Blackfly	*See* Aphids, General list	
Blackleg	*See* General list	
Botrytis	*See* Grey mould, General list	
Carnation rust	Numerous orange spots, later turning brown, develop on the leaves of carnations and other dianthus. Badly diseased leaves become pale and wither	Spray affected plants with copper or thiram fungicides
Carnation tortrix	Greenish caterpillars. Leaves are spun together and eaten or holed blooms, buds and foliage	Spray or fumigate affected plants with derris or HCH repeating at 7–10 day intervals as necessary
Caterpillars	*See* General list	
Chlorosis	*See* General list	
Chrysanthemum aphid, capsid, caterpillar and eelworm	*See* General list	
Chrysanthemum leaf miner	*See* Leaf miner, below	
Chrysanthemum rust	Pale spots which are usually circular, turning brown, develop on the leaves, weakening plants	Remove and burn badly affected stems. Spray with copper fungicide

Table of Ailments Affecting Greenhouse, Frame and Cloche Crops—*continued*

Cause	Effect	Control
Cladosporium	*See* Tomato leaf mould, below	
Common green capsid	*See* General list	
Cuckoo spit	*See* Common froghopper, General list	
Cucumber botrytis	*See* Grey mould, General list	Remove diseased parts
Cucumber mildew	*See* Mildew, General list	Spray affected plants with benomyl at first signs
Cucumber mosaic	Mottled foliage and fruits stunted plants and poor crops	Remove badly affected plants and control aphid to prevent spread
Cutworm	*See* General list	
Dahlia mosaic	*See* Virus, General list	
Damping off	*See* General list	
Earwig	*See* General list	
Eelworm	*See* General list	
Greenhouse red spider mite	Speckled or mottled pale leaves turning bronzed and stunted with reddish or yellowish small insects present. In severe attacks the growing points and leaves become covered with fine webbing	Spray affected plants with derris or malathion. Avoid dry conditions in summer which are enjoyed by this pest
Greenhouse thrips	Flowers and leaves of many crops are speckled, pale and stunted, with small dark insects present	Spray with malathion
Greenhouse whitefly	Many crops are attacked by white flying moth-like insects, causing honeydew and weakening of plants	Spray with derris, HCH or malathion and repeat 7–10 days later
Greenhouse sooty mould	The leaves of plants develop black unsightly growths following attacks by aphids	Spray to control aphids. Sponge and wash thick, shiny leaves
Honeydew	*See* General list	
Leaf miner *See* fig 177	The leaves have brownish or whitish blotches, with white ribbon-like narrow lines	Spray affected plants with HCH
Lettuce problems	*See* Vegetable list	
Lily leaf spot	Red or brown spots on the leaves, increasing in size to form dead patches and weaken plants	Spray with copper fungicide as soon as the spots appear
Lily mosaic	*See* Virus, General list	
Mealy bug	Insects covered with a mealy coating feed on a wide range of crops producing honeydew and weakening plants	Spray or paint affected areas with HCH or malathion
Mildew	*See* General list	

Table of Ailments Affecting Greenhouse, Frame and Cloche Crops—*continued*

Cause	Effect	Control
Millipede	Slow moving creatures with many legs, usually found in soil. Stems eaten at or near soil level and roots also	Dust the soil with HCH
Slugs		*See* General list
Symphilids		*See* General list
Tomato blossom-end rot	The bottom of affected fruits turn hard and black or dark brown, ruining both eating quality and appearance	Remove spoilt fruits. Mulch with peat or similar. Water carefully and avoid dryness at the roots
Tomato blotchy ripening	Fruits develop hard patches like greenback	Water carefully and give balanced high potash feed
Tomato greenback *See* fig 191	The top of the fruits remain green or yellow when the rest is ripe and red	As for blotchy ripening. Grow non-greenback varieties
Tomato leaf mould *See* fig 192	The leaves develop yellowish spots on the upper surface and khaki moulds on the undersides, weakening plants	Spray affected plants with benomyl or copper fungicide. Ventilate freely, weather permitting
Tomato splitting	Fruits crack and split open	Avoid dryness at the roots, and do not overwater, especially after defoliating
Tomato spotted wilt	Affected plants develop spots or blotches on the leaves accompanied by wilting. Young plants may die. Fruits and leaves can become bronzed by this virus disease	Remove and burn severely affected plants. Wash hands and knives before handling healthy plants to prevent the spread of this disease
Verticillium wilt Wilt		*See* Wilt, General list

Table of Ailments Affecting Turf

Cause	Effect	Control
Ants		*See* General list
Chafer grubs	Creamy or whitish grubs with brown heads feeding on the roots of grasses. These grubs weaken turf, sometimes causing dead patches	Water suspect areas with HCH
Corticium	Dead or seriously weakened patches of grass develop. Pinkish moulds with reddish fungus threads among the grass	Water affected patches with calomel solution. Improve aeration and soil drainage

Table of Ailments Affecting Greenhouse, Frame and Cloche Crops—*continued*

Cause	Effect	Control
Damping off	Newly seeded areas form patches where the young grasses die out in the seedling stage	Spray or water affected areas with copper fungicide
Dollar spot	Brownish patches 30–50 mm across which later become bleached in appearance	Water the damaged areas with calomel solution
Earthworm	*See* General list	
Fairy rings	Circles of varying size of vigorous grass, surrounding areas of weakened pale turf which sometimes die off, are features of this problem	In severe cases, remove the affected turf, fork up the ground and water with 2% formaldehyde solution. Re-sow or turf the area three to four weeks later, season allowing
Fusarium	White or greyish patches of mould around pale, dead or dying grass, often appearing in early spring following snow	Water affected patches with calomel solution. Improve aeration and soil drainage
Leatherjackets	Darkish grey-brown leathery grubs which feed on the roots of grasses weaken turf and cause bare patches and withered leaf blades	Water the turf with HCH solution or use chlordane as for earthworms
Moss	Bright or yellowish green carpeting among grass or on bare patches in lawns	Apply lawn sand to affected areas in spring or autumn
Red thread disease	*See* Corticium, above	
Scorch	Brown or bleached areas of withered grass following the application of fertiliser or other chemicals	Water affected areas if there are living grasses present. Avoid feeding lawns when the soil is dry; water first. Take care not to give overdose, by overlapping the fertiliser when using a distributor
Wireworm	*See* General list	

Chapter 11. Tools and Equipment

The items which are discussed in this section are mainly tools and equipment that are in general use in gardens. Unusual or infrequently seen items are not considered here.

Bulb planter This consists of a stainless or hard steel sleeve, attached to a handle. This tool is used for removing small plugs of soil or turf, about 75–100 mm (3–4 in) in diameter and up to 150 mm (6 in) deep, for bulb planting. Keep the sleeve free of hard dried soil to ensure a clean cutting edge.

Capillary bench This is a level shallow tray or trough, which is lined with special matting or sand, on which pot plants are grown. It is designed to enable plants in pots or boxes up to 100 mm (4 in) deep to be watered by capillary attraction. For successful operation, the following points should be observed. Keep the sand or mat lining wet. Ensure that pots and boxes have holes in their bases, and are in close contact with the lining. The moisture rises, like oil in a wick, through the compost in the containers. Green films of algal growth should be removed, to allow the free flow of water.

Capillary matting This is an absorbent material, which is used for lining capillary benches or canals. Matting ensures good contact between containers and has the added advantage of being lighter than sand.

Cloche The main types which are in common use are those listed below.
Barn These are made in various sizes from four sheets of glass or rigid clear plastic, and held together by wires or light metal struts. The arrangement consists of two roof and two side panels.
Tent Each cloche of this type is made from sheets of glass or plastic material in the form of an inverted 'V' and held together by wire, or clips.
Tunnel These are constructed in the form of an inverted 'U', either from moulded units of rigid plastic, flexible plastic, or PVC sheet on wire frames.
General Most cloches in common use are 50 cm (20 in) high or less, and are not usually wider than 60 cm (2 ft). Where one or a number of cloches are used, cover any exposed ends of a run, to prevent draughts and keep covered plants warmer.

For details of the use of cloches; *see* Chapter 4, Greenhouses.

During winter it is important to keep glass and plastic clean, to allow the maximum amount of light to pass through the covering material.

Cultivator A useful hand tool which has three or five rigid tines and is used

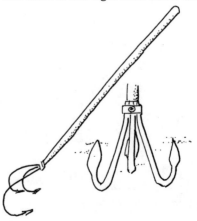

194 Cultivator. Cultivator with head and tines.

169

for breaking up ground, and killing weeds. A cultivator is used by drawing the tines through the soil towards the operator. This implement is effective for creating a deep tilth in spring, in readiness for sowing or planting. It is often better than a hoe for loosening soil between crops on heavy land, particularly for vegetables.

Dibber A short, pointed piece of wood, varying from pencil-thickness to broom handle diameter. These are often home made, and small dibbers are used for pricking out young seedlings such as bedding plants into boxes. Large dibbers are used for planting cabbages and Brussels sprouts into their final positions. A hole of the correct size is made and the roots of each plant are placed in it. The soil is then firmed by levering on one side with the dibber.

Distributor The basic form of small models used in gardens consists of a wheeled box with a regulating mechanism to control the delivery of fertilisers. The most reliable types usually have a spindle or roller feed mechanism at the base. The aim of using a distributor is to evenly apply fertiliser to lawns or soil areas even where quite small quantities of material are involved.

195   Distributor. For spreading fertiliser.

The points to observe are given below.
Cleanliness Make sure the distributor is emptied and well cleaned after use. Fertiliser if left, can corrode metal parts and block up the outlets.
Check the rate of delivery at the start of each application, to ensure that the correct amount is given, and that none of the outlets is blocked.
Avoid doubling the application rate which can damage grass or young plants. This can occur if a second sweep of an application overlaps the first.

Dutch Hoe *See* Hoe, this chapter.

Dutch Light *See* Frame, this chapter.

Edge trimmer A simple mechanical device, consisting of a circle of revolving blades, which shear off long horizontal leaves of grass on lawn edges. Some models are pushed along, others are powered, usually by electric motors. Make sure that the blades are kept sharp and that all moving parts are clean and well lubricated. Check that all electric wires and connections are well insulated and properly earthed before use. Inspect each strip of edging for wire or stones before trimming, to avoid damage to the cutting blades.

Edging iron *See* Half-moon, this chapter.

Edging shears *See* Shears, this chapter.

Fertiliser Spreader *See* Distributor, this chapter.

Firmer These consist of flat, rectangular or circular pieces of wood, metal or plastic with some form of handle. They are used for firming compost in pots, pans and boxes, and leaving a smooth, even surface. Firmers are often home made, usually in various sizes to fit the different kinds of container which are in use.

Flame gun Various models are available and consist of a fuel tank, feed pipe and combustion chamber. These are of

196 Firmers. *Left*: box. *Right*: pot.

197 Fork for turf with interchangeable prongs or tines. *Top left*: solid. *Top right*: slitter tines. *Bottom right*: hollow tines. *Bottom left*: knife tines.

more use in large gardens than small, and are used for burning rubbish, sterilising boxes and seed drills. When using a flame gun for any purpose, take care to avoid pumping up pressure to danger level. These usually operate on vapourising oil or paraffin.

Fork This is one of the most basic and fundamental garden tools and is made in various sizes and shapes to suit many purposes.
Border fork This is usually four pronged, slightly lighter and narrower than the standard garden fork. It is used, as the name implies, for digging or forking borders and in narrow spaces between plants.
Digging fork This is of similar size to the standard garden fork, but the prongs are wider. It is particularly useful for digging stony or clay soils, where normal spade work is difficult.
Garden fork This is the general purpose tool, which can be seen in many gardens, and is used for digging, handling manure, and for solid tine spiking on lawns.
Hand fork A lightweight three or four prong tool often made in stainless steel and which is particularly suitable for use in such as rock gardens.
Hollow-tined fork This usually consists of three hollow tines for the head and is used exclusively for hollow-tine spiking of turf. *See* fig 197 for Turf fork.

Grass hook A cutting tool consisting of a curved steel blade and short wooden or metal and plastic handle. These are made in different weights and sizes and are used primarily for cutting rough grass. The blade should be kept really sharp for ease of cutting, but exercise great care when using a hook. Sweep the blade away from, never towards, the body. Always make sure that pets and children are right out of the way before starting to cut. Never leave these tools lying where they can be fallen on or picked up by children.

Grecian saw *See* Saw, this chapter.

Greenhouse These are constructed of glass or rigid or flexible plastic, and supported by timber, metal and occasionally concrete structures. There are a number of styles of building to consider.
Circular Metal framed houses of this type are becoming popular and are pleasing to look at with a round domed roof.
Lean-to This type consists of a monopitch roofed structure built against a wall, which can provide a good insulation against cold. Ideally, this kind of structure should face south.

198   Greenhouse types. *Left to right*: lean-to; span; three-quarter span.

Mansard Greenhouses of this type have sloping side walls, which are wider at the base than at gutter height.

Span These have pitched roofs of equal size, one on either side of the centre ridge. Where winter cropping is of maximum importance, the ridge should run east-west to obtain maximum sunlight. Houses which are orientated north-south are better for summer crops.

Three-quarter span These, like lean-to houses, are usually built against a wall, but have a pitched roof of uneven size. The shorter roof rises from the back wall to the ridge. With all greenhouses, there should be as few glazing bars as possible allowing at least 60 cm (2 ft) between each. The area of the roof ventilators should not be less than 15 per cent of the floor space.

Tunnel houses These consist of flexible, clear plastic, usually PVC, stretched over tubular supports and secured at soil level. This type of structure is cheaper to buy than conventional greenhouses, but is less suitable for winter cropping with low light intensity and high heat loss.

Grubber A two-pronged hand tool with a bent or curved piece of metal and short handle. To use place the prongs directly under a weed, such as daisy or plantain, levering it out and using the curved piece of metal as a pivot. A grubber is useful for removing the occasional weed from lawns, rock gardens or between paving stones.

Half-moon A tool consisting of a semi-circular steel blade with sharp, curved edge, attached in line to a long handle. This implement is used for cutting and trimming turf. Where straight edges are required, a plank makes a suitable guide for the half-moon which is forced into the turf to cut as needed.

Heating Greenhouses and frames can be heated by various means, none of which is cheap. The principal methods are electricity, gas, oil, and solid fuel. The practical problems of solar heating for this purpose have yet to be satisfactorily resolved.

Electric heating is usually by tubular or fan heaters for space heating, and by warming cables for heating frames, propagators or greenhouse benches.

Gas, oil and solid fuel heating systems require a boiler, hot water pipes or radiators and circulating pump for best results. Although more costly to install initially, the unit heating costs of gas, oil and solid fuel are cheaper than electricity. Solid fuel heating involves disposing of ashes and clinker, which can present problems. Both oil and solid fuel involve providing some form of fuel storage, unlike mains gas.

Portable paraffin and gas burners are popular for greenhouse heating, being comparatively cheap and easy to install. However, where paraffin or gas are burnt indoors for heating purposes, and where there are no flues for fumes to escape, the following points should be observed:

172

use high grade fuels, or fumes harmful to plants can be given off; avoid placing burners too close to crops or damage through overheating can occur.

Hedging shears *See* Shears, this chapter.

Hoes Three main types are in common use.
Canterbury hoe This is a heavy type of draw hoe, but is used like a mattock for chopping and grubbing out weeds.
Draw hoe This is used to chop down weeds, and for earthing up, by drawing loose soil around plants.

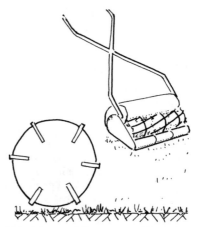

200   Mower. Cylinder type with section.

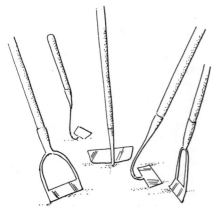

199   Hoes. *Left to right*: Dutch; swan-necked hand; draw; swan-necked; Dutch.

Dutch or push hoe The method of using this hoe is with a push-and-pull action, where the D-shaped blade cuts in both directions. Although this type is excellent on light or medium soils it is less suitable than the Draw hoe for heavy ground.

Hollow-tined fork *See* Fork, this chapter.

Hook *See* Grass hook, this chapter.

Lawn Mower There are various kinds of grass cutter, which operate on different cutting principles.
Cylinder mowers These rely on horizontal cutting cylinders, which have three to

eight knife blades. Three or four-bladed cylinders are used for rough or coarse cutting. Seven and eight-blade cylinders provide a fine, close cut for top quality lawns. These cylinders are mounted on varying types of frame, some having front and rear rollers. Others which have only side wheels are used for rough ground. Some cylinder mowers are pushed and others are motor driven. Cylinders are made in various widths, but 30–35 cm (12–14 in) is wide enough to push. Units wider than the above should be power driven.
Flail cutters This type consists basically of a series of rapidly rotating blades, attached to a powered horizontal spindle, and is used mainly for cutting long grass.
Reciprocating mowers These operate on the principle of a farm reaper with a horizontal arm. This consists of a series of front-facing metal fingers with a long blade. Attached to this blade are a series of triangular cutting knives which move rapidly backwards and forwards. This type is motorised and used on long grass.
Rotary mowers Cutting with this type is by means of, usually two or four, rapidly-spinning horizontal blades, attached to a flat plate or disc. Mowers operating on this principle are always

powered, often self-propelled and are generally used on long grass. Several different kinds of mounting are used. The hover type, which rides on a cushion of air, is popular, particularly for mowing banks. The wheeled, self-propelled mower is also widely used, but the ride-on types are mainly suitable for large areas of turf. Small electrically powered cutters operate on the same principle.

The successful operation of any mower depends on keeping it clean, well maintained and lubricated. The cutting blades should be kept sharp, and all moving parts should be covered with some form of approved safety guard. Never try to alter or adjust any mower while the engine is running or switched on.

201   Rakes   *Left to right*: iron; wire; hand.

Propagator These consist usually of a box-like base with electric cables to provide bottom heat and a glass or plastic cover to retain warmth and moisture. The particular advantages of a propagator are that higher temperatures can be effected at lower cost than heating a greenhouse; that high humidity can quickly be arranged and that two temperature regimes are possible. It is advisable to disinfect the inside between batches of plants, and is necessary where any disease, such as damping off, or Grey Mould has occured.

Pruning saw *See* Saw, this chapter.

Rake There are several variations of the basic pattern.

Aluminium The feature of this rake is its light weight. It is used like the iron variety.

Hand These are small solid tine rakes with a short handle, and are used for removing leaves and loosening soil among bedding or rock plants.

Iron These consist of a comb-like head, with 8–16 teeth, attached to a long handle. This is the general-purpose rake which is used in most gardens to prepare a fine tilth for planting and for seed-bed

preparation. This is also used to break down soil lumps, work in fertilisers, gather up leaves and stones, for final soil levelling and a variety of other jobs.

Rubber Rakes of this type have rubber teeth and are mostly used for gathering leaves.

Spring This rake has wire tines arranged fan-wise. It is used mainly for lawn care. It is excellent for aerating and scarifying turf, gathering leaves and scattering worm casts.

Stainless steel As for iron rake.

Wooden These rakes are usually wider and have longer teeth, which are spaced further apart than on iron rakes. This type is used for gathering long grass, and raking down loose soil before sowing or planting.

Rakes when not in use should be either hung up in safety or placed teeth down to prevent anyone from stepping on upturned teeth.

Roller Although iron rollers were a common sight in large grounds, they are of limited use in small modern gardens especially those with paved foot-paths. Where roller-type mowers are used on lawns and there are no gravel-type paths to maintain, rollers can be hired for a specific one-off job if need be, saving cost and space.

Rotary cultivation A power driven

174

machine with rotating tines attached to a horizontal spindle and used for breaking up the ground, particularly in spring or summer. These are of only limited use in small gardens because they lie idle for much of the time.

Rotary cutter *See* Mowers, this chapter.

Rotorake A powered mechanical turf scarifier which consists of numerous blades attached to a rapidly revolving horizontal spindle. The blades make a series of shallow slits in the ground, aerating the turf and cutting off straggling stems which lie below the reach of mowing machines.

Saws While there are different saws for various purposes, pruning and rough-cut types are most commonly needed in gardens.
Pruning saws have narrow blades for ease of accessibility, and small teeth for producing a smooth finish. Some have curved blades, such as the Grecian type, and others are straight.
The rough-cut type have blades with large teeth, such as Bushman saws, which have a high cutting rate. These are used for cutting down small trees and shrubs.

Paint any saw cuts on growing trees,

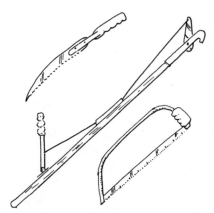

202 Pruner and saws. *Centre*: long-arm pruner. *Top*: Grecian pruning saw. *Bottom*: bow saw.

over 25 mm (1 in) in diameter, with lead paint or bitumen after paring the surface smooth with a sharp knife.

Keep saws sharp and well greased for ease of operation.

See also Tree pruner, this chapter.

Secateurs There are two main types of secateurs in common use: the anvil and the double cut or parrot bill.
Anvil type These have a single cutting blade which cuts through each shoot as it is held in place by the broad anvil side.

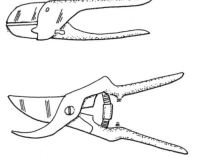

203 Secateurs. *Top*: anvil. *Bottom*: parrot bill.

Double cut (Parrot bill) These have two cutting blades, the edges of which are usually curved. Secateurs of both types can be used for cutting shoots up to a maximum of about 18 mm ($\frac{3}{4}$ in) or less for the smaller models.

Keep secateurs sharp, clean and well oiled. In the interests of safety, these should always be placed well out of reach of small children.

Shears These all operate on the scissor principle, but with variations of design according to the nature of intended use.
Edging shears These usually have long handles, enabling grass cutting to be carried out from a standing position. The cutting edges are straight, unlike those used for trimming banks.
Hedging Shears for this purpose are generally short handled and have notched steel blades for cutting large shoots up to about 15 mm ($\frac{5}{8}$ in) thick. The

204 Shears. *Left:* standard for grass or hedges. *Right:* hand shears for grass.

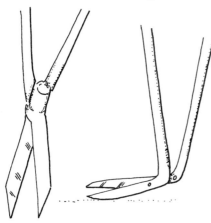

205 Shears. *Left:* long-handled lawn. *Right:* long-handled edging.

blades are often hollow ground, and wavy edged for easy working.

Lawn shears These consist, usually, of blades with long handles, and are used flat on the soil or turf.

Side-wheel mower *See* Lawn Mower, this chapter.

Spade Although made in different sizes and weights, these do not vary to the same extent as hoes and rakes. When selecting a spade, choose one of the correct size and weight for the user. Stainless steel models, though more costly to buy, are often easier to use and take less cleaning. Dirty or rusty spades require far more effort to use than clean ones. Always clean and dry your spade after using and then wipe it down with an oily rag. Border spades are smaller and lighter than digging models, which are usually made in two sizes and known as No 1 and No 2. Another feature which is worth considering is the tread at the top of a spade, only present on some models. This presents a broader edge to boots and reduces undue wear. When digging, press the spade vertically into the soil to ensure cultivation to the maximum depth.

Sprayer These operate either by direct pumping or pneumatically by compressed air. Simple garden syringes and double-action sprayers work by direct pumping. Pneumatic-type sprayers require a pressure chamber of some kind, to contain the compressed air. These are made in various sizes from small hand models to knapsack sprayers. The advantage of the pneumatic type is that once the air pressure is raised sufficiently spraying can proceed without continuous pumping.

When purchasing sprayers of any type, select those which are robustly

206 Sprayers. *Left:* direct-action. *Right:* pneumatic.

made, and constructed of non-corrosive materials.

Where fruit tree spraying is contemplated, extension lances to give additional reach, are really necessary.

When using and mixing sprays, always adhere to the manufacturers instructions. Avoid spraying in wet, windy or freezing conditions and wash hands and face afterwards. Wash out buckets and sprayers after use.

Sprinkler There are various kinds of watering system, involving some type of sprinkler.

Mist unit This consists of one or a number of nozzles connected to a water pipe-line and which create a mist-like spray.

Oscillating sprayer This relies on water pressure to move a perforated pipe backwards and forwards, directing a curtain of fine jets of water in the process.

Pulse-jet This unit is also actuated by water pressure, gradually wetting a circle of ground. Each nozzle releases a jet of water, stops and moves through a short arc, releases another jet, repeating the process until the area is sufficiently wet, when it is manually moved.

Rotary sprinkler These sprinklers send out a number of jets of fine spray from revolving nozzles, often situated at the ends of two pipe arms.

Sprayline Consists of a static pipe with a series of perforations which is connected to a water supply. The perforations are made at different angles to ensure a wide spread of water.

All sprinklers should be checked for blocked nozzles and worn parts.

Steriliser The most convenient method of sterilising soil by heat on a small scale is with an electric steriliser. Proprietary models consist of a well insulated box, heated internally by electric elements. All wiring should be carried out by a competent electrician. The sterilising operation consists of filling the 'box' with sifted moist soil,

switching on the electricity supply until the required temperature is reached. The contents of the box should be spread out on a disinfected surface to cool off rapidly.

Switch A long, pliable fibre-glass rod or bamboo cane, which is used on turf to scatter dew and worm casts.

Syringe A bicycle-pump-like tube with a piston plunger to suck in liquids, which are forced out as a fine spray. Select syringes made of non-corrosive materials for preference. They are used for overhead damping of plants with water, and for applying pesticides.

Tree pruner This tool consists of a metal or timber pole with a cutter head at one end and a handle for its remote control at the other.

The cutter operates rather like the jaws of a pair of secateurs. Is also known as a long-arm pruner, which should be kept sharp and well oiled at all times for best results. *See* fig 202.

Trimmers Three main kinds are used and are usually powered by electric motors. The grass trimmers work on the same principle as the larger rotary mower, with horizontally revolving blades. The hedge trimmer is a small and portable version of a reciprocating mower, and the verge or edge trimmer operates similarly to the grass trimmer, but the blades are vertically arranged.

Trowel A scoop-shaped small planting tool, the best of which are made of stainless steel. As with all tools, clean ones are easy and quick to use.

Turf cutter *See* Half-moon, this chapter.

Turfing iron A kind of flat-bladed spade which is used for lifting turf. Keep this tool clean and greased after use.

Verge trimmer *See* Trimmer, this chapter.

Watering can When purchasing,

choose one made of non-corrosive materials and preferably having a choice of rose size. This enables delicate young plants to be watered with a fine spray instead of being deluged.

Wheelbarrow Where this is necessary, obtain one that is not too heavy to manage. Pneumatic-tyres are worth while in the absence of good firm paths. Keep the barrow clean, especially after handling manure and compost, which dries on hard. Oil the wheel axle occasionally to save unnecessary wear and make pushing easier.

Part Two

Index of Terms and Tasks

Acaricide A chemical such as derris used for the control of parasitic spider mites.

Acid A condition in which the pH level is below 7. Some soils are so described. *See* pH.

Acorn The nut-like fruit produced by mature oak trees.

Adventitious Accidental or unusual, applied to roots, for example, which develop from parts normally above ground, as happens with leaf cuttings or stems when layered.

Aeration A condition of air content or oxygen level of soil, turf or water. Compacted or badly-drained soils containing small or negligible amounts of air or oxygen have poor aeration and are consequently infertile. Pond water needs oxygen for fish to breath and live.

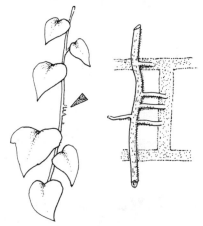

207 Aerial root. Left: an ivy shoot producing aerial roots, *arrowed*. *Right*: a close-up showing stem with roots forcing their way into the joints between brickwork.

Aerial root Some plants, like ivy, have roots emerging from above-ground stems when climbing against a wall and these provide a secure hold. Epiphytic orchids suspended above ground in warm moist conditions obtain moisture from roots in the air.

Aggregate culture Growing plants without soil.

Air-layering A method of propagation in which rooting takes place above ground. Also called Chinese layering. *See* Chapter 2, Propagation.

Algae Minute, often green, plants which can occur as a film on moist tree trunks, wet soil surfaces, on greenhouse staging and on the surface of water in warm, sunlit conditions.

Algicide A chemical used to prevent the growth of, or kill, algae.

Alkaline A condition in which the pH level is above 7. Soils so described usually contain considerable quantities of chalk or limestone. *See* pH.

Alpine Of plants, those which occur naturally between the tree line – the uppermost level of tree growth – and the permanent snow line. Commonly applied to dwarf and hardy plants that are suitable for rock gardens.

Alternate Applied to a branch where leaves or buds occur on opposite sides of the stem, but in alternating fashion. Also used to describe the alternate planting of similar plants in two or more rows.

American Gooseberry Mildew *See* Chapter 10, Problems.

Ammonia An alkaline substance, occuring as a gas or combined with other chemicals to make ammonium salts. Sulphate of ammonia is used as a fertiliser supplying nitrogen to promote rapid growth especially for green vegetable crops and turf. Ammonia gas is given off from rapidly decomposing manure. The roots and leaves of tender seedlings such as cucumbers can be damaged at high concentrations, for example in greenhouses where the ventilators are closed.

Anbury Better known as Club Root. *See* Chapter 10, Problems.

Anemophilous Windloving, applied to plants and trees which are pollinated by wind rather then by insects. Examples include anemonies, sweet corn and willows.

Annual A plant which normally completes its life cycle from germination to seed or fruit production in one growing season. Annuals are subdivided into four main categories.
Hardy One which can complete its life process outdoors without special protection.
Half-hardy This needs protection, either when young or when seeding or fruiting, for successful cultivation.
Tender or greenhouse annual. This type can be grown satisfactorily only under cover for most of its life.
Winter annual One which can be sown in autumn to mature during the following spring and summer. Some kinds of lettuce, clarkia, and sweet peas come into this category. *See* Chapter 5, Flowers and Foliage.

Anther Part of the stamen, or male part of a flower, which normally produces pollen.

Aphicide A chemical used to kill or destroy aphids.

Aphid Various forms of plant 'louse', otherwise known as greenfly, blackfly, aphis or blight. *See* Chapter 10, Problems.

Aquatic Plants that live and grow in water. They are either completely submerged or in part only, with leaves and flowers floating on the surface. Not to be confused with bog or marginal subjects which grow into the air. *See* Chapter 5, Flowers and Foliage.

Arboretum A garden or space allocated to the cultivation, usually of many varieties, of tree. A 'pygmy' arboretum, though similar, contains dwarf or diminutive forms of tree.

Arboriculture The care and cultivation of trees and tree-like shrubs, usually with a decorative, ornamental, or amenity function.

Artificial Processed, man-made or not in a natural form. Artificial fertilisers are processed, concentrated plant foods.

Artificial heat Means other than direct sunheat, such as oil, gas, electricity and solid fuels for greenhouse or other heating purposes.

Artificial lighting or illumination A light source other than natural sunlight. Electric lamps and light bulbs can be used to promote or control plant growth.

Aspect Facing direction. A site or position having a southern aspect, for example, faces south.

Awl-shaped Leaves which are narrow and taper to a point, like those of some conifers.

Axil The angle formed on the upper side where a leaf stalk joins a stem from which growths or shoots often emerge.

Axillary Of the axil. Applied to shoots or buds arising from an axil.

Bacteria Minute organisms some of which are essential for maintaining soil fertility. Peas and beans are able to make use of nitrogen from the atmosphere due to the action of bacteria living in the nodules on their roots. This action improves soil fertility. Under adverse conditions some bacteria are harmful causing diseases of various kinds.

Bag fertiliser Another term for concentrated fertiliser.

Baked Clay or heavy soils which become dried out and hard. Soils are sometimes referred to as being so treated after being sterilised. *See* Sterilisation *also* Chapter 1, Site and Soil.

Ball A mass of soil which clings to the roots of a plant after being removed from a pot or when dug out of the ground.

Balled-and-wrapped Trees and shrubs offered for sale with their roots in a ball with soil attached, and tied up in hessian. They suffer less from drying conditions than those with exposed roots.

Bank Differences in levels can often be overcome by a connecting incline or bank which may consist of turf, rock, plants and/or flowers. Where grass is to be mown or people are to walk frequently slopes should not be steeper than 1 in 3.

Banked Where flower beds or borders adjoin a wall or hedge, banked plants are more effective than where they are all of similar height. A banked effect can be achieved by having dwarf plants to the front and tall ones at the back.

Bare-rooted Young rose plants and shrubs offered for sale in stores and supermarkets wrapped in plastic bags and with little or no soil attached. Soak them in water before planting and keep well moistened to prevent severe drying out later.

Bark A hard woody or corky layer on the outside of tree trunks and large branches. This covering layer develops from the rind or surface 'skin' of young shoots. Bark performs the essential functions of protecting the inner water conducting and cambium (q.v.) tissues

from excessive heat or cold and reducing loss of moisture by evaporation.

Bark-bound Often incorrectly referred to as bark-ringing. A condition in which either the bark is girdled and contricted by, for example, tree ties that are too tight, or the bark itself restricts the upward movement of water from the roots. It should be prevented by regular inspection and loosening of tree ties as the trunks increase in size. Bark may split naturally, or can be assisted by slitting vertically on one side with a sharp knife.

Bark-ringing A method of inducing fruiting in unproductive, over-vigorous apple and pear trees. It consists of removing a narrow circle or two semicircles of bark.

Basal cutting A growth or shoot arising from or near soil level at the base of a plant, or one such shoot which is trimmed and ready for propagation. *See* Chapter 2, Propagation, Cuttings.

Basic slag A phosphatic fertiliser referred to by early writers which is not now widely used in gardens.

Bastard trenching A term previously used for what is now described as double digging. *See* Chapter 1, Site and Soil.

Bed Any small area, regardless of shape, of cultivated ground in gardens. When used for decorative purposes different kinds of flowers or shrubs can be grown in the same bed. Also an area set aside for a single type of vegetable, for example a bed of leeks, onions or asparagus.

Bedding out Planting up/out bedding plants in beds or borders.

Bedding plants Mainly hardy and half-hardy flowering annuals, biennials and perennials. Bulbous plants which are grown for a short season only in beds and borders are also included. *See* Chapter 5, Flowers and Foliage.

Bench heating A heated greenhouse bench or staging. *See* Bottom heat.

Berry A fruit containing one or more seeds encased in fleshy or pulpy tissue which does not open like a pod. Blackcurrants and gooseberries are examples.

Bicolour Two coloured. Mostly used to describe flowers.

Biennial A plant which completes its life cycle, from germination to setting seed or fruit, in two growing seasons. *See* Chapter 5, Flowers and Foliage.

Big Bud A pest of blackcurrants. *See* Chapter 10, Problems.

Bi-generic Hybrid plants which result from crossing two genera together; the Leyland Cypress × Cupressocyparis, for example, a cross between Cupressus and Chamaecyparis.

Binding Organic matter and humus bind sandy soils, preventing wind and water from carrying particles away. Plant roots also have a similar effect.

Raffia, also described as binding, and used for budding and grafting, is being gradually superseded by adhesive tape.

Biological control Natural methods of pest and disease control. Whitefly in greenhouses can, for example, be virtually eliminated by the action of the small parasitic wasp Encarsia. *See* Chapter 10, Problems.

Biotic Related to living organisms, often in a botanical sense. A biotic factor in gardening relates to the interaction of plants on each other.

Bipinnate Leaflets of plants which are divided, and subdivided again.

Black leg A form of stem rot affecting various plants. *See* Chapter 10, Problems.

Black spot A leaf spotting disease of roses. *See* Chapter 10, Problems.

Blade The broad part of a leaf, includ-

ing that of grass. Also knives on a grass-cutting cylinder. Also a horizontally mounted piece of metal used for levelling ground.

Blanching A process of excluding light to improve colour and flavour of crops such as celery, endive, leeks and rhubarb. *See* Chapter 9, Vegetables.

Bleeding Loss of sap or moisture from cut stems or shoots occurring after pruning or injury. Some plants such as vines bleed profusely when pruned at the wrong time just as the sap is rising in spring. Beetroots, if damaged or cut, rapidly lose colour and condition through bleeding.

Blight A general term used to describe the condition of ailing plants. Also the common name of potato blight, *Phytophthora infestans*. *See* Chapter 10, Problems.

Blind Plants which have no growing points. Occasionally occurs with cauliflowers and other seedlings.

Bloom A flower when in full bloom. Also a fine waxy covering often seen on flowers, fruits and leaves. *Cf* Farina.

Blowing soil Light sandy soils when carried away in clouds of dust. These are frequently seen in parts of East Anglia.

Bog plants These have two important features. They occur usually at water margins on wet land. Unlike aquatic plants, which are floating or submerged, they stand more or less out of any pond or river. *See* Chapter 5, Flowers and Foliage.

Bole A clear trunk or main stem measured from soil level to lowest limb or branch of a tree.

Bolting A condition which occurs in flower and vegetable crops when plants produce flowers and go to seed, often prematurely.

Bonsai The art of growing dwarfed and stunted trees in containers by root and stem pruning, and manipulating growth with wires, as originated in Japan.

Border Long narrow beds in greenhouses, also applied to strips of land outdoors, planted with flowers or shrubs.

Botrytis A fungus disease known also as Grey Mould. *See* Chapter 10, Problems.

Bottle gardening Cultivation in which plants are grown in glass or plastic jars, bottles or carboys. Salads and vegetable crops, usually harvested as seedlings can be grown in jars. Ornamental plants which are slow growing can be cultivated in clear-glass containers for decorative effect. *See* Chapter 5, Flowers and Foliage, *also* Chapter 9, Vegetables.

Bottle garden Any bottle or similar container when filled with growing plants or seedlings.

Bottom heat Any form of artificial heating which is applied at or just below root level, usually in greenhouses, frames and propagators. This is frequently employed to speed up the rooting of cuttings, and for forcing or growing early crops. The methods most commonly used include electric soil-warming cables, hot water pipes, and hot beds of fermenting manure. *See* Chapter 4, Greenhouses, Frames and Cloches.

Bottoming The provision of roughage, gravel or crocks in the bottom of boxes, pots or containers for drainage. *See also* Crocking.

Boulder clay A form of fine clay produced, transported and deposited by glacial action. Difficult to work as a soil, inclined to be cold and wet. It can be made fertile by draining, manuring and adding sand or fine gravel to improve aeration.

Bract A modified leaf structure which can be green and leaflike, or be highly coloured and take the place of flower petals, as with poinsettia. Bracts often cover and protect the true leaves and flower buds.

Break Applied to shoots or buds which arise from leaf axils, usually occurring

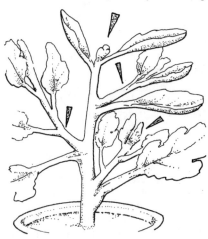

208 Breaks. Side shoots, *arrowed*, which develop from the main are known as breaks and arise below the tip or break bud, *arrowed top*.

after a main growing point has been removed, or naturally after a break bud (q.v.) has formed.

Break bud A terminal bud which if removed encourages breaks, shoots or buds to develop down the stem. Taking or removing a break bud is a common feature of the cultivation of early, mid-season and late varieties of chrysanthemum.

Broadcast Seeds sown broadcast are thinly and evenly scattered in a broad band or patch instead of in narrow rows or drills. Fertilisers when so applied are spread thinly and evenly in similar fashion.

Brown scale A pest often attacking peach trees and other plants. *See* Chapter 10, Problems.

Brutting An old but effective practice of inducing flowering and fruiting, achieved by a form of summer pruning. The new shoots or growths are bent over or 'brutted' and not cut off immediately. The bending reduces the sap flow to the tips causing the flower buds to develop close to the main stem. This enables a tree to still benefit from the manufacture of starch and sugars in the bent over shoots. The brutted ends are cut back in autumn or winter when the leaves have fallen. *See* Chapter 6, Fruits.

Bud An immature shoot, including leaves and/or flowers, which is tightly folded and protected by covering scales. A bud occurring at the extremity of a stem is referred to as terminal. A lateral bud is one which is behind or below the terminal, and usually arises from a leaf axil. Buds vary considerably in shape and size. Those on fruit trees such as apple and cherry can be rounded and plump or thin and narrow depending on whether they are fruit or growth buds. Buds can develop below soil level as in the 'eyes' or hollows in potato tubers, for example.

Budding A method of plant propagation which is a form of grafting. It involves inserting a bud, the scion, behind the rind of a rootstock, to eventually form a graft union, forming one plant out of two varieties – the shoot of one and the root of another. *See* Chapter 2, Propagation.

Bulb A globular food storage structure, consisting of a very short stem, tightly folded leaves and sometimes floral parts. The leaves or leaf are thickened and modified for food storage purposes. A bulb, unlike a corm, consists of successive layers of leaves or leaf scales which cover the stem and embryo flower.

Bulb forcing Growing bulbs to produce out-of-season crops using heat.

Bulbs naturalising Bulbs such as daffodils and snowdrops when planted in grass and left undisturbed to grow and flower naturally.

Bulb planter A tool used for planting bulbs in grass and bare soil.

Bulbil A small, partly-developed or immature bulb. These occur as off-sets at or below soil level. Bulbils can also develop in leaf axils as with some lilies, or in clusters at the end of a stem as in the case of *Allium fistulosum*.

Burr These appear as ugly patches of whiskery outgrowths and are sometimes seen on lime trees. Formerly used to describe the spiny fruits of horse chestnut.

Bush This form of tree has a bole or clear stem of not less than 300 mm (12 in) or more than 450 mm (30 in) in length, supporting a crown of branches.

Low, usually spreading, plants having one or more persistent stems at ground level are described as bush varieties.

Bushel A unit or measure of volume, equivalent to 36 litres (8 gal). A bushel box, formerly used for packing fruit or measuring quantities of soil, has depth and width 250 mm (10 in) by length 550 mm (22 in).

Cactus A succulent plant and member of the Cactaceae – the cactus family. Plants from this group characteristically have fleshy stems and leaves, often accompanied by sharp spines or thorns.

Calcareous Soils containing considerable quantities of chalk and supporting lime-loving plants like cabbage and clematis.

Calcifuge Plants which dislike or are intolerant of chalk or limestone such as azaleas and rhododendrons.

Calciphile or calciphilous Plants requiring chalk or limestone in the soil to promote good growth. Examples include gypsophila and dianthus.

Callus A protective layer which healthy plants produce to cover cut surfaces. Most cuttings form a layer of callus over the base or wound area. Many trees form a callus over the cut surface where branches have been cleanly cut off.

Calyx The protective outer tube-like whorl of sepals usually found in flowers. In buds these cover the petals but are later usually hidden under petals when the flowers are open.

Cambium A layer of cell tissue which lies between the bark or rind and the heart-wood of flowering and fruiting woody plants. The cambium tissue is vital to the success of rooting cuttings, budding and grafting as well as future growth. For a bud or graft to 'take' or form a proper graft union, the cambium layers of rootstock and scion need to be in direct contact. *See* Chapter 2, Propagation.

Cane A stem of raspberry, loganberry and blackberry which are also called cane fruits.

Also, woody stems of bamboo and related plants which when dried can be used to support plants.

Canker Woody stems and bark which are diseased and rotten or have sunken areas.

Also a disease of fruit trees. *See* Chapter 10, Problems.

Capillary action or attraction A natural phenomenon in which water can be held or rise against the force of gravity in soil or certain kinds of woven materials which act like a wick.

Capillary bench A greenhouse bench or staging which is constructed so that plants in containers can be watered from the base by capillary action (q.v.) of compost and/or special matting. Water is held in a reservoir on the bench, topped from a mains supply. A very simple installation can consist of a shallow watertight tray part filled with sand. This is filled with water, level with the surface of the sand. Small pots with holes in the bottom, when placed in the

tray, can absorb moisture from the wet sand. Water is added as necessary to replenish that which is lost from the sand.

Capillary matting Absorbent material used for watering by capillary action (q.v.).

Capsid A common insect pest. *See* Chapter 10, Problems.

Capsule Botanically, a seed case containing usually loose seeds which when mature and dry rattle when shaken.

Carnivorous Applied to plants which can trap and consume insects.

Carpel The combined stigma, style and ovary of a flower.

Catch crop A quick-growing crop taken between clearing one main crop and starting the next.

Caterpillar The larval stage of butterflies and moths, many of which are injurious to garden crops and plants. *See* Chapter 10, Problems.

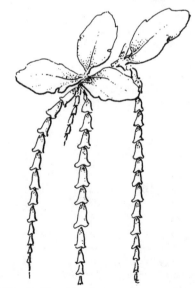

209 Catkins. The flowers of some plants, such as this garrya, take the form of catkins.

187

Catkin A form of flower spike, consisting of uni-sexual flowers with bracts but no petals. These are often pendulous, and wind pollinated.

Centipede A quick-moving, beneficial insect which has, unlike harmful millipedes, two legs per segment. *See* Chapter 10, Problems.

Chafer beetle The larval grubs and adults cause damage to garden plants by feeding on roots and stems as well as leaves and flowers. *See* Chapter 10, Problems.

Check Control, when referring to the use of insecticides and fungicides. A setback to growth or delayed progress.

Chimaera Plants of complex genetic composition, which occasionally gives rise to mutations (q.v.) or sports (q.v.).

Chinese layering *See* Air layering.

Chipping A process of filing, nicking or puncturing the hard outer case of certain seeds such as sweet peas to enable germination to occur readily.

Chlorophyll The green colouring matter found in plants which is essential to the manufacture of starches and sugars in the presence of sunlight.

Chlorosis A condition in which the leaves of plants are or become yellow due to mineral deficiencies, which can often arise on chalk or limestone alkaline soils. Sometimes termed yellows, this discoloration may also be caused by some virus diseases.

Chromosomes Microscopic bodies within plant and animal cells which control or regulate the inherent genetic or hereditary characteristics.

Chrysalis A pupa of butterfly or moth from which a perfect insect should emerge. This stage is intermediate between the grub or larva and the adult butterfly or moth.

Clamp A store made of straw and covered with soil, to overwinter various vegetables. Not much used now except on farms and smallholdings.

Classifications Plants and animals are grouped together according to their relative similarity. Plants for example are classified into natural orders or families. These in turn are sub-divided into genera of closely related species which are further divided in some cases into varieties and thence into forms.

Clay Soils which are described as this are 'greasy', sticky to work, and slow to drain when wet. When dry, clay soils set hard and shrink, leaving large cracks. Clay particles are very much smaller than those of sand. *See* Chapter 1, Site and Soil.

Clay burning The baking of clay over a slow burning fire. The granular baked material is then scattered over the ground.

Click Beetle The adult stage of wireworm, a troublesome soil-inhabiting pest. *See* Chapter 10, Problems.

Climbing plants These can be divided into two categories: self-clinging climbers such as ivy and those which need support like climbing roses. For culture *see* Chapter 5, Flowers and Foliage.

Cloche A low form of protection in which to cultivate out-of-season crops. Cloches of various designs are available. The continuous type, which forms a tunnel of glass or plastic is most popular. The usual methods of construction rely on wires or a light metal framework for support. For amateurs there are three main basic variations of the continuous cloche: the tent type; the barn; and the inverted 'U' tunnel. *See* Chapter 4, Greenhouses, Frames and Cloches.

Clone Genetically identical plants which have been raised vegetatively from a single parent.

Clove Usually a segment of a garlic

bulb, but also occasionally applied to a shallot segment.

Club Root A disease which can attack most members of the cabbage or brassica tribe. Also known as Anbury or Finger and Toe. *See* Chapter 10, Problems.

Clump A small group of trees or shrubs of the same or dissimilar type. A more common application is to a large mass of roots and stems of ageing and undisturbed herbaceous plants.

Coddle To spoil plants by providing unduly warm conditions, overfeeding and unnecessary attention generally.

Collar The base of a plant at or near soil level where stem and roots are joined.

Collar rot An infection of the collar which can be caused by various diseases and results in rotting and decay. *See* Chapter 10, Problems.

Colorado Beetle Striking orange and black striped insect, which attacks potatoes and is a notifiable pest. *See* Chapter 10, Problems.

Compost Any mixture of fertilisers, soil, peat, sand and/or other materials used as a rooting medium, especially for pot or container-grown plants. The mixture used in containers is referred to as potting compost and manure substitute is termed garden compost.

Also the process of making a farmyard manure substitute from vegetable matter waste through to the end product which is a crumbly, brown, earthy material. For details *see* Chapter 1, Site and Soil.

Compound Flowers, fruits and leaves which consist of several similar individual parts. A daisy, for example, has many florets or individual flowers which comprise a compound flower. Mixtures of fertilisers, chemicals and other materials are also described as compound.

Cone A fruit or hard woody seedcase

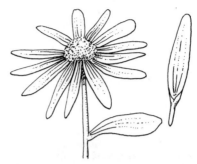

210 Compound flower. Some compound or composite flowers consist of several individual flowers or florets, *shown right*, in one head, like the rudbeckia here.

consisting of a central stem surrounded by scales which protect the usually flattish seeds. These are produced by conifers (q.v.).

Conifer A tree or shrub belonging to a large family of coniferous plants, most of which are evergreen. Most conifers bear cones, but a few produce berry-like fruits. *See* Chapter 7, Trees, Shrubs and Climbers.

Contact insecticide A chemical that can kill insects which are covered or coated with it. Contact insecticide, unlike stomach poisons, do not have to be eaten by the pest to be effective.

Container-grown Any plant which has been raised or grown in pots, tubs or other containers, but with special reference to trees and shrubs.

Cool House Greenhouse conditions usually with minimum temperatures of 4–10°C (40–50°F). *See* Chapter 4, Greenhouse, Frames and Cloches.

Cordon A trained form of plant, which is restricted usually to a single stem, for intensive cultivation. Apples, pears, and tomato plants can be grown in this fashion. Soft fruits such as gooseberries and red currants are sometimes grown as plants having two or even three stems known respectively as double or triple cordons. Cordon apples or pears are usually grown at an angle of about 45° and are referred to as oblique. *See* Chapter 6, Fruits.

Corky Bark Parts of a plant which are spongy and corklike.

Corm A swollen plant storage structure which consists of a thickened plate or stem base usually covered with a paper-like tissue. Buds and roots develop from the tops of corms. These, unlike bulbs, do not have well defined scales like lilies or layers like onions or daffodils.

Corolla The inner part of a flower consisting of an arrangement of petals often highly coloured.

Corona The trumpet or cup part of flowers such as daffodil or narcissus.

Corymb A flat topped head of flowers, held on stalks which arise progressively from a central stem.

Cotyledon True seed leaf or leaves, which are the first to appear and arise from within the seed. Monocotyledonous plants such as onions or grasses produce a single seed leaf, and dicotyledons have two.

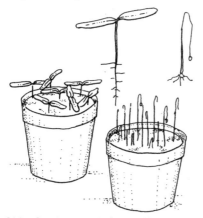

211 Cotyledons. *Left*: seedling dicotyledons, of tomato, showing two seed leaves, unlike the onions, *right*, which are monocotyledons.

Creeper Often applied to climbing plants, but more strictly reserved to describe plants which spread over the soil surface, putting down roots as they grow.

Crocking The process of placing crocks (q.v.) or roughage in containers. This is best carried out by placing concave pieces of crocks face down over the drainage or weep holes. A thin layer of crocks or similar material can then follow, finishing off with the seed or potting compost as required.

Crocks Usually pieces of broken flower pots which are placed in the bottom of containers to provide drainage.

Crop Yield of flowers, fruits, seeds, vegetables or other end result. Plants which are grown with the aim of producing food or flowers are so described in gardening terms.

Cross-fertilisation The fertilising of one flower with the pollen from another. This can be brought about naturally due to wind or insect activity or by human intervention.

Cross-pollination The transfer of pollen from one flower to the stigma of another, often on a different plant.

Crotch The upper angle between a branch and its main stem. A narrow crotch occurs with steeply ascending branches which are inclined to break, unlike those with a wide angle.

Crown A general term with various meanings. A clump of roots, and the collection of shoots or stems at ground level are two of these. Also a framework of branches, shoots or stems of plants or trees.

Crown bud A bud which is 'taken' or retained usually as in chrysanthemum growing. *See* Chapter 5, Flowers and Foliage.

Crown lifting or raising A form of pruning involving the removal of the

212 Crocking. *Left to right*: empty pot with drainage holes; clean crocks placed over holes; final potting, with thin layer of rough peat over the crocks before topping up with compost.

bottom branches of a tree. *See* Chapter 7, Trees, Shrubs and Climbers.

Crown gall A disease which appears as warty outgrowths on trees and woody plants at or near ground level. *See* Chapter 10, Problems.

Crown thinning A form of pruning which consists of thinning out the branches in the crown of a tree. *See* Chapter 7, Trees, Shrubs and Climbers.

Cuckoo-spit A descriptive name for the tell-tale symptoms of an attack by the Froghopper insect which afflicts many cultivated plants. *See* Chapter 10, Problems.

Cultivator A pronged tool used for breaking up and loosening soil.

Curd The white centre of cauliflower, broccoli or suchlike, consisting of masses of immature flower buds.

Cutworm Any soil pest which eats through the tender stems of seedlings at soil level. *See* Chapter 10, Problems.

Cutting back Pruning, especially when new growths are shortened by more than half their length.

Cuttings Pieces of living plants which have been prepared or are being used to increase or propagate plants. These may

consist of leaves, stems, shoots and roots, or parts of these. *See* Chapter 2, Propagation.

Cylinder mower A type of lawn mower which relies on a rotating cylinder of knives to cut the grass.

Damping down Syringing walls and paths in a greenhouse to increase humidity of the air. *See* Chapter 4, Greenhouses, Frames and Cloches.

Damping off A common type of disease which affects seedlings. *See* Chapter 10, Problems.

Damping overhead Similar to damping down, but the plants are syringed also to replenish moisture and increase air humidity. *See* Chapter 3, Plant Care.

Dead-heading The removal of dead or faded flowers. *See* Chapter 5, Flowers and Foliage.

De-barking Removing the bark from fencing posts, plant supports and rustic poles. This eliminates possible hiding places for pests and simplifies the process of applying preservative to prevent decay.

Deciduous Plants, trees and shrubs which shed their leaves in the autumn.

Decorative Some classes of double-flowered chrysanthemums and dahlias which are neither incurving, reflexed nor like pompons.

Decumbent Plants which grow along the ground but produce up-turned tips.

Defoliation A practice used on greenhouse tomato plants, consisting of the removal of the lower leaves as fruits ripen. *See* Chapter 3, Plant Care.

Determinate Botanically, plants such as bush tomatoes where the growing point ends in a flower truss unlike greenhouse or standard indeterminate varieties. Determinate varieties are unable to grow tall because the resultant side-shoots or laterals behave in the same way as the main stem.

Devils Coach Horse The popular name for a black beetle which characteristically arches its back, raising the hind quarters in the air. This strange-looking insect devours many garden pests such as larvae, slugs and snails.

Dibber or dibble A tool used for making holes for setting out plants and large seeds. *See* Chapter 11, Tools and equipment.

Dicotyledon A plant which has two seed leaves in the seedling stage. Examples include lettuce and radish. *See* Cotyledon.

Die-back Diseases known by this name cause shoots and branches to die back or collapse on trees, shrubs and other plants. *See* Chapter 10, Problems.

Digging This is one of the basic fundamental operations in soil management. In essence this task consists of turning over and breaking up the ground to improve soil aeration. The usual hand tools include a spade and fork. *See* Chapter 1, Site and Soil.

Diploid A plant which normally has two sets of chromosomes. This characteristic is important to the fertilisation and fruit set of some varieties of apples, pears and cherries in particular. The

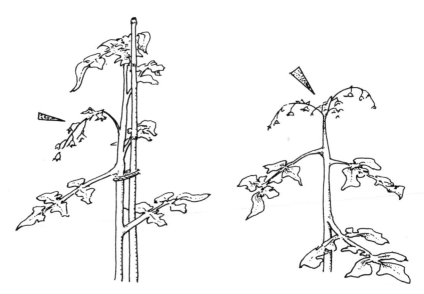

213 Determinate. Bush type tomatoes, unlike tall kinds, produce growing points which end in flowers, *shown right*, and are referred to as determinate. *Left*: a tall or indeterminate type.

number of sets of chromosomes a plant possesses can often directly affect the success or otherwise of plant breeding programmes.

Disbudding The removal of side buds to leave only the terminal or tip buds to develop into large individual blooms.

Disc The flattened or slightly domed 'eye' or centre of daisy-type flowers, which consists of numerous florets.

Disease A true ailment of this type is infectious, unlike disorders, and can, for example with moulds and mildews, be spread from plant to plant.

Dissemination Dispersal, usually of seeds and spores.

Divot A piece of turf, often of irregular shape, which has been displaced usually on soft, wet ground during sporting activities. Frequently referred to in connection with golf-course greens management. *See* Chapter 8, Turf.

Dormant A condition of plants or their respective parts, including seeds, roots and shoots, during their resting period when active growth is at a standstill. Leafless but healthy, living deciduous trees and shrubs in winter are said to be dormant as are seeds and buds before leaves and shoots appear.

Dot plants Specimen or individual plants which are dotted about in bedding schemes, usually to provide height, colour and contrast. Standard fuchsias and pelargoniums are popular plants for this purpose.

Double flowers Applied to blooms which form a mass of petals, and where stamens and other essential floral parts are either concealed or absent. This type of flower is often sterile but retains its petals longer than single flowers making it most useful for display purposes. Carnations, chrysanthemums and roses provide examples of this feature.

Double cordons *See* Cordons.

Double digging *See* Chapter 1, Site and Soil.

Double glazing Greenhouses which have a double skin of glass or plastic with an air space between are described as double glazed.

Drainage The disposal of surplus water, allowing air and oxygen to permeate the rooting medium.
Applied also to movement of cold air.

Drainage system Any arrangement of pits, pipes, ditches or water courses which serves to divert water away from a particular piece of ground. *See* Chapter 1, Site and Soil.

Drawn Plants which are tall and spindly usually in consequence of overcrowding, high temperature and poor light conditions.

Dressing The application of materials such as manure, fertilisers and lime to soil. A base dressing is generally applied before planting, to be followed by top dressing later to give plants a boost during the growing period.

Drill Normally straight shallow furrows, drawn out in readiness for seed sowing, preferably on well-prepared land. Narrow V-shaped drills are used for small seeds, while those that are broad and flat bottomed are more suitable for peas. Also used to describe the process of seed sowing in drills. *See* Chapter 2, Propagation.

Drupe A botanical term for fleshy fruits like plums with hard, stone seeds.

Duster Usually a simple device to apply a thin coating of fungicidal or insecticidal dust or similar finely-divided dry material to plants.

Dutch light A type of frame-light consisting of one large glass sheet in a wooden frame. This form of coverage is very popular particularly with commercial growers. The approximate dimensions are 1.5 m (5 ft) long by 750 mm (2½ ft) wide.

Earthing up Drawing earth around the stems of plants like celery in order to blanch or whiten them.

Also to mound up soil over developing potato tubers to prevent greening due to light, and lessen the chances of infection from potato blight.

Earthworms Soil-inhabiting worms usually found in abundance in manure or compost which improve natural soil drainage.

Earwig A common insect pest of many flower crops. *See* Chapter 10, Problems.

Edging A term with various meanings. The act of clipping grass edges around a lawn using edging shears, or straightening the edges by cutting the vertical edges of turf with an edging iron.

Also plants or materials used to divide flower beds and borders from paths, drives or lawns. Low growing plants such as box and bergenia and bedding subjects such as lobelia and French marigolds can be used as edging plants. *See* Chapter 5, Flowers and Foliage. Kerbs of brick or concrete around flower beds can also be used.

Eelworms Small worms which can cause considerable damage to many garden plants. *See* Chapter 10, Problems.

Elliptical The shape or outline of leaves, fruits or flower beds which are broadly acorn-shaped – oblong with rounded ends of equal radius, in the form of an ellipse.

Embryo A young plant or living organism in the very early stages of development, for example a seed before it becomes fully independent and self-supporting. An embryo garden plant consists of a radicle or embryonic root, a growing point, and seed leaf or leaves.

Endemic Plants which are native to or occur in large numbers in a specific locality or area.

Entire Leaves or petals which have smooth edges that are unbroken by serrations.

Ephemeral A short-lived plant. Weeds, such as groundsel and chickweed are so described, and several generations can arise in a single year.

Epidermis The outer skin or tissues of, for example, leaves and shoots.

Epiphyte A plant which can grow perched on or suspended from rocks, trees or similar positions, putting out aerial roots. This type of plant derives moisture and nutriment from the atmosphere, unlike most land plants which grow in soil or crevices among rocks. Some orchids are epiphytes.

Eradicant Used to describe some forms of fungicide which under certain circumstances can kill the invading fungus which causes disease on a plant. Most materials are, however, preventive in action. *See* Chapter 10, Problems.

Ericaceous Applied to heath plants, heathers and members of the heather family Ericaceae.

Escape A garden or cultivated plant which has become established in wild, natural or uncultivated land. Forget-me-not and poppies are examples.

Espalier A form of trained tree which consists of a central trunk and stem, having pairs of horizontal branches opposite each other. Apples and pears are often trained in this manner when grown against a wall or fence. *See* Chapter 6, Fruit.

Etiolate Plants grown in poor light conditions with pale or white stems and leaves. Shoots which are grown in semi-darkness and are long, thin and spindly with pale leaves.

Evaporation The loss of moisture from plants, soil or ponds into the atmosphere due to the drying action of sun, wind and air currents.

Evergreen Used to describe trees,

shrubs and plants which retain their foliage during the winter, unlike deciduous trees that shed their leaves in autumn.

Everlasting Flowers and individual members or a group of plants which retain their shape and colours when cut, dried and kept in dry conditions. Helichrysum, gnaphalium and statice can be treated in this manner. Sometimes referred to as 'Immortelles'.

Exhibition Varieties of plants which are grown for or are most suitable for show or display purposes, as distinct from average bedding, garden or culinary purposes.

Eye Applied to underdeveloped or dormant buds occurring anywhere on plants, including stems and the sunken buds in potato tubers.

The discs in the centre of some single flowers, such as asters, are also described as eyes.

Fairy Rings A disease affecting turf, appearing first as circles of lush green, later dying out often to leave dead patches. *See* Chapter 10, Problems.

Falls Applied to the pendulous outer petals of flowers such as iris.

Fallow An ancient practice now little used except for cleaning land of weeds before making lawns. In essence, it consists in clearing all vegetation from a plot of ground, which is then hoed and cultivated to kill any weeds while the land is not carrying any crops. *See* Winter fallow.

Family Botanically a group of genera, each of which has similarities with other members within the family. In gardening usage this is applied also to a genus which contains many species. Also loosely used to describe groups of varieties within species.

Family tree A fruit tree consisting of a root stock with two or more scion varieties, removing the need to plant two trees in confined space. This is necessary where one variety of fruit tree needs the pollen of another to set fruit.

Fancy Flowers which are variegated or have irregular colour markings, not usually found on standard or recognised types such as show pansies.

Farina A dust-like or mealy covering on stems, leaves and petals, commonly occurring on some primulas. This gives plants a bluish, whitish or yellowy effect. *Cf* Bloom.

Fasciation A condition in plants in which a number of leaves and stems in particular grow abnormally into one, forming a wide, flat ribbon-like shoot.

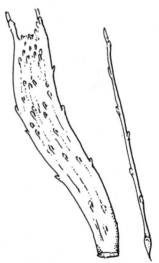

214 Fasciation. *Left*: a multiple stem of willow with many buds, compared with a healthy normal shoot, *right*.

Cucumbers and forsythias occasionally show these symptoms which do not appear to be infectious though the precise nature of the condition remains obscure.

Fascicle A bundle or tuft of leaves or flowers. The flower head of Sweet William, for example, is thus described.

Fastigate Used to describe trees which are narrow in relation to their height, and columnar in shape. Examples of this form include the Incense Cedar and Lombardy Poplar.

Feathered Young trees such as whips or maidens which have shoots growing from their main stems. These feathers are thinned out or removed as soon as an initial framework of branches or crown is formed.

Feather-veined Leaves in which the veins all emerge from the central mid-rib.

Fencing A division or boundary constructed of concrete, metal or timber. Fences consist usually of vertical and horizontal members. Common forms of fencing include chestnut-cleft, close boarded, interwoven, metal rail, palisade, post and rail, and wattle hurdle.

Ferns A large group of foliage plants which can be increased by means of spores, unlike true flowering plants that set seeds. *See* Chapter 5, Flowers and Foliage.

Fertile Plants and flowers which are capable of producing good seed or fruit.
Also soils that are capable of or in the process of producing flowers, fruits and vegetables. *See* Chapter 1, Site and Soil.

Fertilisation The fusion or union of male and female generative cells which results in the formation of seeds and fruits in the case of flowering plants. *See* Pollination.

Fertiliser A material which contains concentrated plant nutrients. *See* Chapter 1, Site and Soil.

Fibre Threads or strands of woody or semi-woody tissue. Fibrous soils contain quantities of root fibre, which serves to prevent compaction. Fibrous peat consisting of roots and moss strands with a minimum of dusty or earth-like material.

Field capacity The water retentive property of soils. It refers to the maximum amount of water that can be retained without being lost through drainage. Heavy or clay loams have a higher field capacity than sandy or gravelly soils.

Filament Usually applied botanically to a fine stalk by which anthers (q.v.) are supported or suspended. Anthers and filaments combine to make up stamens (q.v.).

Fimbriate Any part of a plant, such as leaves, petals and sepals, having fringed margins.

Finger-and-Toe Also known as Anbury and Club Root. *See* Chapter 10, Problems.

Fir Often applied to coniferous trees in general but more specifically reserved for members of the genus Abies.

Firmer Usually a rectangular or circular piece of metal or wood used to firm and level the compost in boxes or pots before seed sowing or pricking out.

Flake Broad streaks of colour as found in some old-fashioned roses and carnations.

Flesh The soft or edible part of fruits such as apples, peaches or pears.

Flora A list or community of plants, usually related to a place, region or time.

Flore-pleno A botanical term applied to double or semi-double flowers consisting of numerous petals, often with the stamens reduced in number or absent. Carnations, dahlias and roses provide examples of this feature.

Floret A small individual flower, such as is found on compound flowers of the Compositae, occurring in chrysanthemums, dahlias and daisies for example. Blooms consisting of numerous florets are referred to as compound flowers.

Florist Cultivated as distinct from wild flowers.

Also one who deals with flowers or plants.

Flower A blossom of a plant which is necessary for the production of seeds and normally consists of the following various parts. Unopened flowers, in the bud stage, are protected by small leaf-like sepals, usually green, but sometimes coloured and known collectively as the calyx. Next the corolla, consisting of the usually colourful petals, opens to reveal the stamens, the male pollen-producing parts. These include the anthers or pollen sacs and the filaments or stalks which attach the anthers to the flower. In the centre is one or more ovaries, each topped by a stigma with a style situated between the two. A stigma, style and ovary are collectively termed a pistil. Plants such as marrow and cucumber produce male and female flowers. The male differs from the female in that stamens are present and the pistil is absent.

Flower drying Any process of removing moisture from and preserving flowers, usually with the retention of the original shape and colour of blooms. Methods used include hanging some kinds of cut flowers upside-down in a shaded, airy place and placing others in containers with drying materials such as silica gel.

Fluid sowing A technique of mixing seeds in a gelatinous fluid and sowing both in drills outdoors. This method can give seeds some added protection and ensure quick germination.

Fluorescent tube A gas-filled glass or similar tube which can be used as a form of electric lighting under which plants can be raised, grown or otherwise illuminated.

Foliage Leaves or leafage as distinct from flowers.

Foliage plants A subject which is

cultivated primarily for its leaves, especially those which are decorative or ornamental. *See* Chapter 5, Flowers and Foliage.

Foliar feeding Preparing and spraying a dilute solution of balanced fertiliser to garden plants. Care should be exercised because some plants can easily be damaged by fertilisers applied in strong solutions or strong sunlight. Droplets of moisture act as a magnifying glass in the sun resulting in severe scorching of plants.

Follicle Botanically, a fruit pod or seed case which opens down one side only when ripe. These can be found among delphiniums and aquilegia.

Forcing A form of cultivation in which many kinds of plants are induced to grow and mature well in advance of their natural season. Rhubarb, lettuce and bulbous flowering plants are usual subjects.

Fork A type of pronged handtool which is made to various forms and designs and has many uses. Varieties are suitable for digging, loosening compacted soil, lifting plants and weeds as well as handling manure, compost and vegetable waste. *See* Chapter 11, Tools and equipment.

Tree stems and branches which divide into two or more growths of roughly equal vigour are said to fork.

Form The smallest group of plants in botanical classification (q.v.), a sub-variety of a variety.

Also used to describe the outline or shape of a plant.

Formal Gardens of a particular style, in which the paths and planting are laid out in regular geometrical pattern, in sympathy more with architecture than nature.

Formalin A soil steriliser also known as formaldehyde. *See* Chapter 10, Problems.

Frame A low form of structure, tradi-

197

tionally made of timber and/or brick, and covered with hinged or sliding 'lights'. Present-day types are constructed of metals or other materials as well as timber and brick. Cold frame is the term used for those which are unheated except by natural sun warmth. A Paris frame consists of one frame inside another, and which proves very useful particularly for rooting more difficult cuttings. Frames can be heated by pipes, warming cables or on hot beds of fermenting straw. Frames can be successfully used as a substitute for small greenhouses for the purpose of raising plants, for forcing and cultivating low-growing crops. *See* Chapter 4, Greenhouses, Frames and Cloches.

Friable Crumbly soils that break down into a fine tilth.

Fringed Applied to fimbriated (q.v.) leaves, sepals and petals, having bristled or twisted margins.

Frond A finely divided and feathery leaf of ferns, but also applied to some palm leaves.

Frost Used variously to describe weather conditions when the temperature is at or below 0°C (32°F) and an action or process resulting from frost. Degrees of frost are a measure of frost intensity.

Fruit In botanical terms a fertilised and developed ovary. In appearance this may appear as a hard dry capsule, a pod seed case containing seeds, a fleshy fruit either encasing a stone or seeds or in which seeds are embedded.

Edible fruits are divided into two categories: culinary, those which are cooked or used in preserves; and dessert, which are eaten raw as a sweet. *See* Chapter 6, Fruits.

Fruit setting sprays A liquid hormone preparation which when sprayed on to tomato flowers, for example, assists the formation of fruit that otherwise might not be produced.

Fruiting bodies The spore-producing heads of mushrooms and toadstools for example.

Fumigation A means of controlling insect pests and some fungus diseases by the use of vapourising materials or smokes containing the active ingredients.

Fungicide A chemical substance which can kill fungi, but also applied to materials which prevent fungal growth and development.

Fungus (pl. Fungi) Members of a large group of non-flowering plants, of which moulds and mildews, mushrooms and toadstools are fairly representative. There are a great many varieties of fungi, but these can be classed into three types according to method of nutrition. Saprophytic fungi such as mushrooms live on dead and decaying matter. Parasitic types which live in or on growing plants and crops include the disease-causing fungi. Symbiotic fungi about which relatively little is known live on or in plants, usually on the roots for the mutual benefit of both fungus and host. Many trees, particularly conifers and certain shrubs, derive great benefit from an association with this type of fungus.

Furrowed Stems and trunks which are so described have parallel, longitudinal grooves running up and down.

FYM A widely-used abbreviation for farm-yard manure.

Gall An abnormal growth which can occur on almost any part of a plant, on leaves, shoots, roots and flowers. The Big bud of blackcurrants or leaf galls on oak, warts on potatoes, or swollen clubbed roots of cabbage are all types of gall. The first two are caused by insects and the others by fungi. Many galls cause little harm, but some, such as Big bud and Club root can be damaging. The swelling or gall is often caused initially by some form of irritation or damage by insects, disease organisms, wind or animals. *See* Chapter 10, Problems.

Garden An area of land, usually close to a dwelling in which flowers, fruits or vegetables are grown. The two main types are formal and informal. Formal gardens are usually symmetrical, of regular pattern with plants often in straight lines, with clipped hedges and straight paths. The informal style consists of plants and planting arranged and grown in a natural unfettered manner, but not necessarily wild and overgrown.

Some well-known kinds of garden include the busy person's garden which is easily maintained; the children's garden or play space which should be colourful, safe, practical and meet the changing needs of its users; the flower garden which should provide colour and scent, and in shaded situations can be a foliage garden.

Flowers and foliage often seem to equate with front gardens, which can be an immense asset to the value of a house while flowers, fruits and vegetables for use in the home are more likely to be grown inconspicuously in the rear garden these days, instead of in separate gardens.

The unfenced open-plan garden is a sign of the times we live in. Rock gardens and those set aside for roses are still popular. The traditional cottage gardens with their old world flowers like columbine, hollyhocks and pinks can still be seen but are fast disappearing. New water gardens today are likely to consist of a formal pool in a flower garden except for those of a favoured few who may be lucky enough to have space and a stream to create something more ambitious.

Genera (singular genus). Botanically these are plant groups consisting of closely related species.

Germination The first stage of the awakening or activating of seeds into growth. This is said to have taken place when shoots and/or roots appear on or from seeds.

Glabrous Leaves and stems which are devoid of hairs and are smooth.

Gland A specialised cell or cells, many of which contain or secrete various substances of an aromatic, fragrant, oily or waxy nature.

Glaucous Blue-green leaves and stems, often with a fine waxy coating of bloom and devoid of hairs.

Globose Trees and shrubs which have a round spherical crown or head of branches.

Glutinous Resembling glue, often of a sticky resin found on Chestnut in spring, for example.

Also used to describe the qualities of wet clay.

Gradient The degree of incline or slope of ground level. Gradients steeper than 1 in 3 – a rise or fall of say 1 m ($3\frac{1}{4}$ ft) in a horizontal distance of 3 m (10 ft), are best avoided when levelling.

Grader A wheeled machine with horizontal blade used for levelling.

Also any device for sorting produce by size.

Grading The process of sorting garden produce such as flowers, fruits and vegetables according to size and quality, and placing these into assorted containers.

Also the levelling of ground, usually the final smoothing out of humps and hollows, using a grader, blade or lute.

Grafting A means of propagation of plants consisting of uniting the roots of one plant – the rootstock – with the shoot of another – the scion.

Graft hybrid A plant, branch or shoot arising from a scion, which combines the characters and qualities of both scion and rootstock. × Laburnocytisus, a graft hybrid between laburnum and

Cytisus, has the habit of growth of laburnum but produces flowers like those of *Cytisus purpureus*.

Grafting wax A sealing compound used to cover the junction between scion and rootstock, to exclude air and prevent drying out until the union is complete.

Grasses A large group of monocotyledonous plants most of which have long narrow strap shaped leaves. In gardening grasses are classified mainly into ornamental and turf. Ornamental grasses are usually allowed to grow and produce their inflorescences (q.v.) without hindrance. Turf grasses are usually mown to create a neat green sward.

Grease banding An operation normally carried out in autumn on fruit trees which consists either of applying a band of special material or grease around each trunk. The purpose of this is to trap the larvae of pests. *See* Chapter 10, Problems.

Green bud A stage of development of apples and pears when the flower buds are visible but not showing flower colour. This is an important time in the fruit growing calendar when certain sprays should be applied to control pests and diseases. *See* Chapter 10, Problems.

Greenhouse A walk-in rigid structure covered with glass or plastic. Those having two skins of glass or plastic are described as double glazed. *See* Chapter 4, Greenhouses, Frames and Cloches.

Green manuring Also known as Sheet composting. This is a practice to build up soil fertility, particularly where FYM, garden compost or organic matter are in short supply. It involves growing a quick crop of mustard or Italian rye grass proprietary mixtures and digging the crop into the ground as a manure substitute.

Grit Fine granular material, which is used in cutting and potting composts, and consists of particles coarser than sand, 2 mm ($\frac{1}{2}$ in) and over.

Growing cabinet A growing case which is lit by artificial lighting for the purpose of cultivating plants out of season.

Growing rooms Indoor space which is illuminated, well insulated and artificially heated, providing a high degree of control for precision in growing.

Growth rings The trunks of certain trees when sawn down expose a series of rings, which are small in the middle and increase in size until the bark or rind is reached. The age of a tree can be fairly accurately gauged by counting the number of rings present.

Ground cover A term increasingly used in recent years. Usually low growing shrubs and perennial plants. These are planted to provide a dense undergrowth between trees and buildings and smother any weeds.

Also, loosely, any plants or planting which provide a green mantle over the ground.

Grub Many forms of larvae, and caterpillars of various butterflies, moths and beetles.

Grubbing A term used among commercial growers, but now increasingly used among gardeners, referring to the clearing out of old trees, roots and woody vegetation.

Guano A form of concentrated organic manure obtained originally from the dried droppings of sea birds. Now applied also to processed fish manure.

Gumming A condition which can occur in many plants where a sticky exudation of resin or gum occurs. In plums and cherries this is quite often prevalent. *See* Chapter 10, Problems.

Gypsophilous Chalk or lime-loving. Plants, which grow and thrive under these conditions.

Habit The natural features of a plant, its size, shape, growth and time of flowering.

Habitat A place or region in which certain plants grow and thrive in the wild state. Also the nature and type of ground in which the plants are found, such as wet or dry, acid or chalk, or woodland or moorland.

Ha-Ha A wall, hedge or fence situated in the bottom of a wide ditch which provides an effective boundary. A well made Ha-Ha should be out of sight when viewed across the top of the ditch. A device formerly much used as a fence to keep out animals especially near large houses, where space allowed.

Half-hardy Plants which are unable to survive outside during winter without protection, or need a longer growing season to develop or flower. The group of plants to which this term is applied include annuals, biennials, and perennials. *See* Chapter 10, Flowers and Foliage.

Half-standard A term used for plants having a shorter length of clear stem than full standards. The length of clear stem varies in the case of a half-standard tree from 1.1 m–1.4 m (3½–4½ ft). With half standard roses this varies from 750 mm–1.2 m (2½–4 ft). Half-standard fuchsias, pelargoniums or other specialist plants should conform to the sizes approved by the appropriate national or local organisation when grown for exhibition.

Hand light A portable cloche, having four sides instead of two only as with the continuous type. Hand lights are particularly useful where plants need individual protection.

Hanging basket A wire, plastic or other form of container in which plants are grown for the effect when suspended from a bracket attached to a wall or ceiling. Very attractive when well made and placed over doorways and arches. Suitable plants for this purpose include many half-hardy annuals and perennials. The baskets should contain a suitable potting or other compost. *See* Chapter 5, Flowers and Foliage.

Hard pan A ground condition in which a compacted or hard layer of soil or material impedes the movement of water or roots. This often occurs where digging or other cultivations are carried out to the same depth year after year. It can also develop where quantities of iron or aluminium accumulate in the ground to form a cement-like layer.

Hardening off A process of gradually conditioning young plants in stages from heated surroundings, as in a propagator or greenhouse, to unheated covered frames and then to open-air positions.

Hardy Any plant which can grow and survive normal outdoor conditions without undue harm the year round. Mild or sheltered situations allow many plants which are border line between hardy and tender, to be grown outside without harm. The converse is also true. Exposed sites on high ground and east or north facing slopes are suitable only for really hardy plants.

Harvesting In gardening terms this includes the cutting, picking, pulling, lifting, drying and storing of flowers, fruits and vegetables. *See* Chapter 5, Flowers and Foliage; Chapter 6, Fruits, and Chapter 9, Vegetables.

Haulm The stems and foliage of crops such as peas, beans and potatoes, but excluding the pods, fruits or seeds for which the plants are grown.

Haw The fruits of hawthorn of any species or variety of Crataegus (quickthorn or may).

Head Usually reserved for a compact cluster of florets or flowers as with chrysanthemums, herbaceous phlox or roses.

Also the crown or framework of branches of trees.

Heading down Cutting back the main branches of a tree to reduce the size of the crown. This consists of shortening all the main branches close to the trunk, unlike crown thinning (q.v.) in which a few only are cut out leaving the remaining boughs uncut.

Heart rot One or more diseases which affect the centre portion or heart of root crops such as beetroot, turnips and swedes.

Also applied to tree trunks which are rotting or rotten.

Heart wood The mature hard core nearest the centre or mid-point of a trunk or branch.

Heating In gardening usually applied to forms of artificial heating used for heating greenhouses and frames. *See* Chapter 4, Greenhouses, Frames and Cloches.

Hedge A continuous row or double line of shrubs planted to form boundaries, providing colour, shelter, and forming a physical barrier to keep out animals. For details and suitable plants *see* Chapter 7, Trees, Shrubs and Climbers.

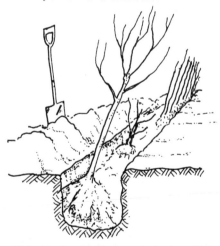

214 Heeling in. Trees and shrubs which cannot be planted in their final positions immediately can be kept in good condition by covering their roots with soil.

Heel A type of cutting which may be soft, semi-ripe, or hardwood and have a piece of older stem attached at the point where the shoot was detached from the parent plant.

Heeling in A process for temporarily 'storing' plants until they can be planted in their final positions. This practice involves digging a hole or trench large enough to take the roots of the plants being 'stored', placing them in the cavity and covering the roots with soil.

Hep The fruit or seed case of roses, though hip is the term more commonly used now.

Herb Botanically, a plant without a woody stem. In garden usage, this is almost exclusively applied to any plant which is used for culinary or medicinal purposes. The group of plants known as herbs may be annual, biennial or perennial. *See* Chapter 9, Vegetables and Herbs.

Herb garden An area or bed used mainly for growing culinary or pot herbs.

Herbaceous Plants which normally die down in winter without forming a permanent framework of branches.

Herbaceous border A flower bed or area which is primarily used for growing decorative or ornamental plants, with the emphasis on herbaceous perennials such as lupins, delphiniums and phlox.

Herbarium A case or receptacle for dried plants, but often used to refer to a collection of dried plants.

Hermaphrodite Botanically, a flower which contains or possesses both male and female parts.

Heterophyllous Plants, trees or shrubs which carry two or more types or shapes of foliage. Many conifers including junipers have juvenile and adult foliage as does eucalyptus. Sometimes these are referred to as dimorphic.

Hide-bound *See* Bark-bound.

Hilum The mark left on a seed of peas or beans, for example, at the point of attachment to the pod or seed case.

Hoary Plant stems or leaves which are thickly covered with whitish hair or down.

Hoe A hand tool used primarily for soil surface cultivations to kill weeds and loosen or stir compacted ground. *See* Chapter 11, Tools and Equipment.

Hollow-tined fork A hand implement similar to a garden fork, but with hollow prongs. *See* Chapter 11, Tools and Equipment, *also* Hollow tining.

Hollow tining A turf care operation in which narrow cores of earth are removed from grass areas. This task can be carried out by means of a Hollow-tined fork (*q.v.*) or machine. *See* Chapter 8, Turf.

Honey-dew A form of sticky secretion which is found on plants usually where aphids (*q.v.*) or greenfly are present.

Hoof and horn A concentrated organic fertiliser which is derived from the remains of animals. It supplies nitrogen for plants when broken down in the soil by bacteria.

Hook A term used for the curved spines or thorns found on some plants such as blackberry.

Also a hand tool with curved blade for cutting grass and weeds. *See* Chapter 11, Tools and Equipment.

Hop manure A by-product of brewing which can be used as a bulky organic manure. Contains little in the way of food value to plants. *See* Chapter 1, Site and Soil.

Horn A term used occasionally to describe any appendage or protuberance from plants which resembles the horn of an animal.

Also the base petals of linaria or aquilegia sometimes called spurs.

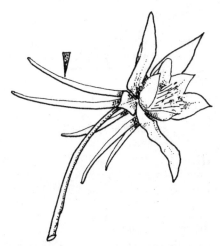

215 Horns or spurs. Flowers such as this aquilegia produce rolled or tubular petals, *arrowed*, which are horn or spur shaped.

Horse manure A popular, but increasingly scarce form of manure consisting of straw and occasionally peat litter, mixed with horse dung and urine. *See* Chapter 1, Site and Soil.

Hose-in-hose A condition in flowers in which the corolla or petals are duplicated and appear as if one bloom is coming out of another. Primulas and polyanthus occasionally show examples of this state which is more common with tubular flowers than those of other shapes.

Host A plant which supports or is affected by a pest or disease parasite. Parasitic plants like mistletoe or dodder need a host for their survival.

Hot-bed A layer of fermenting manure or vegetable material used as a means of undersoil heating for growing plants. *See* Chapter 1, Site and Soil.

Humilis Sometimes placed after a plant name to denote a lowly or low-growing form.

Humus A dark brown residue of granular or crumb form resulting from the decomposition of vegetable remains and animal manure.

Also friable, crumbly, sweet-smelling material found in garden compost or manure heaps. *See* Chapter 1, Site and Soil.

Husk An outer covering, usually hard and dry, surrounding some seeds and fruits, commonly occurring among nuts of various kinds.

Hybrid A seed or progeny resulting from the fertilisation of a flower with pollen from a genetically different plant. A cross-bred type which is not identical with or even closely similar to either parent. *See* Chapter 2, Propagation.

Hybrid vigour Progeny which arise from crossing plants of differing characters and are more vigorous than their parents.

Hydrophytes Plants which live and thrive in water or wet conditions.

Ichneumon Flies A group of insects which are highly beneficial to gardeners because they parasitise harmful pests.

Immortelle A flower or group of plants grown for their usually straw-like blooms which when cut and dried retain their colour. These flowers which are also known as Everlastings include helichrysums, statice and acrocliniums. They are very popular for winter decoration. *See* Chapter 5, Flowers and Foliage.

Immune Botanically, complete resistance to, or freedom from, pests or disease. Certain potato varieties, for example, are immune to Wart disease.

Impatient A term used less than formerly, plants that are intolerant of even small variations in temperature or moisture. Saintpaulias for example, resent water on the leaves and pelargoniums can quickly succumb to overwatering.

Imperfect Flowers or parts of plants which are incomplete or lack certain organs. Flowers without stamens are examples of this. *See* Perfect flower.

Impervious Clay soils which do not allow water to drain away.

Impregnate A condition which occurs when chemicals and fertiliser become mixed with soil or other materials. Soils which are saturated with a solution of chemical steriliser are said to be impregnated.

Inarching A method of propagation, also known as 'grafting by approach', in which both stock and scion are grown side by side after grafting. The plants are grown on their own roots until a graft union has formed.

Inarticulate Botanically, stems or shoots without joints.

Incinerator A form of receptacle in which garden refuse is burnt. They are usually constructed of metal in the form of a perforated box or wire bin on legs.

Incised Leaves with deep and regularly toothed margins.

Incomplete Flowers lacking some essential part such as stamens or stigma. *See* Imperfect.

Incrustation A visible film or covering of lime, grit or chemical on the surface of leaves.

Incubation A term often used by scientists in connection with the development of disease spores and the eggs of insects. It refers to the period of time which elapses between the depositing of a spore or egg and the growth of fungus bacteria or the emergence of an insect.

Incurved Flowers, such as some chrysanthemums, where the florets or petals curve upwards towards the centre.

Indefinite Plants of a climbing or trailing habit which do not stop stem elongation at a pre-determined height or length, but continue to grow. Greenhouse varieties of tomato, unlike outdoor bush types, continue their upward growth in good conditions and are so described.

Indeterminate Plants which produce flowers from the leaf axils instead of terminally at the growing tip. *See* Indefinite.

Indigenous Plants native to or originating from a place, region or particular soil type.

Infection An area of plant or plants affected by disease.

Infectious The capacity of a disease to infect or transmit harmful organisms from an affected plant to another which is healthy.

Infertile Plants fail to produce fertile seed for various reasons. Pollen may not be produced; it may occur in the wrong place at the wrong time, or be unsuitable as a fertiliser, as occurs with some kinds of fruits.

Inflorescence The arrangement or grouping of flowers on a plant. There are two main types, known as determinate and indeterminate (q.v.). The first forms a flower or cluster at the growing point or lip. Those of the second type are produced in or from the leaf axils. Some of the more usual arrangements are catkins, corymbs, cymes, panicles, plumes, racemes, umbels, and whorls. The shape of an inflorescence is a useful aid to plant identification.

Informal Plants and flowers used for example in floral arrangements where the effect and attractiveness is not conditioned by rigid symmetry and regularity. *See* Garden.

Inorganic Strictly, a substance which contains no carbon in its composition. Fertilisers derived from rocks or chemical salts without any animal or plant remains are examples of this type of material.

Insect A term used loosely in gardening for any small creature such as flies, caterpillars, grubs and beetles.

A true adult insect characteristically has a body in three sections, consisting of head, thorax and abdomen, and six legs. One or two pairs of thoracic wings complete the main features.

Most members of this group pass through three or four stages during their life cycle. Many start at the egg stage, hatching out into larvae, usually grubs, caterpillars or maggots (which is the first stage for some). Next comes the pupal stage, when the larvae become encased in a chrysalis or pupa. Finally they emerge as adults. Examples of mature insects include beetles, butterflies, moths and flies.

Insecticide Any material which is used to kill insects. Ideally these should be harmless to people, plants and beneficial creatures. *See* Chapter 10, Problems.

Insectivore An animal or bird such as hedgehog, swallow or centipede which devours insects.

Insectivorous Plants, which capture and consume insects for their nutrition. Native plants such as butterworts and sundews are examples of this group of plants. Tropical plants like the nepenthes and pitcher plants are well adapted for this purpose. Insectivorous plants have various mechanisms for trapping insects. These range from folding leaves to sticky fly-paper-like leaf surfaces, and one-way traps, preventing the insects from escaping once inside.

Intensive culture Sometimes referred to as intensive cultivation. Any method of growing where very high yields are obtained. The aim is to obtain the maximum cropping level from an area of land. Greenhouses, frames and cloches are usually a feature of this system where rapid growth and heavy crops are expected.

Intercrop The sowing or interplanting of a quick growing crop such as lettuce or radish between rows of slower-growing subjects. The aim is to harvest the short term crop, leaving space for the long-term subject to mature.

Internode The length of stem between two leaf joints.

Intermediate An intermediate house is maintained at a minimum temperature of 10°C (50°F) and is warmer than a cool house, but cooler than one providing tropical or stove conditions. *See* Chapter 4, Greenhouses, Frames and Cloches.

Introduced Plants which have been brought in from another place or region or which are new to cultivation. Plant raisers, nurserymen and distributors are credited with introducing new varieties. This occurs after they have raised new stock and offered these for sale.

Irishman's cutting A type of cutting with roots attached at the time of preparation. *See* Chapter 2, Propagation.

Iron Sulphate A chemical used for the control of moss in turf. *See* Chapter 8, Turf.

Irrigation A practice of correcting water deficiency, usually in soils, but also applied to any form of watering plants. The three main methods used in gardens are overhead, surface, and sub-irrigation. Overhead consists of applying water in fine droplets over the plants. Surface involves delivering water at or near soil level but keeping the foliage dry. Sub-irrigation consists of re-plenishing moisture by means of underground pipes, a method used almost exclusively for soilless cultivation.

Japanese garden A form of garden which has the character of those found in Japan. The type of plants, their method of use, together with the use of lanterns, water, rocks, stepping stones and timber bridges in an unmistakably oriental way are hallmarks of this style.

Joint A node or swollen point of junction between a leaf and stem, which is particularly evident among grasses.

June drop Some fruit trees, apples in particular, shed immature fruits in June, or thereabouts and this acts as a form of natural thinning process.

Juice The liquid or sap which is contained in most parts of growing plants but particularly in ripe fruits.

Jute A fibre obtained from a tropical plant and used in the making of matting and twine for garden purposes. Its soft nature makes it excellent for tying plants, but man-made fibres have superseded it today.

Juvenile A botanical term for forms of growth which retain or revert back to seedling type foliage. This is frequently found in junipers and some conifers.

Kainit A mineral used more in farming than gardening as a fertiliser. This material contains chlorides of potassium and sodium as well as magnesium sulphate. The potassium part is valuable, but care should be exercised in the use of kainit because crops like gooseberries are sensitive to sodium chloride or common salt and chloride forms of potash. Excellent for salt-loving crops like beetroot.

Katabatic wind A downhill flow of cold air on frosty nights.

Keel A ridge or projection found on some seeds.
Also the boat-like petal found beneath the stamens and stigma of each pea flower.

Kelp A term used for seaweed which is a useful alternative to farmyard manure. This material contains nitrogen, potash and many trace elements which are essential for healthy plant growth and development. *See* Chapter 1, Site and Soil.

Kernel Inner portion of a nut within its shell, but also the inner portion of any seed, including the embryo.

Key The winged seeds of trees such as ash also the samarae of maple and sycamore.

Knee Any angular or sharp bend in any stem, shoot or root. This can be caused by injury or adventitious growth (q.v.).

Knot The swelling of stems, particularly at the nodes or joints of grasses.

Also the hard circular areas in sawn timber.

Labellum The lip-like and usually largest and lowest petal of an orchid.

Also the lip of labiates (q.v.) such as sage.

Labiate Flowers having two lip-shaped petals, an upper and lower. This is characteristic of the Labiatae family which includes plants such as mint, sage, and salvia.

Lacewing-fly A group of several species, most of which have a pair of large iridescent wings. The larvae which emerge from the stalked eggs feed on aphids and on the whole are beneficial in gardens.

Lactescent Plants like lettuce and euphorbia which produce a whitish, milky fluid when cut or damaged.

Ladybird A group of small beetles which are particularly useful to gardeners. The adults and larvae feed on aphids, considerably reducing their numbers. The red form with black spots is more conspicuous than the black, red-spotted types.

Lamellae The gills on the undersides of mushrooms and similar or related fungi. These comprise a series of plates which protect the spores.

Lamina A term given to the main blade, functionally the most important part of a leaf.

Lanceolate Leaves which have a long narrow lamina, slightly wider at the base than the tip. Leaves of this type are widest at the centre, tapering to a point at each end.

Landscape Gardening This involves the various aspects of design and layout of gardens, including the placing and arrangement of plants.

Larva The caterpillar, grub or maggot of an insect. The larval phase is the first stage after the hatching out of an egg, in the development of an insect.

Latent Hidden plant characteristics which are revealed only following plant breeding and hybridisation.

Latent buds or bulbs are those which exist in a dormant or quiescent condition ready to start into growth when the conditions are right.

Lateral A secondary growth or shoot arising from a main stem, usually from a leaf axil (q.v.). Lateral buds are those which can form on a leader, or shoot, but are situated beside or below the terminal buds.

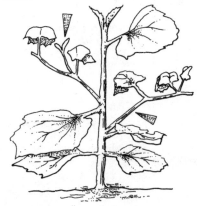

216 Laterals. *Right*: a lateral shoot, *arrowed*, grows from the main stem. *Arrowed left* is a sub-lateral which arises from a lateral.

Latex A white milk-like juice which is exuded from the cut stems of some plants such as poinsettia. This occurs particularly when cuttings are being taken and prepared.

Lawn An area usually of closely-mown turf or grass sward providing a useful surface for walking or playing on and for appearance. A well-kept lawn provides an excellent foil for flowers, shrubs and trees. Chamomile and other carpeting plants are sometimes used instead of grass for lawn making.

Lax A habit or characteristic of various plants, which is evident by an open, spreading arrangement of shoots or branches.

Layer A young plant which is being layered or has been propagated by layering.

Layering A reliable method of increasing plants vegetatively by pegging down pliant stems into some fine soil. This encourages the shoots to form rooted layers which can then be severed from the parent plant and transferred elsewhere. *See* Chapter 2, Propagation.

Leaching Plant foods are said to be leached out of the land in areas of high rainfall. This washing out, usually of nutrients, is caused by repeated percolation of rain water through soils.

Leader A central main stem or leading growths which form the principal branch framework of plants, shrubs and trees.

Leaf Regardless of shape or life-span, these are essential to the well-being of plants. In sunlight, green leaves synthesise starches and sugars that are needed for growth and development. In addition to this manufacturing role, leaves help to reduce the temperature especially in warm weather by increasing evaporation. Plants can also obtain water and nutrients through their leaves. Leaves are simple structures compared to flowers and consist of a protective outer covering with conducting strands and cells inside. The outer coat is perforated with breathing pores or stomata, mainly on the underside. These pores open and close according to the plants' needs. The conducting tissue, or veins, convey nutrients, water and sugary sap or manufactured products as required. The cells within the leaves contain the vital green chlorophyll.

Leaf classification Groupage of leaves according to shape, for identification purposes.

Leaflet One of several leaf blades from a compound leaf. A pinna from an ash leaf is an example of a leaflet.

Lean Undernourished plants and impoverished soils. Extra manure and fertiliser usually can and will induce more vigorous growth in these conditions.

Lean-to Greenhouses and frames having a high wall for one of the sides and a mono-pitch roof or light.

Leatherjacket The destructive soil-inhabiting larva of the Crane fly. *See* Chapter 10, Problems.

Leathery Leaves and other parts of plants and animals having a tough hide or skin-like texture.

Leeward A sheltered position in the lee, protected from the wind by plants or structures.

Leg A short length of stem between ground level and the lowest branch of gooseberry bushes, for example, when grown as stools. *See* Stool.

Legume A seed pod of peas and beans, for example.

Members of the Leguminoseae family which includes peas, beans and lupins are also collectively known as legumes.

Lepidopterous Resembling butterflies and moths, having hairy or scale like wings. The term is derived from their group or family name Lepidopterae.

Lesion An area of injured or infected leaf root or other tissue which is not functioning normally. Particularly damage caused by disease organisms.

Levelling A process involving gradients and levels. The object of levelling is to accurately determine levels to ensure that land is contoured as needed and that drainage systems can work. *See* Chapter 1, Site and Soil.

Lichen A form of vegetation which grows on stones, rocks, tree trunks and walls in damp situations. It usually consists of a fungus growing on algae, and may be grey, green, bluish-grey or grey-green, brown, yellow and orange.

Lift Where plants are being set out in new positions some are dug or 'lifted' out of the ground before the move. *See* Chapter 3, Plant Care.

Lighting Can be used horticulturally to regulate plant growth and development. Fluorescent lighting tubes can accelerate seedling growth when correctly used. Low light intensity can delay flowering in chrysanthemums when applied at the correct stage of development and where given for the necessary duration. *See* Chapter 4, Greenhouses, Frames and Cloches.

Lights Glass or plastic clad timber or metal covers used for protecting plants. A garden frame consists essentially of a box-like base which is covered with a light or lights of varying size. *See* Dutch Lights, *also* Chapter 4, Greenhouses, Frames and Cloches.

Liliaceous Members of the lily family, the Liliaceae.

Limb A branch, usually of fairly large proportions on trees.

Lime Horticulturally, loosely applied to lime compounds, consisting of the oxide, hydroxide and carbonate of calcium. *See* Chapter 1, Site and Soil.
 Also a variety of tree.

Lime Sulphur An effective fungicide, which also has some insecticidal value. *See* Chapter 10, Problems.

Lime test There are various ways of testing soil for its content of calcium compounds, but two main methods are in use. One simple method consists of mixing soil with an indicator liquid which changes colour according to the amount of lime present. The colour of the liquid is then compared with those on a graduated scale and can be read off at the point where the colours match. In an equipped laboratory more sophisticated methods are available, including the use of a calibrated electric pH meter. *See* Chapter 1, Site and Soil.

Limiting Factor Rapid and balanced plant growth can proceed only when all the basic conditions are satisfied. As soon as one or more of the requirements are lacking growth slows down or ceases. The unsatisfied need, such as lack of water or plant food is known as a limiting factor. The main limiting factors are correct levels of temperature, moisture, air, light, food, space, and pollution.

Linear Long, narrow strap-like leaves.

Ling A popular name for heather.

Lip The petals of flowers with a corolla consisting of an upper and lower petal.

Liquid feed Any form of liquid nutriment for plants *See* Chapter 1, Site and Soil.

Liquid manure A feed for plants, obtained by soaking manure in a tub of water and applied when it is the colour of weak tea. A practice now largely superseded by the use of liquid fertiliser.

Loam An ideal type of soil consisting of coarse and fine sand, silt and clay, together with organic matter and nutrients. Loam soils are classed as light when sand predominates, heavy when clay dominates, and medium when intermediate between the extremes. *See* Chapter 1, Site and Soil.

Loam stack A heap of turfy loam, stacked in layers to mature in readiness for use in seed and potting composts.

Lobe A rounded segment or section as on flower petals or leaves.

Loggia An open-sided but covered room, usually opening onto a garden terrace.

Long-day Summer-flowering subjects which bloom during the long days of summer. These are light-responsive plants which can flower only with difficulty, if at all, in short days when daylight is only of 8–10 hours' duration.

Looper A type of caterpillar which is characteristically seen in the form of a loop. Most are destructive.

Loose Plants of an open lax habit (q.v.).
Soils which have been recently dug and cultivated and which are often uncompacted and puffy.

Lop To cut or saw off, usually branches or limbs of trees.

Lush Plants which have made excessively vigorous, rank growth.

Lute A simple garden tool, used for spreading soil or soil-type mixtures thinly and evenly on or over turf. The operation is sometimes referred to as luting.

Macro-element Nitrogen, phosphorous and potassium which are needed by plants in larger amounts than, for example, boron and manganese which are referred to as trace or micro-elements.

Maculate Spotted or speckled plants. The markings are usually on the flowers or leaves.

Magpie moth An attractive insect seen quite frequently in gardens, but the caterpillars are pests.

Maiden Trees usually in their first season after budding or grafting before their first pruning.

Maincrop Types or varieties of plants which provide the greatest yield within their respective groups. Generally, these kinds require a longer growing season than early or second-early varieties.

Male Flowers or plants of which the female parts are absent. In male flowers, stigmas, styles and ovaries are lacking. Cucumbers, and marrows, produce male and female flowers on the same plant. Some hollies carry male and female flowers on separate plants and are termed male or female respectively.

Mammillaria A group of cactaceous plants many of which are domed or hemispherical in outline.

Manure Usually bulky organic matter consisting of a mixture of animal and vegetable residues. These are less concentrated in their feeding value than fertilisers but they still provide essential elements and are very valuable for improving the organic matter content of soil.

Marbled Plants such as cyclamen varieties which have variously mottled leaf markings vaguely similar to that seen on some forms of marble.

March Moth A fairly common pest on fruit trees, causing considerable defoliation on apples and pears.

Margins The borders or edges of ponds, pools and water courses.
The edges of leaves, petals and other broad floral structures are also so described.

Marginal Plants which grow or thrive in or near the water's edge.

Marl A type of clay earth which contains a high proportion of chalk and is mainly used for 'digging in' to improve sandy soils. It is also used as a light dressing for cricket squares.

Marling A process of applying marl,

either by digging in or by spreading thinly as a top dressing in dust form over grassed areas.

Marrowfat A type of pea also known as wrinkled. These are considered to be the best flavoured varieties but are slightly less hardy than the rounded seeded kinds.

Mast The nuts or fruits of beech, oak and similar trees.

Mastic Various preparations which usually contain resin, wax and some solvent, which when made up into a putty-like consistency, can be used as grafting wax.

Similar types of materials are used also as putty when glazing greenhouses and frames.

Mats and matting Usually of hessian, these are used mainly in connection with frames and turf culture. Mats can be used to cover frame lights on frosty nights, or during periods of severe weather to give added protection for the plants inside. The task of placing these in position is referred to as matting.

Another type of mat, which is used occasionally on high-quality lawns is a flexible, close-mesh type of chain or drag mat. This is pulled behind the operator, scattering worm casts and spreading and working in top dressings. *See* Chapter 8, Turf.

Meal Some organic fertilisers, which have a granular or fine dusty texture, are referred to as meal; examples include bone, fish and hoof meal.

The leaves of some plants are described as mealy when coated with a fine, whitish dust or farina, which can occur naturally or be a symptom of disease.

Mealy bug An insect pest which is characteristically covered with a whitish fluff or mealy coating. *See* Chapter 10, Problems.

Membrane A thin protecting layer of tissue covering or dividing any part of a plant. The covering skin around un-opened daffodil buds is an example.

Mendelism The laws or principles of genetics as outlined by Gregor Mendel and adopted by many plant breeders and hybridisers.

Mercury vapour tube A type of fluorescent lighting tube which is used mainly in commercial establishments to supplement natural daylight. During winter when the hours of sunlight are short and the intensity of light is low plants can be much more rapidly under these tubes.

Merit Garden-worthy plants are awarded a Certificate of Merit by the Royal Horticultural Society. This is the second highest award in the R.H.S. scheme of certification, the highest being the First Class Certificate. Not all plants are submitted for consideration by plant breeders, and there are other reliable and important award schemes both nationally and internationally.

Meta A type of slug killer, and an abbreviation for the chemical name metaldehyde. *See* Chapter 10, Problems.

Metamorphosis The transformation of a pupa or chrysalis into the adult insect.

Micro A prefix to denote anything small or on a small scale.

A micro-climate is very local and the climatic conditions within an area of a garden, or even a part of one are so described. Conditions within a greenhouse for example are sometimes referred to as a micro-climate.

Trace or minor elements which are essential for plant growth, but needed only in minute quantities are termed micro-elements.

The term micro-species has been coined for plants having differences even within a species.

Midge A group of dipterous flies, having one pair of wings. Many of this type of insect are injurious to garden plants.

Midrib The main vein or central thickening, usually of leaves, dividing the lamina or leaf blade in two.

Mid-summer growth Occasionally taken into account when assessing the age of a tree by counting the annular rings when sawn down. With some species two rings represent one year's growth, the narrower being the Mid-summer growth.

Also growth which takes place in late summer.

Mildew A type of fungus disease which affects many kinds of plants, and takes various forms. *See* Chapter 10, Problems.

Millipede A group of creatures which are often harmful to garden plants. Characteristically these have four legs to each body segment. *See* Chapter 10, Problems.

Mist propagation A method of rooting cuttings and raising plants under intermittent or almost continuous fine mist. Bench or undersoil heating is one of the features of the system. *See* Chapter 2, Propagation.

Mite A group of small, often minute, creatures which feed on plants. The red

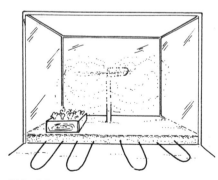

217 Mist unit. Cuttings root quickly in the mist-like conditions, with bottom heat. Note the electric warming cables.

spider mite which can be very damaging especially to indoor plants is a member of this tribe. *See* Chapter 10, Problems.

Mole A nocturnal, burrowing creature which throws up mounds of fine earth causing considerable annoyance and sometimes damage. *See* Chapter 10, Problems.

Mono A prefix meaning one, having many applications. Monocarpic flowers have a single carpel; monocotyledons, such as onions and leeks have a single seed leaf.

Monoecious Plants which bear both male and female flowers, unlike dioecious plants which are either male or female.

Moraine Geologically this is a deposit of gravel and small particles, occurring near the edge of a glacier.

In gardens it is a layer of chippings in or near a rock garden and planted with alpine or rock plants.

Morphology The study of the outline or form of plants, as distinct from anatomy or the inner functioning.

Mosaic In gardening a virus disease which affects many kinds of plant. The symptoms appear as a mottling and blotching on the leaves. *See* Chapter 10, Problems.

Moss One of a group of lowly plants which are normally found in boggy or moist, and usually shaded, places. Some species invade lawns and present difficulties. *See* Chapter 8, Turf. Live moss is used in some orchid composts and for propagating purposes.

Moss rose A type of old-fashioned rose which is outstanding for scent. The stems are densely covered with thorns.

Moth Members of the insect family which are closely allied to butterflies. Moths are mainly nocturnal and visit pale-coloured or white flowers, which are open during the hours of darkness.

Mother plant Plants which are the seed bearing parents. With crops like carnations which are increased by cuttings some plants are grown for the sole purpose of producing propagating material.

Mottled Umber Moth One of the family of winter moths which can cause considerable damage to fruit trees. *See* Chapter 10, Problems.

Mould Many kinds of fungal infection. Some common examples include greymould or botrytis which can affect the flowers, fruits and leaves of many plants, blue mould on ripening fruits and the Khaki-coloured patches of tomato leafmould. *See* Chapter 10, Problems.

Mowing An essential operation in the care and maintenance of fine turf areas, consisting of removing the top growth to the desired level. *See* Chapter 8, Turf.

Mulch A layer, usually of loose material placed on the soil surface around plants to conserve moisture and smother weeds. A dust mulch is created by loosening soil around plants by hoeing, taking care not to injure plants.

Multi A prefix signifying many, such as multi-flora meaning many flowered.

Multi-dibber As the name implies, this is a device which consists of a number of dibbers. This type is often used to make the holes in compost for seedlings. It can save considerable time in pricking out and raising bedding plants.

Muriate of potash A fertiliser consisting mainly of potassium chloride, and very useful for crops such as asparagus and beetroot. *See* Chapter 1, Site and Soil.

Mushroom An edible fungus which can be grown indoors in darkness as well as outdoors. A member of the order Agaricaceae and which has gills on the underside of the fruiting heads.

Mushroom headed Some forms of tree which resemble a giant mushroom in outline, when viewed from the side.

Mushroom spawn Pieces of organic matter through which or in which the root-like strands of mushroom mycelium (q.v.) have permeated. Mushroom spawn is planted or sown as necessary to start off crops. *See* Chapter 9, Vegetables.

Mutable Plants which are constantly changing in their character and habit.

Mutant A part or whole plant which has spontaneously developed a new feature. Also known as a sport, this type of change occurs among chrysanthemums where it is not unusual to find a change of flower colour, sometimes only a single bloom on a plant. These sports often produce new varieties.

Mycelium The root-like growths of fungi which ramify through the soil or through the cell tissue of their host to obtain food and nutriment. Unlike green plants, which manufacture starch and sugar in sunlight, fungi have to obtain all their requirements by other means through the mycelium. When this root-like structure is sufficiently developed and an adequate food supply is available, fruit heads such as mushrooms form.

Mycology The scientific or systematic study of fungi.

Myrobalan A popular name for the cherry plum, *Prunus cerasifera*, which is used as a root stock for plums. This is also useful for hedges and screening in gardens which are large enough to accommodate it.

Native A plant which grows and thrives in its place, area or region of origin.

Natural A natural garden is informal, without regularity or straight lines or geometric patterns. Man has not interfered with Nature in such settings.

213

Natural break Some varieties of early-flowering chrysanthemum produce side growths without being stopped or having the growing points removed. Any shoot which arises in this manner is referred to as a natural break.

Natural order Closely related plants are grouped in their natural orders.

Natural selection A random system of plant breeding which is largely or completely uncontrolled and unregulated by any pre-planned hybridisation programmes.

Naturalised Plants once introduced, but now growing wild in new areas.

Naturalising A practice of setting out plants in wild or near natural surroundings. One of the best known examples is planting bulbs such as daffodils and crocus in grass or turf.

Neck The length of stem between roots and leaves: the piece of stem just above an onion bulb is called the neck, as is the piece of stalk immediately below a daffodil flower. Blooms are said to neck when they fall over, a weakness in certain varieties of zinnias, and a characteristic of over-crowded flowering plants.

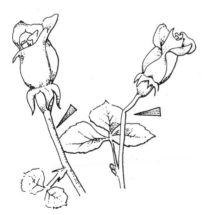

218 Neck. Weak stems, *arrowed right*, result in blooms flopping over, unlike those with strong stems *arrowed left*.

Necrosis A condition of plants in which dead and dying areas of tissue appear.

Necrotic Plant leaves, stems and other parts when sunken, dead or cankerous areas are evident.

Nectar A sweet liquid which is secreted by nectary glands in flowers.

Nectary A gland situated usually close to the throat of a flower and secreting a sweet liquid that is much sought by insects.

Needle Long, narrow needle-like objects, in particular the leaves of conifers such as pines, firs, spruce and juniper.

Nematode Small worms, many of which are parasitic on garden plants. Eelworms which are among the most deadly pests belong to this class of creatures. *See* Chapter 10, Problems.

Netted Some kinds of melons, so described because ripe fruits have an exterior net-like ribbing.

Netting Mesh netting is used to protect seeds, plants and fruits from birds and animals.
Also the veins of leaves.

Neuter A flower having neither male nor female organs and unable to produce seed.

Neutral Soils which are neither acid nor alkaline, and have a pH level of 7.
Also subdued quiet tones, such as browns and olive green.

Night flower Blooms which open or remain so during the hours of darkness. These are often popular with moths and other night-flying creatures.

Night temperature When applied to greenhouse plants such as tomato, cucumber and melon, the minimum degree of warmth during darkness which is needed for satisfactory growth.

Nitrate Fertilisers which supply nitrates, a form of nitrogen which is readily taken up by plant roots. Nitrate is usually combined with other elements to produce a valuable salt. Potassium nitrate is a fertiliser, widely used for making liquid feed. Other salts include ammonium and sodium nitrates. These are readily soluble and can easily be lost in soil drainage water. Some soil bacteria are able to synthesise nitrate, providing valuable nutriment for crops.

Nitrogen One of the most important elements in plant nutrition. This is necessary for the functioning of every living cell. Excess nitrogen causes rank, vigorous growth, delays fruiting or flowering and pre-disposes plants to disease. A deficiency will stunt growth, and cause early flowering and under-sized crops.

Nitrogen assimilation/fixation The process of obtaining nitrogen from the air carried out by some soil bacteria. Certain plants such as peas and beans enrich the soil due to the nitrogen fixation which occurs within the nodules on their roots.

Nitrogenous fertilisers Nitrogen-rich materials which supply needs for

219 Nodes. The space between the leaf joints, or nodes, *arrowed*, is an internode. Some cuttings such as clematis are prepared by cutting at this point.

this element. These substances can be in liquid or dry forms.

Node The point where leaf and stem meet often resulting in swollen joints, as with some grasses and dahlias.

Non-resistant Plants which have no resistance to some pest or disease.

Nursery Beds or areas set aside for the purpose of raising young plants of any kind.

Nutrient Any substance, usually in solution, used as a feed for plants.

Nutrient film technique A recent development designed to enable plants to be grown without soil or granular aggregates. At present this system consists of one or more shallow channels or canals in which plants are grown. Dilute nutrient solution is fed to these from a tank and surplus liquid is returned to the reservoir and re-cycled as necessary. The canals are usually lined with capillary matting or similar material.

Nutrition All aspects of feeding plants.

Nymph An immature stage of an insect before undergoing the final transformation.

Oak apple Also known as Oak gall, a condition usually of oak leaves, which appears as marble-sized swellings and are caused by one of a number of insects. These galls, pinkish or reddish, flushed green in summer, turn brown in winter.

Obtuse Any blunt-ended leaf, lobe or petal as distinct from an acute or sharp point.

Off-set A swollen stem, bulb or short growth which is formed beside the base of a parent plant at or near soil level.

Omnivorous Insects or other pests which attack and devour all plants indiscriminately.

Opposite Botanically, the arrangement

of leaves where these occur in pairs on opposite sides of a shoot or stem.

Optimum Conditions which are conducive to the most favourable type of growth. The best form of growth, taking all relevant factors into account.

Orbicular Circular or discoid leaves, lobes or petals and spherical or globular berries and fruits.

Organs Specialised tissues which have some particular function such as stamens, stigmas, styles and ovaries.

Organic Derived from living matter. Chemically, carbon-containing materials are so described.

Organism Any independent animal, plant or insect, from single-celled algae to highly developed living forms. A term more frequently used in the context of lower, less specialised living material such as fungi, bacteria and disease-causing bodies.

Osmosis A process which enables plants to take in moisture. In the case of roots, water can pass from the surrounding medium or soil, through the cell walls into the sap-conducting cells and through the plant.

Ovary The swollen female reproductive organ in the pistil or gynaecium of flowers which develops into the seed case.

Ovate Leaves, petals, fruits or any objects which are egg-shaped in outline.

Ovoid Similar to ovate, anything which resembles an egg in appearance, but with one end noticeably more pointed than the other.

Oxygen An essential element required by living organisms. This occurs in gaseous form in the atmosphere, combines with hydrogen to form water, and is converted into starch, sugar cellulose and other vital materials by plants.

Oxygenate To release pure oxygen into water, soil or other medium, enabling living plants to breathe.

Oxygenator Aquatic plants which give off oxygen to aerate and oxygenate water.

Paddy's cutting *See* Irishman's cutting.

Palmate Leaves having several lobes which are joined to a central vein, such as maple and sycamore.

Pan A hard or compacted layer, usually of soil. Sometimes referred to as a hard pan, or chemical pan when the condition is caused by a deposition of iron or other constituent of soil.

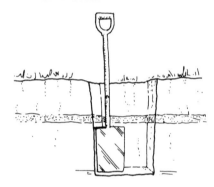

220 Pan. Compacted layers of soil, which are often thin as shown here, prevent heavy cropping, but can easily be broken up when digging.

Panning The process of forming a pan as for example by cultivating the ground in wet conditions.

Pappose Plants, leaves, buds and stems which are covered with dense silky hairs.

Pappus (Pl. Pappei) A hair found on some plants, including thistle, which serves as a means of seed dispersal. They usually occur in tufts.

Parachute The specialised hair device which aids seed, for example of dandelions, to disperse. The name is a reference to the resemblance of the hair arrangement to the cords of a parachute.

Parasite A fungus, bacterium or insect which feeds on another organism for its sustenance.

Parted Leaves or petals which have a cleft or division to form lobes.

Parterre A level area of ground which consists of several distinct beds. Each one of these is a self-contained compartment, usually surrounded by low-growing edging such as box.

Parthenocarpic Fruits which develop without fertilisation.

Parthenocarpy Botanically, the capacity or process whereby fruits and seeds are formed without fertilisation of the pistil in flowers. Greenhouse cucumbers are said to show parthenocarpy, producing parthenocarpic fruits.

Parthenogenesis The production of living young without the sex process taking place. Many aphids or greenfly give birth to several generations of their young when conditions are favourable during the summer months.

Patch plants Annuals which are sown in drifts or patches, in beds or borders for colour and effect.

Pathogen A disease producing organism.

Pathogenic A member of a group of pathogens, or the conditions created by, for example, harmful fungi and bacteria.

Pathology The study or science of diseases, usually prefixed by the word plant in gardening.

Path A walkway or link between two or more points for the use of pedestrians. The type and construction details vary.

Peach Leaf curl A disease which affects peaches and apricots, causing severe deformity. *See* Chapter 10, Problems.

Peat Partially decomposed plant remains. Two main types are recognised, namely moss or sphagnum peat, and sedge peat. Fibrous granular peat is widely used in potting composts, as mulches, and for digging into the ground as a manure substitute.

Peat Moss A sphagnum type of peat which is obtained from moss which accumulates to a considerable depth in moist situations. This is usually more fibrous and acid than sedge peats, which consist mainly of grass, sedges, rushes and leaves. Moss peats are more resistant to decay and are ideal for potting composts.

Peat wall A form of low retaining wall, consisting of blocks of peat one on top of the next to retain a growing medium, usually peat-based. They are used mainly in situations where the natural soil contains excess chalk or limestone, which is unsuitable for some acid loving plants, such as calluna and cassiope.

221 Peat wall. Plants such as acid-loving heathers can well be grown in beds of acid-rooting medium, held in place by peat blocks, *arrowed*, even where the subsoil is chalk or limestone.

Pedate Leaves which are shaped like, or have the outline of, a bird's foot.

Pedicel A short stalk or stem which bears an individual bloom of either solitary or compound flowers.

Also, (often spelt pedicle) a fruit stalk of apples, pears, plums, etc.

Pedology The science or study of soils.

Peduncle The main stalk of single or compound flowers.

Peel The rind or outer skin of fruits. Sometimes also the rind or pliable bark of young stems.

Peltate Leaves where the stalk or stem is connected to the leaf blade centrally instead of the more usual one side or tip.

Pencilled Petals, mainly, which have grey or black parallel lines or markings at or near the margins.

Pendent Flowers, fruits and shoots which hang down. Plants which display this feature are described as pendulous.

Perch A soil condition in which waterlogging occurs on a piece of high ground. More strictly it is a perched water table, caused usually by a saucer-shaped depression in clay and overlaid by soil. The water is unable to drain away through the layer of impervious clay and causes wet conditions.

Perennials Plants which grow and flower for three or more years, either indoors, or in the open air.

Perfect Any flower and other parts of plants which consist of or contain their full complement of functional organs. Perfect flowers include sepals, petals, stamens and pistils.

Pergola A covered walkway consisting of horizontal timbers supported on uprights forming arches and covered with climbing plants.

Perianth The covering or envelope of a flower which consists of the calyx sepals and corolla petals. These give protection to the reproductive floral organs of stamens and pistils.

Perpetual Certain types of plant which have a more or less continuous habit of flowering, such as carnations and roses.

Persistent Stems, leaves and other parts of plants which remain and function during winter, for example, when others are dormant. Evergreen leaves and woody stems are examples of this habit.

Pesticide Any material or substance which serves to control, kill or contain the spread of pests.

Pests *See* Chapter 10, Problems.

Petal One of the corolla segments of a flower which is usually highly coloured and consists in fact of specialised leaf tissue.

Petal fall Fruit trees are said to be at this stage when 90 per cent or more of the blossoms have shed their petals. This is a critical period in some fruit spraying programmes.

Petaloid Petal-like, applied usually to highly coloured bracts or sepals which, in the case of poinsettia, closely resemble true petals.

Petiole A stalk which carries or supports a leaf.

pH A scientific term which is used to express a degree of acidity or alkalinity. In gardening it is mostly applied to soil. It uses a scale of measurement which ranges from 1–14, with 7 being neutral. A pH of 6 is slightly acid becoming increasingly so with decreasing numbers. Soils having a pH of 8 are alkaline, and are increasingly more so as numbers approach 14. *See* Chapter 1, Site and Soil.

Phosphate Materials which contain the element phosphorous which is essential for plant growth and development. Fertilisers which contain this substance are referred to as phosphatic.

Physiology The study of function and purpose of plant systems.

Picotee Blooms which have narrow bands of different colour on the petal margins but are otherwise single colour.

Pick-axe A hand tool for breaking up hard ground and digging out tree roots.

Pig manure *See* manure, *also* Chapter 1, Site and Soil.

Pilose Leaves or plants which are covered with soft down or hairs.

Pinching out Several operations which involve the removal of growing points, buds and side shoots. These include stopping, side shooting, and disbudding. *See* Chapter 3, Plant Care.

Pinetum An area of land devoted to the culture of conifers.

Pin-eyed Flowers devoid of stamens. Primulas often develop this type of bloom, as distinct from the thrum-eyed staminate male form.

Pink bud A condition of apple trees when the majority of the flower buds begin to show colour, but before they open fully.

Pinna The main leaf divisions, which may be further divided and subdivided, occuring among ferns.
Also a single leaflet of a pinnate leaf.

Pinnate A compound leaf which consists of pairs of leaflets on either side of the main rib. Ash is a common example.

Pip A seed of fruits such as apple and pear, as well as those of citrus.

Pipe heat A form of artificial heat suitable for greenhouse and frame.

Piping A type of cutting which is broken or snapped off the parent plant without using a knife or cutting instrument. Carnations and pinks are examples of this.

Pistil The female or seed bearing part of a flower consisting of stigma, style and ovary. The style is sometimes much shortened.

Pistillate Female flowers in which male organs are absent.

Pits The sunken areas which sometimes develop as a result of disease on leaves, stems and fruits.
Also holes which are dug when tree planting.

Pitchers Pitcher-shaped sacs which are formed by certain insectivorous plants. These sacs or receptacles contain fluid at the base into which insects fall and are dissolved by various means, providing nutriment for the plant.

Pitcher plants Any member of the group of plants which bear pitchers. Two main families which fall into this class are nepenthes and sarracenia.

Pith The inner whitish, often soft, tissue in the centre of shoots such as elder.

Planting A process of setting plants out in beds or borders. The term is usually prefixed by a word denoting the method used. *See* Chapter 3, Care.

Plash A method used for revitalising old and/or neglected hedges by part-cutting through the stems and laying them in the row either horizontally or obliquely. Also known as hedge laying.

Plastic Any substances, but including soils which are moist or wet and mouldable which will retain any shape they are formed into.

Plastics Rigid or plastic substances, which have many applications in gardening. Clear forms are used as glass substitutes for covering greenhouses, frames and similar structures. Pots, boxes, tools and other equipment are made of these materials.

Pleached Trees and shrubs which have their limbs and branches trained to intermingle with similar plants to form living walls and arches.

Plume Feather-like arrangements of flower inflorescence, as with some grasses.

Plumose Most forms of foliage which are light and feathery in appearance.

Plunge To sink pots up to their rims in soil, peat, sand and similar material for stability, and to reduce watering.
Also to bury containers of bulbs in

similar materials while roots form.

Pocket A hole or hollow in which plants are or can be set out, particularly used in connection with alpines and rock plants.

Pods The seed case, particularly of dehiscent plants: peas and beans are typical examples.

Pollard Trees that are given a particular form of pruning, usually consisting of lopping the limbs into a small crown. *See* Chapter 3, Plant Care.

Pollen Fine granular dust-like material released by the male flower organs, the stamens, which is essential for seed formation.

Pollen compatibility Where the pollen of one variety of apple, for example, enables another to set fruit successfully, it is said to be compatible. When the pollen of one variety fails to assist another to set fruit or seed it is said to be incompatible.

Pollination The process of transferring pollen to the female stigma. Some flowers such as those of marrow, need to be pollinated to enable fertilisation and fruit formation to take place. *See* Chapter 4, Greenhouses, Frames and Cloches.

Pome An apple shaped fruit or one which is similar.

Pond weed A group of plants which are commonly found in ponds, lakes and water courses, sometimes causing considerable nuisance.

Population A collective group of plants, insects or animals in any particular location, place or area.

Post-emergent Spray applications of weed killer which are given after weed growth emerges above ground.

Potash Fertilisers or other materials which contain quantities of potassium.

Potassium An element which is essential to plant nutrition and the manufacture of sugars and starches by green leaves. Potassium increases the general efficiency of plants, balances up the softening effect of nitrogen, improves winter hardiness and the colour intensity of flowers and fruits.

Pot herb Originally plants and herbs which are cooked in a pot. Occasionally applied to herbs that are grown in a pot.

Pot-pourri An assemblage of rose petals other flowers and leaves which retain their perfume when dried. These can be used to scent rooms and linen.

Potting The operation of placing plants or bulbs in pots or similar containers. *See* Chapter 2, Propagation.

Potting compost A rooting medium for container-grown plants.

Potting off Transferring pricked out seedlings or cuttings from boxes or trays into pots.

Potting on The process of moving plants which have outgrown small or medium sized pots into progressively larger sized pots.

Potting up Lifting plants from beds or borders and setting them out in pots.

Predator Animals or insects which prey on others. Some are beneficial to gardeners by killing harmful pests.

Pre-emergent Weedkillers which are applied before crops, seedlings and other weed growth appear.

Pricking off (or pricking out) Transferring seedlings from the seed box, pot or pan into pots or spacing them out in boxes or trays.

Primary Those parts of a plant which appear first. A primary shoot is the main shoot which first arises from a seed.

Profile A vertical soil section such as that which is exposed when a hole is dug in the ground.

Proliferate A rapid multiplication of plants, fruits or even cells, particularly with some diseases.

Proliferous Bulbous growths on the fronds of embryo ferns where spore cases would normally occur.

Also a form of increase by shoots and suckers.

Propagating frame A box or frame which is covered with a frame light of glass or plastic and used for raising plants. These are usually constructed to provide higher levels of temperature and humidity than is economic or practical in the whole of the greenhouse.

Propagator *See* Propagating frame.

Propagation The increase or multiplication of plants by any means, including seeds, spores and vegetative methods such as cuttings. Chapter 2 is devoted to methods of propagation.

Prostrate Creeping or sprawling plants which grow close to or on and over the ground, such as creeping juniper.

Protected cultivation Any form or method of cropping which involves the use of cover, such as greenhouses, frames and cloches.

Protozoa A collective name for minute animal-like creatures or microbes which live in films of moisture in soil and elsewhere. When present in large numbers soil fertility is diminished and soil sterilisation becomes necessary.

Pruniform Plumlike or plum shaped.

Pruning The process of shortening or removing shoots and branches to regulate growth and cropping. *See* Chapter 3, Plant Care.

Pruning, extension A system of pruning in which not more than one-third to one-half of the total number of shoots are shortened. *See* Chapter 3, Plant care.

Pruning, spur A method of pruning wall-trained and other intensive forms of fruit tree, in which all shoots are shortened.

Pseudo-bulb A thickened bulb like stem section consisting of an internode which may develop in various orchid species.

222 Pseudo-bulbs. *Left,* single and *right,* multi-jointed pseudo-bulbs or thickened stem of orchids.

Pubescent Plants, leaves and stems which have a downy or silky covering of hairs.

Puddling Natural pools or ponds can be made watertight by making a clay lining which is worked or puddled into a soft consistency to prevent water draining away.

Also the effects of cultivating very wet soil when it is churned up into mud.

Also the working or kneading of grafting wax.

Pupa The stage intermediate in the life cycle of an insect, between larva or grub and the final or perfect adult.

Pustule A form of wart-like swelling which can appear on most parts of any plant. These are usually a disease condition. Such excrescences frequently burst to release either powdery spores or wet slime, infected with living organisms.

Pyramid Trees which are trained and pruned in the shape of a cone and usually have one central stem. *See* Chapter 3, Plant Care.

Pyriform Trees, fruits and flowers which resemble those of pear are described as pyriform.

Race A group of plants descended from the same ancestor and having many similarities.

Raceme An inflorescence of flowers which are carried on a long single stem to which they are attached by pedicels (q.v.) or stalks. Examples include lily of the valley and hyacinth.

Radial Tissues which are arranged in a circle, or radiate from a central point, like the florets of a daisy flower.

Radicle The first or main root of a seedling, supporting the seed leaves or cotyledons with the upright shoot or plumule (q.v.).

Rake An important garden hand tool consisting of a comb-like head with metal, wood or rubber teeth attached to a long handle. *See* Chapter 11, Tools and Equipment.

Raking Using a rake usually to level and crumble or break down soil to remove loose grass, leaves and debris and to scarify turf.

Rambler *See* Rose classification.

Ramify To form branches or branching in a network, applied to roots of trees and plants.
Also applied to the invasion of soil or plant tissue by fungal mycelium threads.

Rammer A shaped piece of wood which is used for working and firming the soil around the root ball of plants being potted on (q.v.).

Range A covered area, such as greenhouse or frames.

Ratoon A clump of plants, such as bamboo, which have been cut back almost to ground level. The operation of cutting back is sometimes referred to as ratooning.

Raw Uncooked or unprepared in the case of fruit and vegetables.
Manure, when it is fresh and undecomposed.
Seeds when in the natural state and not specially treated as are those which are sold in pelleted form.

Ray The group of outer rings or rows of florets of composite flowers such as daisy, single dahlias and chrysanthemums which consist of two types of flowers – florets of the ray and those of the disc or eye. *See* Compound flower.

Reagent A chemical which is used to test the qualities or properties of substances; for example, the feeding value of soils, or their pH level.

Receptacle Botanically the head of a flower stalk to which the various floral organs are attached.

Reciprocating Mechanical devices which operate on a backward-and-forward motion. Lawnmowers or grass cutters which use knives that move very quickly from side to side.

Reclaim The operation of returning disused or neglected land back to cultivation.

Recurvate or recurved Petals of some flowers such as lilies curve backwards and down. *See also* Reflexed.

Reflexed Similar to recurvate (q.v.), but even more downward or backward bending or curving.

Regular Flowers which are symmetrical in shape and with petals of equal size. This type of bloom can be equally divided by an imaginary line running through the centre point.

Remontant Plants or varieties which produce flushes of flowers at intervals during the growing season.

Reproduction The increase of plants by seeds and spores as well as by vegetative propagation, such as cuttings, layering, budding, and grafting. *See* Chapter 2, Propagation.

Reserve garden A nursery plot. An area of ground set aside for the purpose of raising and growing young plants until they are ready for setting out.

Resin A sappy fluid, waxy or glutinous substance produced by certain plants, in particular by conifers. Some resins are aromatic and pleasantly scented, such as Canada balsam.

Respiration In plants, *all* living cells respire or breathe, unlike animals which have lungs.

Rest A stage or condition in seeds or plants in which little or no outward signs of growth or movement are apparent.

Resting period A period when seeds or plants are dormant, such as during winter. Various broad-leaved trees which have shed their leaves in autumn provide examples of plants at rest and in their resting period.

Resurrection plants A group of plants which have the capacity to wither and shrivel during drought and then apparently come to life with the return of moist conditions. The two best known examples include: the Rose of Jericho, *Anastatica hierochuntica* and the Resurrection Plant, *Selaginella lepidophylla.*

Retaining wall A wall which separates ground at different levels to contain the soil and prevent spillage from the upper to the lower levels. Retaining walls are usually required where the gradient of soil banks are likely to be steeper than 1:3. This represents a vertical rise of 30 cm (12 in) for each 90 cm (36 in) of horizontal distance.

Retardant A material or process which prevents or delays the growth or development of plants, disease or other organisms. Practical applications of these materials include the use of maleic hydrazide to slow down the growth of grasses on steep banks and inaccessible places where mowing is a problem. Retardation of growth by cold storage, for example, of prepared crowns of lily of the valley, enables these to be forced at any time of the year. Various chemical sprays slow down and retard the growth of diseases and mosses.

Reticulated Any form of markings or venation (q.v.) of flowers, leaves or fruits which are net-like. Some varieties of melon produce fruits with such markings and are referred to as net or netted types.

Reversion A virus disease of blackcurrants, also known as nettle leaf, in which the leaves assume the appearance of those of nettles and cropping almost ceases. *See* Chapter 10, Problems.

Reverted Plants which have produced a branch or shoot of a primitive or original type. Variegated trees and shrubs regularly revert and produce a green shoot unmarked with any variegation.

Also blackcurrants with reversion disease (q.v.).

Revolute Leaves which are rolled back at the margins to form a narrow, almost tubular arrangement, as in rosemary and some heathers.

Rhizome An underground stem which is used by many plants as a natural means of spread, as in some kinds of iris and couch grass. These produce buds below the soil surface at the nodes unlike true roots which develop buds only when cut or damaged.

Rhizomorph A root-like strand of compact or close fungal mycelium which occurs in some soils ready to attack and infect susceptible plants. *Armillaria mellea*, the Honey Fungus, which can be devastating among trees and shrubs, can form these, to produce black or dark brown strands.

Rib The central or main vein in leaves which is usually thicker than the surrounding tissue or leaf blade.

Riddle A sieve consisting of box-like sides or circular rim with a wire-mesh base, which is used for riddling (sifting) soil or other material.

Ridging A form of digging which consists of throwing the soil into ridges, to expose the maximum surface area to the action of frost, wind and weather. *See* Chapter 1, Site and Soil.

Rind The surface or soft bark of young wood or branches which is pliant enough to fold back when cut for budding or other purposes.

Also the skin of citrus fruits such as orange and lemon.

Ringing *See* Bark-ringing.

Ripe Fruits, usually, which are at the right stage of maturity for eating.

Also, shoots which have hardened and lignified, a condition normally reached by new growths in late summer or autumn. The hardening process is known as ripening.

Riser The vertical face stone or brick between two steps in a flight.

Rock garden An area of ground which consists predominantly of rocks and is planted with alpines and similar subjects. For construction, *see* Chapter 5, Flowers and Foliage.

Rock Garden moraine A deep, well-drained bed of fine chippings and similar granular material prepared for and planted with alpines and rock subjects.

Rogue A plant which is not true to type and is inferior or has reverted.

Roguing The process of weeding out diseased and unwanted plants.

Roller Various kinds of roller are used in gardening. Iron and wooden types are needed to consolidate turf areas especially when sowing or laying areas to grass and in spring after severe frosts. *See* Chapter 8, Turf.

Roller blinds Lightweight slatted timber, nylon or other materials are wound on rollers to provide shading for plants in greenhouses and frames.

Roof garden An area of roof which is used or set aside for the cultivation of plants. *See* Chapter 5, Flowers and Foliage.

Root The downward growing, usually underground, branches of plants which obtain moisture and sustenance as well as providing anchorage. Adventitious roots are those which develop from cuttings and from above ground stems of layers and some climbing plants like ivy. Aerial roots are similar to adventitious forms, but usually remain suspended in the air obtaining moisture from the atmosphere instead of soil or compost. Fibrous roots are usually fine and much branched, providing the main source of nutrients and water. Tap roots are the main, first-formed underground stems of plants, providing anchorage

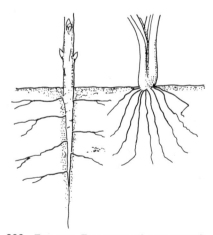

223 Tap root. Two types of root occur in garden plants. *Left*: tap root. *Right*: adventitious.

and support. Secondary roots which obtain most of the plants nutrients arise from the tap roots.

Root crop Vegetables and other food plants which produce swollen roots or stems at or below soil level, such as beetroot, carrots, parsnips and potatoes. *See* Chapter 9, Vegetables.

Root cutting A small section of root which is used for raising certain types of plants with fleshy underground stems. *See* Chapter 2, Propagation.

Root hairs Very fine feeding hairs which develop just behind the root tips.

Root knot An ailment of tomatoes, chrysanthemums and cucumbers, when the fine roots of affected plants form knots. It is caused by Root-knot eelworms. *See* Chapter 10, Problems.

Root nodules Small nodules on the roots of peas, beans and related plants which can enrich crops and soil. These swellings contain considerable numbers of a particular kind of bacterium which can fix nitrogen from the atmosphere. This type of partnership is not enjoyed by other commonly-grown crops.

Root pruning Is occasionally carried out with plums and cherries to induce fruitfulness where trees are excessively vigorous. *See* Chapter 6, Fruits.

Root rot A condition of roots in which they are diseased and rotting. The causes of this are numerous. *See* Chapter 10, Problems.

Root run This is the area and extent of a plant's root system. The run is measured as the volume from the base of the stem to the extremities of the root tips at the surface by the maximum depth.

Root system This is the branching network, ranging from the thickest tap root down to the finest root hair.

Root undercutting *See* Pruning, root.

Rosaceous Members of the rose family and flowers which are rose-like.

Rose classification A system of grouping similar types and kinds of roses together. *See* Chapter 5, Flowers and Foliage.

Rose stock The roots of one variety of rose supporting the top of another as with budding or grafting. The top portion is referred to as the scion. There are several types which are suitable for use as root stock many of which are selections from the wild dog rose, *Rosa canina*. *See* Chapter 5, Flowers and Foliage.

Rosette A circular rose-like arrangement of petals or leaves.

Rot, rotting Conditions of plants in varying stages of decay due mainly to disease. Various types are recognised, such as dry or wet rots of potatoes, black rot of pelargoniums and white rot of onions.

Rotary Rotary cutters are grass cutting machines which operate on the principle of quickly rotating knives attached to a horizontal spinning disc. *See* Chapter 8, Turf.

Rotary cultivators have revolving tines to break up the ground. *See* Chapter 11, Tools and Equipment.

Rotation A sound garden practice of growing a succession of different crops on the same plot each year so that no piece of ground becomes unproductive. This can occur through continuous cultivation of the same type of plant on the same land, either through build up of disease or depletion of nutrient. Examples include a three or four course rotation commonly used when growing vegetables. *See* Chapter 9, Vegetables.

Rotavation A system of soil cultivation using rotary cultivators. *See* Chapter 1, Site and Soil.

Rough Soil which has been dug over, usually in autumn or winter, and is not finely broken down by forking and raking. In this state the land is improved by weathering.

Sawn timber which has not been planed smooth is described as rough cut.

Crops which are of poor quality or troubled by pests and diseases.

Rugose Leaves or other tissues which are furrowed or wrinkled, such as primula or foxglove foliage.

Running to seed A condition of plants such as lettuce or beetroot when they send up a flower spike and cease to crop well.

Runner An embryo or young plant formed at the end of a stem or stolon, which is attached to, and produced from, the parent. Strawberries are usually increased by this means.

Russet Fruits such as apples which develop a rough surface but are not necessarily inferior to smooth-skinned varieties. It is included in the name of some apple varieties which develop this feature.

Rust A name given to various plant diseases which produce a characteristic rust-like reddish, yellow or ochrous dust or pustule on leaves and stems. *See* Chapter 10, Problems.

Rustic Usually occurs as rustic work and is used to denote garden structures, such as pergolas or furniture which are made of unplaned timber.

Saddle graft A form of grafting where the stem of the scion is cut out to form an inverted 'V' shape nick. *See* Chapter 2, Propagation.

Sagittate Leaves which are arrow-shaped with two back-pointing lobes as with sagittaria.

Salad plants This is a group of esculent plants which are usually eaten uncooked or cold. *See* Chapter 9, Vegetables.

Salt Common salt or sodium chloride, as well as other combinations of elements such as sulphate of potash.

Samara A winged nut-like fruit usually borne by trees and shrubs such as members of the maple family, including sycamore.

Sand A crystalline inert material that is found in fertile soils and is an important ingredient of potting composts. It does not normally contain many nutrients but contributes to the physical condition of the soil or compost. Of the two generally recognised grades, coarse and fine, the former is favoured for compost purposes. Sand consists principally of silica or silicon dioxide. *See* Chapter 1, Site and Soil.

Sandstone The parent rock from which sand is derived as a result of weathering. An attractive natural material used in the construction of rock gardens and retaining walls, but less durable than limestone.

Sanitation felling A forestry term which came into prominence as a result of Dutch Elm Disease. It involves the cutting down and burning of diseased trees and shrubs to prevent spread of infection.

Sap A juice or juices which occur in the stems and leaves of living plants.

Sapling Seedling or young trees before the heart wood becomes hardened.

Sappy Growth consisting of soft, rank leaves and shoots that are inclined to be attacked by pest and disease.

Saprophyte Various organisms which feed only on dead plants and trees.

Sap-wood Soft, tender shoots which have not become lignified and hardened. Shoots at this stage are suitable for soft- or semi-ripewood cuttings.

Savory or savory herb A member of a group of plants or herbs which are or can be used for culinary purposes. Examples of this include mint, parsely and sage.

Saw There are many designs of this

cutting instrument which in the garden is mainly used for pruning and lopping trees. *See* Chapter 11, Tools and Equipment.

Scab The symptoms and disease organisms which attack potatoes, apples and pears.

Also any pitted, sunken or diseased leaves, fruits or plants. *See* Chapter 10, Problems.

Scale Small leaf-like structures found on the outsides of buds which protect the unopened leaves within. Similarly, flattened small leaves, often pointed and adpressed to the stem of shoots. These occur on many conifers, such as Lawson Cypress and various Junipers. Scales can serve as food storage organs in some bulbous plants such as daffodil.

Scale insects A group of creatures, many of which are harmful to garden plants. These appear as brownish or greyish scales on leaves and stems. *See* Chapter 10, Problems.

Scandent Climbing, clinging or growing through and up, of plants of ascending habit.

Scape A leafless flower stalk, such as occurs with some primulas.

Scarify An operation involving vigorous raking of turf to tease out old grass and let air circulate more freely. *See* Chapter 8, Turf.

Scion The part or plant which forms the upper or top section of a graft union consisting of stock and scion.

Scion rooting A condition of budded or grafted plants in which the scions or top parts form roots, thus losing the benefits of the stock or root varieties.

Sclerotium A resting form of some fungus diseases appearing as dark or black pin-head size dots among mycelium.

Scolytus The generic name given to a group of bark-boring beetles, one of which is the main transmitter of Dutch Elm Disease.

Scorched Leaves, plants and seedlings which appear damaged, almost as if seared or burnt by fire. Strong sun, wind, drought and spray damage are common causes of this condition. Scorching is the process during which this type of damage occurs.

Scree An area or pocket of well-drained chippings found either naturally in mountainous areas or in man-made rock gardens. Similar to moraine (q.v.), and usually containing some soil to sustain plants.

Scree plants Those occur naturally on or in scree beds.

Screen A hedge, trees, wall or other barrier which serves to hide an ugly view, to provide shelter and protection usually from wind, to be a physical barrier, and to act as a foil for flowers and plants.

Scrub Stunted trees, shrubs and plants which usually provide incomplete ground cover, often appearing in cold, exposed positions or on high ground.

Scythe One of the oldest and best-known types of grass cutting implement. Single and double-handed versions are used but are now seen mainly in country districts.

Seaweed Sea-inhabiting plants of all types. In coastal areas where this is available it is gathered, stacked, and composted for use as a manure substitute.

Secateurs A group of pruning tools. Two main types in regular use are the parrot-bill type with curved cutting blades and the anvil type. *See* Chapter 11, Tools and Equipment.

Second soil Potting composts which are being used again, sometimes with disappointing results.

Secondary Any growth or development which commences after the initial or primary organs are developed. In dry seasons potatoes occasionally develop swellings or secondary growths on the tubers if there is wet weather during summer before the foliage dies down.

Seed A dormant embryo plant developed as a result of fertilisation of the female part of the flower.

Seed bed An area of ground which is prepared for seed sowing. This involves breaking down the soil into a fine state, and ideally eliminating weeds, pests and diseases. *See* Chapter 1, Site and Soil.

Seed box A wooden or plastic container in which a suitable compost is placed and on which seeds are sown. The standard sized seed box or tray is approximately 350 × 200 mm and 50 mm deep (14 × 8 × 2 in).

Seed coat The protective skin or layer immediately surrounding individual seeds.

Seed drill An implement or device used for seed sowing.
Also a shallow furrow or row in which seeds are sown.

Seed leaf A cotyledon or initial leaf, appearing singly as monocotyledons, or in pairs as dicotyledons. These are the first emerging leaves to show above ground with some exceptions.

Seedling An immature plant which is raised from a seed as distinct from one which is increased vegetatively from a cutting.

Seed protectors A contrivance used to prevent birds and animals from eating seeds and damaging seedlings. These often consist of a light metal framework, covered with fine wire mesh netting.

Seed raised Plants raised direct from seed as distinct from those increased vegetatively by cuttings, layering, budding or similar.

Seed vessel The seed case, pod or envelope.

Segment One of a number of similar parts or sections, such as petals of flowers and cloves of garlic bulbs.

Selective weed killer A material or substance used to kill weeds in a crop without harming the cultivated plants, such as could be used on daisies in lawns.

Self Flowers of a single colour.

Self fertile Plants and varieties which do not need the pollen of another for fruit and seeds to develop.

Self sterile Plants and trees which need to have their flowers pollinated by another suitable variety to enable fertilisation to take place. *See* Chapter 6, Fruits.

Semi-double Flowers which expose the stamens in the centre or eye and have several outer rows of petals. In double flowers the place of the eye is covered by petals, whereas those which are single have only a single row of petals surrounding the disc or eye.

Sensitive Plants which produce some visible response to touch. The Sensitive Plant, *Mimosa pudica*, lowers its leaves into a drooping position when the leaves are touched. The leaves of some insectivorous plants close when an insect alights, thus trapping it in an enveloping leaf.

Sepal One of a group of protective leaf-like structures on the outside of developing flower buds and collectively known as the calyx. On some plants these are highly coloured as with clematis, but most are some shade of green.

Sequence Colour arrangements of flowers in beds or borders where the shades range in stages from light to dark or are set out in contrasting groups.

Sessile Fruits and flowers which are stalkless, being positioned flush on a shoot or branch.

228

Sets Small part-grown bulbs or bulbils of plants such as some onions and shallots which are stored during winter in a dried dormant state. These are planted out in spring to grow and develop to maturity usually in the same year. *See* Chapter 9, Vegetables.

Shade A form of blind, screen or paint-like substance applied to glass during summer to protect seedlings and tender plants from intense sunlight. These can be placed over or on greenhouses, frames and cloches. The task of applying this cover is known as shading.

Shade plant Trees and shrubs which are grown as nurse or cover plants, providing shade and shelter.

Also any plant which needs or grows well in shaded situations.

Shanking A condition found among grape vines which results in shrivelling and loss of fruit, but is not due to any particular disease. *See* Chapter 10, Problems.

Shears Scissor-like hand tools used for cutting grass, hedges and shrubs. The two main types recognised are ordinary and long handled, the latter being suitable for edging. *See* Chapter 11, Tools and Equipment.

Sheath A protective covering often found at the base of leaf stalks among grasses, consisting of a short tubular sleeve.

Sheep manure The droppings from sheep are sometimes used by gardeners in country areas to make liquid manure, but is a practice which is rapidly falling into disuse.

Shell The hard exterior covering of various creatures such as snails.

Also the husk or outside of some nuts.

Shelter *See* Screen.

Shelter belt A line of close planted trees and shrubs which serve to reduce or eliminate the ill effects of wind on plants behind the belt, in the lee of the prevailing wind. Large scale wind belts on farms occasionally consist of several rows of plants.

Shield budding A method of vegetative increase consisting of placing a scion bud on a root stock to form a graft union. This practice is widely used in the propagation of roses. *See* Budding.

Shingle Usually rounded, water-worn stones found on the sea shore or in river beds. Fine grades are used for working in and lightening heavy soils. *See* Chapter 1, Site and Soil.

Shoddy An organic, slow-acting nitrogenous manure that is obtained as a by-product of the woollen industry. The value of the clippings depends largely on the quality and wool content. *See* Chapter 1, Site and Soil.

Shoot Any growth that is slender, usually starting in the process of emergence from the stem, crown or ground.

Shovel A spade-like tool having a larger but lightweight blade with up-turned edges. *See* Chapter 11, Tools and Equipment.

Shreds A form of fumigating material consisting of combustible shreds which have been impregnated with an active substance. These materials are suitable for indoor greenhouse use and, according to the ingredients employed, can control pests and diseases.

Shrivelling Leaves, shoots and fruits which are withering and becoming wrinkled. A condition which often occurs in hot weather when plants wilt for lack of water or are subjected to hot drying winds and strong sunlight. Disease and injury can also have similar effects.

Shrub A plant which is smaller in size than a tree and characteristically has more than one stem arising at soil level. *See* Chapter 7, Trees and Shrubs.

229

Shrub list *See* Chapter 7, Trees and Shrubs.

Shrubbery A bed or border which is planted exclusively, or mainly, with shrubs.

Shyness A condition, usually problematic, of plants. Shy rooting is a reluctance of cuttings or other plants to form roots. Shy flowering and shy fruiting denote a similar reluctance to produce flowers or fruits.

Sickle A grass or weed cutting hand implement with a curved cutting blade. *See* Chapter 11, Tools and Equipment.

Side graft A method of grafting which is often used with conifers. *See* Chapter 2, Propagation.

Side-wheel mower A type of grass cutter or mower having wheels positioned on the sides and a light roller either leading or trailing. *See* Chapter 5, Turf.

Sieve and sifting *See* Riddle.

Silica An inert substance, consisting of the elements silicon and oxygen, which are the main consitituents of sand.

Silk The term normally used for the tassle or stigma (q.v.) on sweet corn.

Silver leaf A disease of plums and cherries. *See* Chapter 10, Problems.

Simple Whole or undivided leaves.

Single Flowers which have a single outer circle of petals or florets around the eye or disc.

Site An area of land or ground delineated by boundaries, on which buildings and other features are positioned.

Situation A site and its surroundings with all the attendant features, influences and circumstances.

Slasher A type of long-handled hedge knife which is used for the purpose of trimming hedges and similar.

Sleepy Seeds and plants which show few if any signs of growth and movement as found during the resting season. Extremes of temperature can bring about induced dormancy for example in lettuce seed which are then said to be sleepy.

Slip A popular word for cutting.

Slug A group of soil-inhabiting pests which can attack most tender or succulent garden crops and young plants. *See* Chapter 10, Problems.

Snag A short, usually sawn-off stump left on a tree trunk which to lessen the chances of disease should be cut back flush with the main stem.

Snail Similar to slugs (q.v.), but with a hard protective covering. Birds, particularly thrushes, feed on these. *See* Chapter 10, Problems.

Soil A mixture of mineral and organic matter, water and air spaces, the qualities and properties of which vary according to the relative size and proportions of the constituents. *See* Chapter 1, Site and Soil.

Soil classification Practical gardeners differentiate between soil types mainly according to their texture as follows: clay; heavy loam; medium loam; light loam; peat, fen or moss soils; chalk or limestone soils; sands; gravels, and stony soil. *See* Chapter 1, Site and Soil.

Solar heating A system of obtaining heat or energy from the sun while it is shining and retaining this for heating or lighting purposes.

Soluble A substance that can be dissolved in a solvent liquid. The fertiliser, sulphate of ammonia, is soluble in water. Fertilisers need to be soluble in water rather than any other medium if they are to be of any value to plants as they can take up only watery solutions.

Solvent In gardening, a liquid or fluid, such as water, turpentine or paraffin which can dissolve various substances, such as fertilisers and other chemicals.

Soot A black or dark grey substance usually in powder form when dry. Domestic soot, obtained from chimneys of private dwellings, contains small amounts of nitrogen and potash. This makes a useful fertiliser when well weathered – exposed to the air for six months. Fresh soot, however, can scorch tender young plants. *See* Chapter 1, Site and Soil.

Sour A term used for acid soils with a pH level below 7 and for most purposes in need of liming. *See* Chapter 1, Site and Soil.

Sowing An operation involving the placing of seeds in or on a suitable rooting medium to enable them to grow and develop. *See* Chapter 2, Propagation.

Spade A digging implement used for cultivating or draining soils on a small scale. Large medium, border and schlick types are available. *See* Chater 11, Tools and Equipment.

Spathe A bract which surrounds and envelopes an inflorescence such as the petal-like structure of arum or zantedeschia.

Spathulate Leaves or other structures which are rounded at the tip and tapering at the stalk, with a hollow spoon-shaped blade.

Spawn A piece of mycelium, which is used to start off a mushroom crop.
    Also raspberry suckers.

Spear A shoot or growth which in the case of sprouting broccoli consists of flower buds, small leaves and a length of stem.

Specimen An individual plant which illustrates characteristics of its variety. A single tree planted in an expanse of grass would do this to advantage and might be described as a specimen.

Sphagnum A type of moss, which when partly decomposed forms the basis of moss peat which is commonly used for garden purposes. *See* Chapter 1, Site and Soil.

Spike An elongated inflorescence on a long axis to which stalkless flowers are attached.

Spiker An aerating implement used on turf. Hand versions are like a garden fork with either solid or hollow tines. More sophisticated mechanical models are available for large areas of grass.

Spiking The operation of driving tines into turf to reduce soil compaction and improve aeration and drainage.

Spine A thorn such as occurs on rose bushes.

Spire A tapering pointed tip of a plant, like the top of a narrow conifer.

Spit A spade depth of 250–300 mm (10–12 in) usually of soil.

Sporangium A spore case or sac of fungi or ferns containing spores.

Spore A small structure which is a means of reproduction in ferns, fungi and lower plant forms. These minute spores germinate and grow rather like seeds of higher plants.

Sport A mutation is a plant, shoot or other issue, which differs from its parent plant. This spontaneous character change without raising plants from seed is termed sporting.

Spray A group of flowers on a single stem.
    Also a chemical mixture in liquid form for application to garden plants to control pests and diseases.

Sprayer An appliance to deliver a spray in the form of a fine mist to protect plants.

Spraying The operation of mixing, and applying chemical sprays to control pest, disease and weeds. *See* Chapter 10, Problems.

Springtail A whitish pest sometimes found in greenhouse soils.

Sprinkler A name given to a watering appliance to deliver water to crops as and when needed. *See* Chapter 11, Tools and Equipment.

Sprout A fresh growth or shoot which arises from a seed, root, stem, or any other part.

Spur Short lengths of growth or twig-like shoots particularly on fruit trees. Fruit spurs carry flower buds and fruits and are the main source of crop on many varieties of apple and pear. Spur-like tubular projections on flowers such as aquilegia.
Spur pruning A method of pruning to retain and develop fruit spurs.

Squarrose Plants which are covered with or have many scales.

Stage or staging Greenhouse benching on which plants are placed.
 Also the process of setting up a show exhibit.

Stag-head An arboricultural term for a tree condition when the tips of shoots and branches die. Affected trees in

224 Stag-head. Old trees which are dying back or with root rot, show characteristic dead tips of branches.

summer have leafless 'stags horns' rising out of the leafy crown.

Stake A substantial tree support as distinct from sticks or bamboo canes.

Stake and tie The process of providing and fixing any supports, thick or thin, to which plants are tied or secured for support.

Stalk The means of attachment or support for flowers, fruits and leaves.

Stamens The male floral organs, consisting of anthers or pollen sacs and the filaments which attach them to the flower.

Staminode Male flowers which have stamens but no female organs.

Standard Any tree having a clear trunk or main stem from soil level to lowest branch of 1.1–2.15 m (3 ft 6 in–8 ft). Four types of standard are recognised according to their length of clear stem as follows: Half standard 1.1–1.4 m (3 ft 6 in–4 ft 6 in). Three quarter standard 1.45–1.6 m (4 ft 6 in–5 ft 6 in). Standard 1.7–1.85 m (5 ft 6 in–7 ft). Tall standard 1.85 m–2.15 m (7 ft–8 ft).

Standard petal The largest or upright petal in flowers of the pea family.

Starting The process of providing seeds, plants and cuttings with the necessary conditions for growth.

Station A hole or position in which a plant is set or seed is sown.

Steeping The process of watering plants in containers by standing them in shallow water; soaking seeds in water before sowing, or trees and plants before setting them in their final positions.

Stellate Star-shaped.

Stem The main axis, or one of several, which provides the frame to which leaves, flowers and other organs are attached. The recognised different types are arboreal or arborescent, meaning tree-like; climbing; creeping; herbaceous, meaning soft and non-woody; prostrate, or lying on the ground; twining, to support ascending plants, and underground.

Stem rooting Stems which form roots above ground where, for example, they may be in contact with moist soil. A useful means of plant increase. *See* Chapter 2, Propagation.

Steps A useful garden device for practical and ornamental purposes to overcome changes of level. Stone, brick and concrete provide durable surfaces for formal settings.

Sterile Flowers which fail to produce viable pollen or are unable to set seed.

Also plants which for other reasons are unfruitful.

A flower which cannot set seed on its own but does so with pollen from another is said to be self-sterile.

Sterilisation A process of disinfection, usually applied to soil or other rooting medium. This involves the use of heat or chemicals to control pests, diseases and weeds. *See* Chapter 1, Site and Soil.

Stigma The part of the pistil or seed-producing organ which needs to be dusted with good pollen to enable fertilisation to take place.

Stimulant A substance or condition which causes or brings about a burst of energy, growth or excitement. Heat, light, moisture and fertilisers come within this category although an excess of one or more can be harmful.

Stipe The stalk of any fungus such as mushrooms and toadstools.

Also the leaf stalk of ferns.

Stipule A small leafy bract which occurs usually in a pair at the base of a leaf stalk at or near the junction with the stem.

Stock Any plant which is budded or grafted and used as the root.

A group or race of plants having the generic name of Matthiola, and including Ten-week and Brompton Stocks for example.

Also all plants in a batch, group or garden. Plants set aside for propagation by means of cuttings are referred to as stock plants. *See* Chapter 2, Propagation.

Stolon A stem, shoot or runner which grows on or over the soil surface.

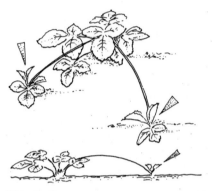

225 Stolon.

Stoma (*pl. Stomata*) A breathing pore or opening on leaf surfaces which enables fresh air to enter and allows surplus moisture and gases to escape.

Stomach poison A chemical insecticide which relies for its effectiveness on being eaten by chewing and biting insects, cf. Contact Insecticide. *See also* Chapter 10, Problems.

Stony Soils which contain a high proportion of stone or rock particles over 40–50 mm (1½–2 in) in size.

Stool A plant root retained usually for propagation and production of cuttings of such as chrysanthemums.

Also any plant with a short stem, such as Gooseberry. *See* Chapter 2, Propagation.

Stopping The process of removing the growing points of shoots and side

233

growths to encourage breaking and control or to regulate cropping.

Store Any method of keeping plants or crops in good condition until required for use.

Stove Plants which require tropical or sub-tropical growing conditions for success.

Strain A group of plants within a variety which differ in certain respects from others within the same variety.

Strap A narrow piece of textile or plastic that is used for tying up trees.
Also long narrow leaves.

Strata (singular, stratum) Layers of the earth's crust.

Stratification A method of treating seeds before sowing to encourage quick germination. This consists of subjecting seeds to cold conditions before sowing in the usual manner. *See* Chapter 2, Propagation.

Straw The stems and leaves of grasses and cereals, and also the haulm (q.v.) of peas and beans. Cereal straw has many uses in gardening, from composting to frost protection. *See* Chapter 1, Site and Soil.

Streak A condition sometimes found among tomato plants, chrysanthemums and dahlias in which streaks or stripes of different colouring appears. This is often accompanied by stunting and distortion. A virus disease referred to as streak is known to cause these symptoms.

Stringless High quality celery and French or climbing beans when stringiness is absent.

Strip The harvesting of any crop in which all the flowers, fruits or vegetables are cleared at one gathering.

Strip cropping Growing crops in narrow strips where cloches are used, to avoid unnecessary handling when moving them from one crop to another.

Stump A sawn-off tree with a length of trunk showing above ground.
Also a short length of branch attached to a trunk.

Style The central part of a pistil or connecting piece between stigma and ovary.

Sub A prefix used to denote below or under.
Sub-alpine applied to plants found lower or closer to sea level than true alpines.
Sub-irrigation, applied to methods of watering where moisture is supplied from below ground.
Sub-shrub is a plant bordering between herbaceous plants and shrubs.
Sub-soil consists of the material under the top soil.
Sub-tropical plants grow and thrive at temperatures below those needed for tropical subjects.

Suberose Cork-like, applied to bark or tissue with similar qualities.

Succulent Plants having little or no tough fibrous tissue, such as salad crops.

Succulent plants Some plants that are closely related to cacti and have fleshy

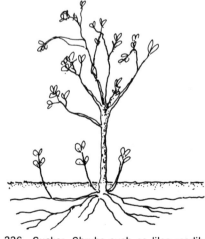

226 Sucker. Shrubs such as lilac readily send up growths as do some rose stocks.

stems and leaves. Crassula and kalanchoe provide examples of this group.

Sucker A growth which arises at or near soil level, especially from the root stocks of a budded or grafted plant is an example of this. Apples, plums, lilacs and roses quite often produce them.

Sulphates A term applied to a large group of salts, many of which are fertilisers, or used by plants. They include sulphates of ammonia, iron, magnesium, manganese and potash. See Chapter 1, Site and Soil.

Sulphur The flowers of sulphur, which consists of the element sulphur, and is widely used as a fungicide. Liver of sulphur or potassium sulphide is also used as a fungicide. Flowers of sulphur is sometimes used to correct the pH level of soils and composts, to make them more acid. See Chapter 1, Site and Soil; also Chapter 10, Problems.

Summer fallow A soil cleaning operation, consisting of cultivating bare soil to kill weed growth before planting trees or making lawns.

Summer pruning A practice of shortening and cutting out new seasons growth during summer on wall-trained and intensively-grown trees and bushes. See Chapter 3, Plant Care.

Summer wood Growths which develop during mid-season after the initial branches are formed.

Sun-blind A lath or roller which can be lowered or raised to shield plants from intense sun.

Sundial A form of garden ornament with a central projection which casts a shadow on a calibrated table, enabling the hour of day to be calculated.

Superphosphate A fertiliser containing phosphate in a fairly soluble form. See Chapter 1, Site and Soil.

Supplementary illumination Artificial lighting using fluorescent tubes or coiled bulbs to control, regulate and improve plant growth under difficult conditions.

Surface caterpillars Grubs and caterpillars which conceal themselves just below the soil surface by day and attack crops usually at night. See Chapter 10, Problems.

Surround Any form of edging which encloses an area of ground. This can be a raised kerb, hard surface, grass or planted strip, or low wire, wrought iron or timber division.

Sward A grassed or turfed area of ground.

Swath or swathe The width of cut of a mower, cutter or sweep of a scythe.

Symbiosis A condition in which one organism lives in or on another, to the mutual advantage of both.

The bacteria which live in the root nodules of members of the pea and bean family are a good example of this.

Syringe A tubular piston-type pump which draws in water or liquid as the handle is pulled to its full extent. When the handle is pushed down the liquid is forced out as a fine spray or mist. This is used for damping down or spraying.

Systemic Chemical sprays which are carried from one part of a plant to another. These substances move in the sap, from the roots to the leaves, for example. See Chapter 10, Problems.

Take, taking A process in propagation. Taking cuttings consists of: selecting and removing suitable shoots or growths from a parent plant; trimming; preparing, and inserting the cuttings in pots or containers. These are then placed in warm, moist conditions as needed for rooting.

Gardeners are said to 'take' a chrysanthemum bud when the buds below the terminal bud are removed, leaving the tip bud to flower. *See* Chapter 2, Propagation.

Taken Cuttings have 'taken' when roots are formed.

Tap root *See* Root.

Tar distillate A product or products obtained from the distillation of tar. One of the applications is as insecticidal winter sprays for fruit trees.

Tar fillis A type of twine or yarn treated with tar derivative and used for tying plants.

Tar oil wash A type of insecticidal spray that is used mainly on fruit trees, and is applied in winter during their dormant period. *See* Chapter 10, Problems.

Temperate Plants which originate from these zones of the world, from both northern and southern hemispheres.

Temperate house A greenhouse which is maintained at a minimum temperature of 10°C (50°D).

Tender Plants which need warm conditions especially in winter and protection from wind and severe weather. Of course, plants which are considered tender in northern climates may be perfectly hardy in southern areas.

Tendril Slender twine-like organs without buds or shoots which are used by some plants as a means of support. In sweet peas these are situated at the ends of the leaves and wind round any object that is close by.

Tentacle A type of glandular hair found on some insectivorous plants such as sundews, Drosera.

Terminal Growths occuring at the leading tips of shoots and stems. Terminal buds develop on the leading main shoots.

Terrace A level piece of ground which drops down to lower land on at least one side. Creating one or more terraces is an effective way to lay out sloping ground.

They are often treated in a formal manner with regular or geometric shaped beds.

Terrestial Plants which live and grow in soil as opposed to aquatic or epiphytic subjects which live in water or on trees or elsewhere with their roots suspended in water or air.

Tetraploid Having four sets of chromosomes in genetical composition. The significance of this condition is perhaps greatest where the problem of fruit pollination needs to be considered.

Thallus A leafy, plate-like structure which develops from the spores of lower plants such as mosses and ferns.

Thermometer A registering instrument for measuring temperature. Various types available, including the conventional rod type; the bi-metallic dial; and the maximum and minimum type, which records the highest and lowest extremes over a period of time.

Thicket Close-growing clumps of plants making dense undergrowth.

Thin, Thinning An important operation of removing overcrowded seedlings leaving strong plants spaced sufficiently far apart to develop into good quality crops. *See* Chapter 9, Vegetables. Various fruits, including apples, pears, plums, peaches and grapes, are thinned to enable them to swell, develop and ripen satisfactorily. *See* Chapter 6, Fruits.

Thrips A small insect which can spoil various crops causing spotting and mottling of flowers. *See* Chapter 10, Problems.

Throat The inner surface of tubular flowers near the base of the petals.

Tie The operation of securing plants to supports from the tying of seedlings to split canes, to fastening trees to their stakes with straps.

Till To cultivate the soil.

Tilth A condition of soil and depth of cultivation. Land with a fine tilth has been well worked and broken down into a fine or granular crumb consistency. Ground with a deep tilth has been broken down to a considerable depth. *See* Chapter 1, Site and Soil.

Tine A prong or spike attachment for cultivating or aerating soil and turf. Spring tines are sometimes fitted to mechanical rotavators to cultivate the soil for planting. Solid or hollow tines are fitted to forks or aerating machines to aerate turf and relieve ground compaction.

Tissue A section of cellular material, usually living, consisting of a few or many cells thickness.

Toadstool Fungi which produce fruiting heads on stalks in a similar manner to mushrooms.

Tomentose Plants which have a dense covering of short hairs.

Tongue graft One of the most popular forms of grafting, consisting of a sloping cut, which is 'nicked' in the centre on both stock and scion. Also known as splice, or whip-and-tongue graft. *See* Chapter 2, Propagation.

Top-draining A practice of digging shallow channels or ditches to remove and drain away surface water. *See* Chapter 1, Site and Soil.

Top-dressing The application of manure, compost or fertiliser to the soil surface around plants.

Sometimes also used for the practice of mulching. *See* Chapter 1, Site and Soil.

Topiary The art and practice of trimming hedges in the shape of animals and other creatures.

Topping *See* Stopping.

Total weedkiller A chemical or mixture, which kills all or any vegetation and is harmless to none.

Toxic Any poisonous substance which can kill or harm plants, animals and people.

Also plants which contain or produce toxic substances.

Trailing Procumbent or prostrate plants which produce shoots that grow on or close to the ground without readily forming roots.

Training Any process involving the pruning, tying or other manipulation of the shape or form of plants.

Transpiration The natural process of exhaling moisture through the pores in plant leaves.

Transplant The operation of digging up, moving and setting plants in fresh positions, as from a nursery bed to final place.

Trap Any device which retains or captures moving animals, insects or other objects. Various types are used to kill or catch vermin and insects.

Also a sediment trap or catch pit as used in a drainage system to prevent the blocking of pipes with mud and similar material.

Trays Shallow boxes, often with raised corner pieces, to allow them to be stacked one on top of the other and still allow air to circulate.

Tread To consolidate loose soil by treading the ground heel-to-toe fashion.

Tree banding A process of either placing a band of sacking, or applying a gelatinous substance around tree trunks to trap or prevent harmful insects from ascending or descending. These bands are usually placed 450–900 mm (18 in–3 ft) above ground.

Tree bark protector A process similar to tree banding (q.v.) but consists of applying a coat of compound onto tree trunks to discourage animals like rabbits from eating and removing the bark.

Tree cement A dark coloured or black

material which is used for covering wounds and filling cavities to prevent fungal and insect attack.

Tree guard A plastic metal or wire mesh shield which is placed around, but does not touch, the tree trunk, to physically prevent animals and people from damaging the bark.

227 Tree guard. Three commonly occurring types of guard are *left to right*: plastic wrap-round, against rabbits; metal collar, against vandals; and wire, stock proof type.

Tree pruner Any pruning tool especially those with long handles intended for tree work. Long-arm pruners, long-handled loppers or parrot-bill pruners and heavy duty secateurs are some of those tools used.

Tree surgery An aspect of tree care that involves the cutting back, thinning out or removal of branches and limbs; the cutting out of dead and diseased wood; cleaning out; draining and filling cavities. *See* Chapter 7, Trees, Shrubs and Climbers, *also* Chapter 10, Problems.

Tree type Two broad divisions are recognised: deciduous and evergreen; most of the latter are conifers. *See* Chapter 7, Trees, Shrubs and Climbers.

Tree, Weeping A form of tree which has pendulous or drooping branches and shoots such as Weeping Willow. *See* Chapter 7, Trees, Shrubs and Climbers.

Trellis A form of light structure or screen consisting usually of crossed timber laths, leaving squared or diamond-shaped openings. Trellis provides a useful support for plants to climb up or be tied to.

Trench, trenching A form of digging, which involves the excavation of one or more trenches. *See* Chapter 1, Site and Soil.

Tribe A group, family or race of plants having several similar features.

228 Tree habit. Trees grow naturally into different shapes some of which are shown here. *Left to right*: columnar, fastigate, pyramidal, rounded or globose, and weeping.

Trim To cut, clip or lightly prune shrubs, plants, grass and trees. *See* Chapter 3, Plant Care.

Triploid Plants which have three sets of chromosomes.

Trowel A small hand tool primarily used for planting out part-grown seedlings and cuttings. *See* Chapter 11, Tools and Equipment.

True Plants which are representative of their group or variety in all respects.

Truncate Any form or shape which has a blunt end, appearing almost as if cut off, as with some leaves.

Trunk The main stem of a tree.

Truss An umbel of flowers, those inflorescences where the flower stalks arise from a common point such as with rhododendron.

Also a cluster of flowers or fruits, of tomato for example.

Tub A container or receptacle made usually of wood, or sometimes of wooden or plastic barrels, in which plants are grown in soil or water.

Tube The throat or neck of some flowers.

Tuber A swollen and thickened storage organ. A stem which has eyes or buds and usually occurs below soil level as with potato and Jerusalem artichoke.

Tubercle A small swelling, such as an immature tuber.

Tufa A type of soft rock or stone, consisting of chalk or calcareous material and often of irregular shape. This weathers readily and is used in rock garden construction.

Tunicated Bulbs which have an outer membrane of loose skin, such as onion.

Turf An area of ground covered with mown or grazed grass. A piece of turf consists of a layer of soil held together by a mass of grass and roots. *See* Chapter 8, Turf.

Turf beater A piece of wood, attached to a handle, which is used for firming and levelling turves during lawn making. *See* Chapter 8, Turf.

Turf drain A form of draining in which stone or gravel filled trenches are covered with a shallow layer of soil and turf. *See* Chapter 1, Site and Soil.

Turf rake A type of wire rake that can be used to scarify and aerate turf. *See* Chapter 11, Tools and Equipment.

Turf perforator A device used for aerating turf by making holes with spikes. *See* Chapter 11, Tools and Equipment.

Turfing iron A flat bladed tool which is used for lifting turf. The handle is angled to avoid the need for the user to bend too steeply. *See* Chapter 11, Tools and Equipment.

Twig Any short piece of branch or shoot usually consisting of ripened woody growths.

Twiner Climbing plants which twist their stems around any nearby object for support.

Twitch One of the various names that are used for couch grass, *Agropyron repens*.

Type Plants which are true to type are representative of their species or genus.

Umbel A type of inflorescence in which flowers are borne, in flat or domed heads, parachute-fashion on short stalks. These originate at a common point on the main flower stem. Hedge parsley is an example.

Undergrowth Vegetation under the branches of trees or shrubs.

Underplant To grow garden plants beneath a canopy of foliage of taller subjects. Growing crocus or daffodils among trees or shrubs is an example of this.

Unisexual Plants and flowers which produce either male or female organs, but not both.

Unseasoned Branches or shoots which consist of 'green' or unripened, immature wood.

Vapour A gaseous form into which liquids and some solids pass when heated. Various types of soil steriliser insecticides and fungicides which can be vaporised give excellent control in enclosed situations like a greenhouse.

Vaporiser A device used for heating vaporising chemicals to control greenhouse problems.

Vapourer Moth The caterpillars of this moth are very destructive to various garden plants. *See* Chapter 10, Problems.

Variation Plants which differ from the usual form, colour or habit.

Variant A sport or mutation – plants which differ from the usual as a result of some spontaneous change.

Variegated Plants which have leaves of two or more colours. Hollies provide many examples of this with green and gold, green and silvery white, and other combinations.

Variety Any plant which merits recognition and differs from its type species distinctly in colour or form.

Vascular The conducting tissues of plants of the group of vascular plants which have well defined fibre and circulating systems for food and water unlike some of the simple forms of lowly plant life.

Vegetable A crop, or part of a plant, such as root or leaf, which is used for culinary purposes, excluding fruits.

Also any plant form in the plant kingdom. *See* Chapter 9, Vegetables.

Vegetable garden An area of ground which is used primarily or exclusively for the cultivation of vegetable crops.

Vegetable forcing The production of out-of-season food crops, usually with the aid of a greenhouse or other form of shelter and protection. *See* Chapter 9, Vegetables.

Vegetative propagation The raising of plants from cuttings; budding grafting; layering or any method which involves 'taking' and rooting a piece of plant as distinct from increasing plants by seeds. *See* Chapter 2, Propagation.

Vein A thickened often prominent part of a leaf such as the mid-rib, providing conducting tissue, to convey food and water as needed.

Venation The arrangement of leaves within the bud.

Ventilation Air circulation, which can be by natural air currents or assisted by fans in greenhouses.

Ventilator The most simple form consists of a window frame which can be opened or shut at will. In greenhouses these are usually sited near the roof ridge and on the sides.

Verge trimmer A mechanical device for cutting the edges of lawns, consisting usually of a number of revolving blades. *See* Chapter 11, Tools and Equipment.

Vermin Any animal or bird which is harmful to garden crops. Common examples include mice, rats, rabbits, and sparrows. *See* Chapter 10, Problems.

Versicoloured Plants having variously coloured flowers with an irregular arrangement of tone and shade.

Verticillium A troublesome wilt disease which can affect various plants such as tomatoes, carnations and dahlias. *See* Chapter 10, Problems.

Virus A disease causing organism, which can be transferred by insects or on hands, knives and sap. Normal sprays are of no use against these organisms. *See* Chapter 10, Problems.

Vista An outstanding view seen through an opening or along an avenue.

Wall gardening A branch of gardening involving the culture of plants on or walls. *See* Chapter 5, Flowers and Foliage.

Wardian Case A form of elegant glass box or case in which plants are grown. It enables tender plants to be grown in otherwise draughty or unsuitable positions indoors.

Wart disease A serious disease of potatoes. Fortunately there are varieties which are immune to this ailment. *See* Chapter 10, Problems.

Water barrow A wheeled form of water carrier or cart consisting of a light frame on wheels with a tank. *See* Chapter 11, Tools and Equipment.

Water garden An enclosed area of ground, in which water or water features are prominent. *See* Chapter 5, Flowers and Foliage.

Water roller A type of garden roller which can be filled or drained of water as necessary to regulate the weight. *See* Chapter 11, Tools and Equipment.

Watering Water can be applied in three basic ways: overhead, low level and from below. *See* Irrigation. Watering by capillary attraction consists of placing container grown crops on damp sand or similar and the water rising up by capillarity provides the moisture needed. *See* Chapter 3, Plant Care.

Watersprout A vigorous vertical shoot arising from a branch or trunk as the result of hard pruning, and which is usually unproductive.

Water table The level below which all spaces between soil particles are filled with water. This level varies according

229 Watersprouts. Trees which are severely cut back often produce vigorous upright growths, as *arrowed*.

to rainfall, climate and soil drainage.

Waterlogged Ground which is saturated with moisture and has water lodging on the surface.

Wattle A form of interwoven shoots or lath fencing which is useful for protecting plants from wind and for screening.

Wax Various leaves and fruits are covered with a bluish or whitish bloom or wax. *See also* Farina.

Sealing compounds placed round plant grafts are described as grafting wax.

Weather The ageing or mellowing of soil, stone or rock.

Webbing The mass of fine strands which are created by Red Spider Mites in severe attacks.

Weed A plant which is growing in the wrong place. *See* Chapter 1, Site and Soil. *Also* Chapter 8, Turf.

Weed cutter A device used for severing and removing weeds from ponds and water courses as well as on firm ground.

Weed eradicator A rod or roller type of device which is used to smear or inject weeds with a chemical to kill them. *See* Chapter 11, Tools and Equipment.

Weed extractor A pronged hand tool used for levering weeds out of lawns, rock gardens and between paving stones.

Weed host Weeds or wild plants that can be attacked by, or harbour, pests and diseases harmful to cultivated crops.

Weedkiller Chemicals, usually, which are used specifically for the purpose of eradicating weeds. *See* Chapter 10, Problems.

Weeding fork A two, three or four-pronged handfork used primarily for digging out weeds. Various types are available in different sizes and with short or long handles. *See* Chapter 11, Tools and Equipment.

Weeping Plants having a drooping or pendulous habit.

Weevil Various biting and chewing small beetles. *See* Chapter 10, Problems.

Whetstone Originally a type of stone used for sharpening hooks and scythes. Nowadays a stone-like composition is more usual.

Whorl A circular arrangement of flowers, leaves or other organs where the stalks radiate like spokes of a wheel.

Wild garden An area of land which is enclosed and where the plants and planting are informal and unregimented, retaining a natural rather than a man-made appearance. *See* Chapter 5, Flowers and Foliage.

Wilt A condition of plants, leaves and shoots when drooping occurs, for lack of water, by injury or through a disease condition which can be caused by a number of organisms. A typical symptom is for diseased plants to wilt from the base upwards. *See* Chapter 10, Problems.

Wind pollination The natural process of pollen disposal by wind. Many trees, grasses and crops such as sweet corn are pollinated by this means.

Windfall Fruits such as apples which can be picked off the ground, having been blown from the tree by wind.

Window box A rectangular container, in which plants are grown, and which rests on, or is supported by, brackets, close to a window-sill.

Windscreen A row or lines of trees and/or shrubs which are grown to protect plants and provide shelter from wind.

Wing, winged Seeds which have a membraneous keel attachment, such as those of sycamore. These keels enable seeds to be carried over considerable distance by wind.

Winter annual A summer or autumn-sown annual, or a biennial treated as such, which is overwintered to flower the following year. *See* Chapter 5, Flowers and Foliage.

Winter crop Any crop such as Brussels sprouts, which matures and is harvested during the winter months.

Winter fallow The practice of leaving land vacant during winter. *See* Chapter 1, Site and Soil.

Winter garden Originally applied to a large glass structure which was kept frost free to enable the cultivation of flowering and other plants during winter. Now used mainly to describe an enclosed area planted to provide colour and interest mainly during winter. *See* Chapter 5, Flowers and Foliage.

Winter greens Vegetable leaf and shoot crops such as broccoli, Brussels sprouts, cabbages and kale, all of which are members of the brassica family.

Winter wash Chemicals which are sprayed onto dormant trees in winter and the practice of applying them. The plants most commonly given this treatment are fruit trees and bushes.

Winter pruning The winter treatment of trees, shrubs and bushes which differ from that given in summer. *See* Chapter 6, Fruit.

Wireworm The larval stage of Click Beetle and which is a troublesome pest in soil. *See* Chapter 10, Problems.

Wire netting Wire mesh of various gauges is widely used for plant protection and support. *See* Chapter 10, Problems.

Wire stem Damping-off in seedlings, caused by various disease organisms. *See* Chapter 10, Problems.

Wood ash The remains of wood after burning which contains potash and other elements necessary for good crops. *See* Chapter 1, Site and Soil.

Woodland garden An enclosed and/or secluded area which is devoted to the cultivation of trees and woodland plants such as rhododendrons.

Woolly aphid A pest which occurs on fruit trees, appearing in cracks in bark and resembling tufts of whitish cotton wool. *See* Chapter 10, Problems.

Work, worked The operations of budding and grafting. Plants are described as having been worked when budded or grafted.

Also, soil which has been cultivated.

Worm *See* earthworm.

Wound Any area of a plant which is not covered with bark or hard external tissue, providing a ready means of entry for disease organisms. The base of cuttings or sawn-off tree limbs provide examples of this.

Wrinkled Any part of a plant which has crimpled and wrinkled surfaces. Some varieties of garden peas which have seeds with raised and netted venation are so described.

Yard gardening The cultivation of plants in courtyards and similar spaces. The expression is used less now than formerly.

Yield The final or ultimate weight or equivalent of crop.